Words for Today
2011
Notes for daily Bible reading

Words
for today ■■■■ *2011*

Edited by Nicola Slee

International Bible Reading Association

Words for Today aims to build understanding and respect for a range of religious perspectives and approaches to living practised in the world today, and to help readers meet new challenges in their faith. Views expressed by contributors should not, however, be taken to reflect the views or policies of the Editor or the International Bible Reading Association.

The International Bible Reading Association's scheme of readings is listed monthly on the Christian Education website at www.christianeducation.org.uk/ibra_scheme.php and the full scheme for 2011 may be downloaded in English, Spanish and French.

Editor: Nicola Slee
Cover design by Christian Education, showing a detail from the Holm Window, Wellington Cathedral of St Paul, New Zealand. Photo by Nicola Slee.

Published by:
The International Bible Reading Association
1020 Bristol Road
Selly Oak
Birmingham B29 6LB
United Kingdom

Charity number 211542

ISBN 978-1-905893-28-7
ISSN 0140-8275

Typeset by Splash! Creative Design Ltd
Printed and bound in the UK by Mosaic Print Management
www.mosaicpm.com

Contents

Editorial

This year's cover shows a detail from the Holm window in Wellington Cathedral, New Zealand. The window depicts St Paul (patron saint of the cathedral) and various symbols of the Holm Shipping Company, within a mass of swirling blue and green waves. The sea, of course, is a central reality for the peoples of Aotearoa, New Zealand and the surrounding Polynesian islands. New Zealanders, like Brits, are island people, never far from the sound and sight of the sea, historically dependent on the waves for travel and transport, for industry and food – and, in more recent times, for leisure and tourism. I was fortunate to spend a three-month sabbatical in the outskirts of Auckland during 2009, living, worshipping and working at the Anglican retreat centre of Vaughan Park. My scholar's studio was about 100 yards from the shore, and every day I walked the beach, usually several times, relishing the varying colours, moods and sounds it manifested in all weathers and at different times of day and night. Although it was a different sea from my native waters of North Devon (where I was brought up), there is something about a beach that feels like home to me, and, as I walked the beach at Long Bay each day, I had a sense of being connected to family and friends back in the UK.

The sea is a central image in the scriptures for the all-pervasive, powerful and mysterious presence of the Spirit. Both feared and held in awe by the Israelites, the sea was to them the source of their livelihood, but also the place of potential chaos, destructive and overwhelming. In our very different time and place, the sea can still be a terrifying force, as floods and tsunamis remind us. Rising sea levels and the melting of the icecaps are potent symbols for us today of potentially cataclysmic changes happening within our earth. We urgently need to pay attention to the life of our oceans and to read the signs of the times therein. The Spirit still speaks through wave, water, flood and disaster, if we can but hear her voice.

This year's notes are, as ever, varied and challenging, and I am glad to have a number of new writers from New Zealand, representing different parts of Maori, Polynesian and Pakeha cultures. As you read and encounter new voices alongside more familiar ones, may you be refreshed, doused, even drenched, by the active power and presence of the Spirit at work in the scriptures, in human lives and in the whole creation.

Nicola Slee
Editor

Prayers

Protect me, O Lord;
My boat is so small,
And your sea so big.

Traditional Breton fisherman's prayer

Wake us up, God,
with your life-giving water.
Splash our faces
with the cold of your truth
which can make us gasp and catch our breath.
Draw us deeper
into the depths of your ocean
where we may learn to swim more freely in your waters.
Surprise us with creatures and beauties of the deeps
which enlarge our vision and kindle our adoration.
Fill us with a sense of urgency
to protect and preserve the powerful life of your oceans
and of your earth.

Nicola Slee

Heavenly Father,
whenever we are in danger
of being possessed
by the selfish materialism of our time,
remind us again that your way,
the way that enables us
to drink the enduring water of life,
is a way of loving self-giving,
which calls us to help satisfy
the hunger and thirst
of others of your children
with material needs far greater than our own.

Edmund Banyard

How to use a 'quiet time'

Pay attention to your body Take time to slow down, consciously relax each part of your body, and listen to your breathing for a while.

Use silence to relax and empty your mind of all that's going on around you. Know that God's loving presence encircles you, your family, your community and the world. Learn to enjoy God's presence.

Have a visual focus – a cross, a plant, interesting stones, pictures or postcards. . . Create a prayer table on which to display them with other symbols.

Read the **Bible passage** for the day several times, perhaps using different translations, and then the notes. Allow the words to fill your mind. Try to discover their message for you and the world around you.

Listen Remember that the most important part of prayer is to hear what God is saying to us. God speaks to us through the words of scripture, the daily news, and often through people around us.

Include the world Hold the news of the day in your mind. Enter the situation of those you hear or read about and try to pray alongside them and with them.

Pray without ceasing Prayer is not only 'the quiet time' we set aside. It becomes part of the whole of life, a continuous dialogue between God and ourselves, through all that we do and think and say: a growing awareness of the loving presence of God who travels with us and never leaves us.

Acknowledgements and abbreviations

IBRA gratefully acknowledges permission to reproduce extracts from the following:

GNB   *Good News Bible* (The Bible Societies/Collins Publishers) – Old Testament © American Bible Society 1976; New Testament © American Bible Society 1966, 1971, 1976.

NIV   Scripture quotations taken from *The Holy Bible, New International Version* © 1973, 1978, 1984 by International Bible Society. Used by permission of Hodder & Stoughton Limited. All rights reserved. 'NIV' is a registered trademark of International Bible Society. UK trademark number 1448790.

NJB   Taken from the *New Jerusalem Bible*, published and copyright 1985 by Darton, Longman and Todd Ltd and Doubleday & Co. Inc., and used by permission of the publishers.

NSRV   *New Revised Standard Version* © 1989, Division of Christian Education of the National Council of Churches of Christ in the United States of America.

REB   *Revised English Bible* © Oxford University and Cambridge University Presses 1989.

RSV   *The Holy Bible, Revised Standard Version* © 1973, Division of Christian Education of the National Council of Churches of Christ in the United States of America.

The Message: Scripture taken from THE MESSAGE Copyright 1993, 1994, 1995, 1996, 2000, 2001, 2002. Used by permission of NavPress Publishing Group.

John Henson, *Good as New* (O Books, 2005).

Note
BCE   Before the Common Era. BCE and CE are used by some writers instead of BC and AD.

God still speaks

1 God's word at work in the world

Preparing for the week

'This is the Word of the Lord' are dangerous words if you are holding the Bible in your hand, especially if you have been reading a passage about the Israelites slaughtering their enemies. Idolatry is the practice of offering worship to someone or something in the place of God. The Bible can become an idol. The Bible itself encourages us to listen to God speaking in the physical and natural world, through the words of the prophets interfering in politics, and above all, in the good news of God's offer of life in all its fullness and, supremely for Christians – in 'the Word made flesh' – Jesus himself.

The 'This' can be a mind-numbing curtain-fall to the reading of scripture, carrying overtones of 'this and not that', excluding other forms of God's expression apart from the big book. It threatens even the special place of Jesus as the living Word. It directs the mind away from the possibility of God speaking through science, art, music, literature, pop culture and personal relationships. God is not to be so confined! The words 'This is the Word of the Lord' are best replaced by such words as 'Praise God who speaks to us'. Better still, why not let the scripture speak for itself?

At the beginning of this New Year, our readings from scripture will seek to alert our senses to God's many lines of communication.

Notes based on the *New Revised Standard Version* and the *Good As New* version by

John Henson

John Henson is a writer, conference speaker and 'Inclusive Church' promoter. He is best known for *Good as New* (O Books, 2005), his radical retelling of the Christian scriptures.

**The call to
trust**

Hebrews 1:1–12

*Up to now, God has always spoken to our people
by means of special agents, each with their own
way of putting things. But recently God has
spoken to us by means of a human personality,
someone so close to God as to share
responsibility for everything, including the
physical universe. This person is like a picture of
God thrown in big lights on a screen, or a lifelike
sculpture, and speaks the words the world needs
to stay in existence.*

Good as New, p. 432

The best bet for the author of Hebrews is Paul's
friend Priscilla (of the double-act 'Cill and Will').
The reason why this is taking so long to be
accepted is two thousand years' monopoly of
leadership and scholarship by male Christians. Cilla
was a Roman aristocrat who appreciated Greek
culture and wrote good Greek. Her letter to Jewish
Christians shows the influence of Plato's phil-
osophy, as does the Gospel of John. The beginning
of Hebrews is very like the opening of John. Both
celebrate God speaking by means of a human
personality. This idea was familiar to the Greeks
and Romans but was difficult for the Jews. Jews
believed God communicated by means of agents.
These might be prophets, or superhuman beings.
Cilla tells us that in Jesus God communicates with
us directly, person to person, sharing our human
existence. Later she will explain how God experiences every aspect of our lives in Jesus.

Thank you, God, for speaking to us right where we are.

John Henson   God still speaks

Jesus thought highly of 'Voice', the anonymous prophet recorded in Isaiah chapters 40–66. His pitch was the exile, when the flower of Hebrew leadership and intelligentsia were captives in Babylon. Babylon was soon to fall to the Persian conqueror Cyrus, who would allow the Jews to return home. The prophet had been made a slave, castrated, scantily dressed with his buttocks exposed, to become a eunuch in the house of a courtier. He was highly gifted, writing poetry that he sang as he played a small harp. He surmounts the experience of bitterness with a message of confidence in God. He brings together three ways in which God speaks: in the cosmos (verse 13); in the progress of history (verses 14–16) and in relationship with a community (verses 17–21).

God has not spoken in secret

Isaiah 48:12–21

Christian thinking has neglected the God of history and the God of the physical universe, catching only a fraction of God's revelation. God is not only God in the time capsule we have made for ourselves. God is God of everything that exists. If we took that on board we would exploit our environment less and respect it more. We would not treat animals as inferior beings. We would honour not just the lives of Christian saints, but the ancestors from whom we have evolved over millions of years, as well as our cousins from other cultures and religions. Cyrus was not a member of 'God's chosen people', but God was revealed through him.

God, help us to tune into more channels.

God still speaks   John Henson

God's power to speak and save

Isaiah 46:3–13

The Jews in exile encountered the full force of an idolatrous religion and a hedonist culture. For some it was highly shocking, for others alluring. Though the images of the gods were expensive to make and heavy to carry, and could impress by their size and glitter, they did nothing for the life of the worshipper. The culture they symbolised was that of brute force and the pursuit of material wealth and pleasure. In contrast, the God of Israel had no image. Instead of the size and impressiveness by which so often we human beings forge our values, this God has personality.

God is the mother who cradles the child who has emerged from her womb. God is the modern father who shares in the parenting. Our parents grow old and we have to learn to do without them. God continues to act the ideal parent into our old age. It is a beautiful picture.

Some people today reject the idea that God is personal. God is some kind of impersonal force. But I believe a god without personality represents regress not progress. The danger is a spirituality that is materialism in disguise. God is more than personal, but not less than personal. God speaks and we can listen. God cuddles us like a mum or dad when we need it, and we can feel those arms around us and sense that they are eternal.

Thank you, God, that though you are beyond our imagination, you are not beyond our touch.

Here the prophet uses anthropomorphic language. That is, he describes God in language of human understanding. Some say this should not be done. God is indescribable. What's this about God going through divorce proceedings, or having creditors? What sort of hand does God have? Yet this is the language the prophet uses. It is not just a matter of using poetry to convey truth (though poetry being allusive can open doors that cannot be opened by logic). It is a matter of translating God's communication into language human beings can understand.

God teaches us to hear and speak

Isaiah 50:1–11

It may not be possible to understand a Russian novel to the full unless you are able to read it in the Russian language. But a good translator will do their best and may come close. We do not say that because the Christian scriptures were written in Greek, no one of another tongue can hope to grasp their message. The reason human beings with the gift translate what is meant by God into human language is because they have experienced God speaking and want others to experience God speaking too. This is why I, one of many, have devoted much of my life to translating the Christian scriptures into language that people today can understand.

My father preached at my ordination on verse 4 of today's reading. The Hebrew means not 'teacher' but 'one who is taught'. Translators must not only know the text, they must continually listen to the audience.

Give me the tongue of one who is being taught.

God still speaks   John Henson

Listen that we may live

Isaiah 55:1–7

'You don't get something for nothing!' Consumerist society is anxiety ridden. Was that really a bargain or have I been swindled? That expensive item, could I have got it cheaper somewhere else? The prophet stands in the Babylonian marketplace and sets out in song God's stall. Free gifts for all!

This is the New Testament gospel in the Hebrew scriptures. Stop trying to get, to achieve, to impress. God has something better on offer. God offers friendship, for ever and a day. You can have a relationship with God, just as David did. David behaved very badly at times. But he and God remained mates to the end.

It's up to you. If you wish an end to the hunger you express in desire for things or the admiration of others, then this is it. Let the things of God be your favourite food and drink. Sounds too good to be true, which is why the offer is so rarely taken at face value, even by religious people. Especially not when it comes to God's offer of forgiveness. God stipulates no demonstrations of remorse or promises of future good behaviour. Just come home! Christendom has never been happy with God in this respect. If God won't do it, we will. We'll make them miserable! Longer sentences for criminals! But stop to think how we would like to pay the full penalty for our wrongdoing, and perhaps we will then be grateful God is the way God is!

God, I accept your offer.

John Henson   God still speaks

The prophet goes on to explain why God offers everything for free. God does not look at things the way we do. Once we understand that God's love is unconditional, we realise that rules like the Ten Commandments are a grateful response to God's way that we have adopted for ourselves. There is everything right with responding to God with controlled behaviour to keep our selfishness at bay, as long as we realise that God's love is of a higher order than something we can earn and elicit by what we do. God loves people who do not keep our rules. Rules may be amended, improved, scrapped. But since God's thoughts and ways are always higher than ours, they can never be permanently codified or tied up in a creed or rulebook.

Because of our experience of God in Jesus, we know that the 'Word' referred to by the prophet is love. He is not suggesting that this word is irresistible, though God has eternity within which to work. The picture of the rain falling and teasing out growth in shoot and bud is a gentle one. God co-operates with the farmer and invites but does not compel the hungry to eat.

Again we see that the sphere in which God operates is not one of narrow religiosity or human arrogance. The mountains sing and the trees applaud. Firs and bramble bushes respond to God's word.

All creatures of our God and King, lift up your voice and with us sing.

Creating abundance for the people

Isaiah 55:8–13

God's word is fulfilled

Zechariah 1:1–6

Zechariah is a bit of a comedown from 'Voice' (as the prophet of Babylon called himself in Isaiah 40:3). Zechariah was part of the fulfilment of Voice's prophesy. Some keen Israelites returned to Jerusalem and established something like a devolved state. This didn't happen by God waving a magic wand. Voice needed to get others to share his vision, organise interest groups and lobby politicians at the Persian court. God works in co-operation. If we don't do our part, nothing gets done. God also works with all levels of competence. Voice is a high point in the Hebrew scriptures: Zechariah is a poor successor.

Voice portrays God setting out a free banquet, inviting all to come. Zechariah reverts to a God who will 'only return to you if you return to me'. The words are similar to Voice's words perhaps, but the tone is very different. We are back to a peevish, threatening God, courtesy of God's less spiritually discerning prophet. The window Voice opened to the refreshing view of the New Covenant was shut again. The God of the restored Jewish community would not be the inclusive God who, according to Voice, would welcome those of other nations and sexual variants into the full privileges of the covenant (see Isaiah 56). Voice is the Hebrew prophet who most looks forward to the coming of Jesus. His hopes are still some way from being fully realised in the Church.

God, attract my attention to the highest expressions of your word.

John Henson   God still speaks

God still speaks

2 Pay attention!

Preparing for the week

When I was at college preparing for the ordained ministry, our talents as preachers were tested among the churches. How they suffered! We were supposed to be like the prophets, bringing a message. Alas, we knew a bit of Greek, but little about life. My parents lived in Bovey Tracey on the edge of Dartmoor. My father was minister of the Baptist church, and I sometimes preached for him. More often I preached at the little branch church up the valley in Lustleigh. It always seemed to have a membership of about three ladies in their eighties. I went back ten years later and there were still three ladies in their eighties, only a different three. But what I remember most was what confronted me when I went into the pulpit. In front of me next to the Bible were the words 'Sirs, we would see Jesus' (John 12:21, King James Version).

This week we continue to explore through scripture what is meant by God's word. The expression 'Word of God' carries with it many possibilities. We find that some of these occur frequently, and that God still speaks in those ways today. But those old ladies were so right. There is one way above all that God speaks to the Christian and that is through Jesus – by looking at him as much as by listening. If you forget about him when you are preaching, then however hard you thumb or thump the Bible, the message will be out of true.

Help us to see Jesus.

Notes based on the New Revised Standard Version and the *Good as New* version (O Books, 2005) by

John Henson

For John's biography, see p. 1

Let me hear what God will speak

Psalm 85: 8–13

This psalm seems to be a form of worship for a gathering of those Jewish people who had returned from Babylon to Jerusalem. As today, such forms of service would be worked out by a priest, probably in conjunction with musicians and songsters. We presume the priest had also listened sensitively to the concerns of the worshippers. When anyone produced a piece of work of this kind that was deemed suitable for regular worship, it would have been copied out and preserved. It has a recognisable liturgical form. It begins with grateful acknowledgement of what God had done in the past (verses 1–3). Then follows a plea for God's forgiveness in view of the people's fear of God's wrath. The restoration of right relationship with God is on offer. Health and vitality will flow to the community (verses 4–7). Then the opportunity is given to a prophet to speak. Maybe it was Zechariah or Haggai (verses 8–9). Finally, the priest pens a few words of blessing for the people before they leave, which probably he will say himself (verses 10–13). The people will leave with a sense of confidence that God is again with them and on their side, and with a challenge to righteous living.

We are familiar with this kind of pattern. We must not forget our spiritual pioneers who realised the necessity for well thought out worship that would answer the needs of the worshipper.

Let me be ready to hear what God will speak.

It is unlikely that Paul wrote 1 & 2 Timothy. The Greek is different from Paul's, and so is the theology. Someone attached Paul's name to their work. In the ancient world this would have been regarded as an act of humility. The works include snatches from personal letters Paul wrote to his friend. Maybe it was Timothy himself who wrote the letters to other Christian leaders. As Paul included Timothy in the authorship of his letters, why might not Timothy have ascribed his work to Paul, his teacher?

Learn from scripture and example

2 Timothy 3: 10–17

Today's chapter ends with words which have been misused to argue for the infallibility of the Bible. The Bible as we know it had not even been compiled when 2 Timothy was written. 'All scripture' means 'all sacred writing', and should include not only ancient Hebrew and early Christian writings, but also all other sacred writings since those times. No sacred writings are infallible. They have been inspired by God's Spirit and written down by human beings. They are all useful. All we have to do to turn any good book into God's words for today is to ask the question 'What would Jesus make of this?' Then use the Spirit's gift of imagination. She inspired the writer in the first place. In that way God has spoken to me through John Bunyan, C S Lewis, J K Rowling, Philip Pullman and *Torchwood*!

Remind me, Spirit of God, that the only person you can do nothing with is the person with a closed mind.

God still speaks   John Henson

We must pay attention

Hebrews 2:1–4

So we need to keep aware of this new way God is speaking to us, otherwise we will lose all sense of direction. People always get into trouble when they ignore what God's agents tell them. If we take no notice of this new venture on our behalf, we're asking for big trouble. The Leader announced a fresh start for the world. Those who got the message passed it on to us. God has backed up their report by being active in events, helping us to do amazing things and discover new talents from God's Spirit.

Good as New, p. 433

Cilla is not at her best when she sounds the note of warning. But listen to what she says here. Ignorance and prejudice are not your fault *unless* you cling to them after enlightenment has been proffered. Then you are in grave danger.

Sometimes the message we learn from scripture is what not to do. Cilla was a fan of Jesus. She wanted to share him with others. It came as a shock that some did not respond to her zeal. Where she failed to enthuse, she then tried to frighten. This is never very effective. It shows lack of empathy for the reluctant convert, who may need space. Perhaps the word of God in this scripture is that we should not allow what seems failure to seduce us into negativity.

May I treat others not as recipients of my opinion but as those who may correct it.

John Henson   God still speaks

Today, if you hear,
Don't plug up your ear;
You did, once and more,
In desert days before.
Though helped for generations,
You people tried my patience.
I swore to every one,
'You'll miss out on the fun!'

Be willing to listen

Hebrews 3:7–14

Keep thinking about that word 'today' in the song. We're business partners of God's Chosen, but only provided we have the same confidence in the firm at the end as when we joined! When the song condemns those who were deaf in olden times, who do you think it refers to? It must have been God's former partners from Egypt. Moses was in charge of them. After forty years, God was fed up to the teeth with them. Because of the things they did wrong, some never got out of the desert alive.
Good as New, p. 435

Some Jewish Christians were hankering after yesterday. Cilla tells them, 'Today' is the buzzword. God promised the Israelites a holiday at the end of their journeys, what is meant by 'Shalom' (peace within and without). They lost out on points! Today's offer is a partnership with God, based not on points but on trust – our confidence in God and God's confidence in us. As business partners with Jesus, God trusts us to be creative. Shalom is not hereafter but in the trust.

Help us face the challenge of today.

God still speaks   John Henson

I AM has sent me to you

Exodus 3:13–18

We have been thinking about God's word. But God is more than word. God is 'Being'. God has a name and relates to those to whom the name is revealed. The Hebrew 'Yahweh' means 'I am', 'I am who I am' and 'I will be who I will be'. 'I am' is the unchangeable, eternal nature of God. 'I am who I am' means God beyond human understanding. 'I will be who I will be' means God the 'living God'.

God is not static but kinetic. That which is living grows and moves, as Genesis 1 makes clear. God enjoys being alive. Every stage of evolution is a new thrill. God has no intention of getting bored or being a bore. God called Abraham to adventure. God calls Moses and the Israelites to freedom. They are not on their own. God is in on the action!

God hates to see people enslaved and instigates a liberation movement. God is doing this all the time in a world where there are so many types of slavery. God has agents everywhere, but needs more. God needs to get more involved in freeing those trapped in the sex trade against their will, those who are economically and socially trapped and those who cannot get over past mistakes, waiting for someone to befriend them. And perhaps we should add 'those who are trapped by inflexible forms of religion and belief that, instead of liberating the soul, make it prisoner'.

Help me, Living God, to set people free.

In the beginning God spoke. This is just like God – part of the way God is. Everything there is comes from God speaking; otherwise there would be nothing at all. God speaking brought into being the life and intelligence we all share . . . The one who made the world appeared in the world, but the world paid no attention . . . From his superstore we have received one good gift after another. Moses gave us rules and regulations: Jesus, God's representative, gave us true love. No one has ever seen God, but the one faithful likeness who shares God's nature has shown us what God is like.

Good as New, p. 82

In the beginning was the Word

John 1:1–18

These words, which open 'Good News from Sources Close to Jesus', sum up our thinking these last two weeks. God speaks, God communicates, God relates – in the universe, in life and intelligence, and through special messengers like 'John the Dipper'. Supremely, God speaks by means of a human personality, someone who speaks to us not only in words but also in the flesh. In Jesus we get to know God as far as it is possible for humankind to know the unknowable God. Jesus is like the son who is a spitting image of his father, or as Cilla puts it, 'like a lifelike sculpture' (*Good as New*, p. 432). It is only through Jesus that we come to know that the essential nature of God is love, and what true love is.

Teach us, God, to test every word against your Word Jesus.

God still speaks   John Henson

Attitudes to suffering

1 From anger to trust

Notes based on the New Revised Standard Version by

Geoffrey Herbert

Geoffrey Herbert is a retired Anglican priest in Birmingham, UK, now with a ministry of listening and speaking about our spiritual journeys. He is a grandfather. He occasionally writes poetry and includes some in these notes.

Preparing for the week

This Sunday starts the Week of Prayer for Christian Unity (in the northern hemisphere). That seems odd when our theme is suffering, but Christian divisions and conflicts have produced a lot of suffering. Conflicts between religions do too. So that kind of suffering will never be far from our thoughts this week, alongside all the rest.

In our Bible passages we draw on the Old and New Testaments. Our attitudes and beliefs about our afflictions have traces of both: we can't assume that, as Christians, we have somehow 'grown out' of the Old Testament. At times it can give voice to our feelings as well as to deep faith. Look at Lamentations 3:4–15 – the words could be written by someone in depression or with a terminal illness today.

Christians also draw on a message of hope like that found in Revelation 21:1–4, but the road to that kind of hope often passes through dark places. This week we shall look at some waymarks on the road, not hurrying on to shallow con-solation. The Lord has a real hope in store for us because Jesus has walked our way and shares our hardest times. That blessing often comes not in trite words but after a struggle like Jacob's (Genesis 32:22–31).

This very human psalm is full of the anger of the abandoned faithful, like Job's. Often, taking the funeral of someone who has suffered terribly or died young, I have voiced this kind of anger on behalf of a family feeling a huge sense of assault and injustice. Grief and anger are two sides of the same knife-blade. The psalms of searing hurt give us permission to confront God with our anger and ask 'Why?'

Having it in for God

Psalm 44:13–26

Psalm 44 and others like it take us beyond our own anger, justified though that may be. They come from the Exile in Babylon, when Jewish thinkers agonised over why God had allowed the destruction of Jerusalem and its temple. Again and again they refer to the derision and shame that they feel. This is horribly close to what the descendants of the Exile must have felt in the cattle trucks and the concentration camps – a sense of being unjustly rejected and also treated as trash by those who saw themselves as the master race. Palestinians no doubt feel something akin to that today.

In my own country there are many people who feel belittled and even scorned: the poor, the disabled, and those who come from other cultures, particularly those who feel at the mercy of the powerful or ignored by the privileged.

Bring before God your own questions 'Why?', and also someone you know who feels rejection and scorn as in Psalm 44.

Attitudes to suffering   Geoffrey Herbert

'May they rot in hell'

Psalm 73:1–20

Another human psalmist! He says what he feels he ought to think, but is aware that hard realities make him waver (verses 1–3) and undermine his belief that God looks after good people (verses 13–14).

He sounds like a brother of Job, protesting his innocence and sense of injustice, but switches to being a Job's comforter in saying piously that the self-satisfied and arrogant will come to a sticky end. They can do of course – the Hitlers, the Saddams – yet so often, like fat-cat bankers, they seem to do very well for themselves. What do you think?

I can't stop thinking of a woman who was trafficked into Britain by a powerful and respected man in her country assuring her that it was all legal, and who was then abandoned to a nightmarish network of ruthless men who exploited her in many terrible ways. They all profited and she was wrecked. All she has is the knowledge of her innocence, her love for her children for whom she did it all, and her faith.

May her abusers be 'destroyed in a moment, swept away utterly by terrors' (verse 19)! But then another prayer comes: for them to be faced with what they did, really see it, and give up an evil way of life that is destroying so many. And of course the other prayer is for her healing and her home-coming: in that there will be resurrection, because she has walked the way of Jesus.

Pray your own prayer.

Geoffrey Herbert   Attitudes to suffering

Ruth vows to stay alongside Naomi, who feels abandoned by God: a vow in the dark, whose power is not in a guaranteed outcome but rather in simply offering real friendship.

Finding our Naomi

Ruth 1:1–18

The woman I mentioned yesterday has been befriended. The terrible wounds can't be wiped away; the only healing at present is from the love that stays alongside, and then from a canny practical help in piloting her through a legal and human minefield. Both are like Ruth's tenderness and calculating resourcefulness (read the rest of the story). This befriending is being repeated again and again in other situations, but not nearly enough. Any of us may need it, too.

That befriending is one sort. Another is when sufferers befriend their own demons and the demons of those who have afflicted them. Jesus wanted to know the names of demons, and he knew that they wanted somewhere to live – no hate there, but a strange kind of care. That whole way of thought is alien to many in the West (though not in other cultures). To me it speaks of a need to face, to identify and to care for the torment that is in us. That's a long journey: it may take a short time or a lifetime. The woman I've mentioned is on it, and again Jesus shares it and has gone on ahead.

The first kind of befriending may help the second. It's all about acceptance.

Lord, help me to befriend others and myself.

Attitudes to suffering   Geoffrey Herbert

New sight makes an apostle

John 9:1–17

'What have I done to deserve this?' is a frequent response to affliction. Jesus' reply would be, 'Nothing, but it has happened so that God's works might be revealed in you.'

The story has deep layers. The title 'light of the world' echoes John's prologue in chapter 1; the mud from dust echoes God's creation of Adam (Genesis 2:7); the blind man 'washing' himself may signify baptism; the Greek 'sent', translating 'Siloam', perhaps echoes 'sent' in verse 4; also it has the same root as 'apostle' – the man will become an apostle for Jesus. In the sequel to today's story he progressively increases in courage to witness to Jesus, moving from 'a prophet' in verse 17 to a recognition of Jesus as Son of Man in verse 38, using the words 'Lord, I believe' and worshipping him.

Truly God's works are revealed in this man's healing. All healings have that possibility. My heart disease was substantially 'healed' by a bypass operation over twenty years ago: seven years after it I had to take early retirement because symptoms returned, but since then I have had a new ministry in spirituality for over ten more years. I really believe the whole of this is healing, even though I still have heart disease. I wholeheartedly thank God.

We can all look in our suffering for the silent work of God in transforming us and making us into apostles for Jesus.

Lord, give us new sight.

Geoffrey Herbert   Attitudes to suffering

Paul is in an anti-boasting mood: people in his church are challenging his credentials and quoting their own dramatic spiritual experiences. He says, in effect, 'I've had my own spiritual peaks, but I don't boast about them.' Then he tells the story of some affliction that he has which God hasn't cured. This, he says, is where true spiritual power is – in our weakness, the way of Christ's own suffering.

We and people we know or hear about all have times like this – times of helplessness, loss, pain, fear. They are pits of darkness. When we're in one, it feels like Gethsemane, a place where we desperately don't want to be. Yet, even in there, crying out like Jesus or Paul, we may be able make our own song:

The song of weakness

2 Corinthians 12: 1–10

The Pit
Heart of darkness,
strange place where fear lives
and looks back at me with compassion,
the face of blood and thorns
and, incredibly, smiles.
The Pit which I must revisit
for my hope and what love I have to give,
to join in the song of weakness
and the prayer for deliverance from evil,
the Compline at the day's rest,
the new day's root in this night,
the necessary little dying
as far as I can bear it,
dark double edge of trusting.

A Muslim neighbour of ours, in great suffering, prayed to God, 'Show me your mercy, whatever happens.' I was humbled, and felt he was singing the song of weakness.

Pray that man's prayer.

Attitudes to suffering   Geoffrey Herbert

The song of weakness goes on

Romans 8:18–28

Another poem, a fragment:

Stay here
don't force yourself, though
be as kind as you need
and as tough as you need
to stay here a while
be compassionate towards your core
your tender wobbly hermit core
love it
let it be loved
let it love
by any touch
yours, hers, his, theirs, its
hold out your hand
into the tunnel
towards the child
the laughter
the tune

As Paul says, in all suffering, despite the futility and anger, there is a great hope. It has to do not only with our own little bits of suffering, but is a share in the groaning and birthing of the whole created order. In God's strange way an ultimate deliverance waits on our obedience and endurance. We and all suffering things are on the cross and in that is the great hope.

This is an eternal song. It starts in our time, our bodies, our groaning. It is the song of the Spirit in us, beyond words, not in our control or effort, like a childbirth straining to happen. In a way we just have to let it happen, learning when to rest and wait; in another way we have to go with it, learning when to 'push'.

Lord, make us tender to ourselves as you are to us. Open us to the 'now' of our sufferings, and in your good time disclose to us the hope that hides there, for us and everything.

Geoffrey Herbert   Attitudes to suffering

Attitudes to suffering

2 Your will be done

Preparing for the week

It is very hard for believers, those who are faithful to God, to face up to difficulties and obstacles in life. Health problems, crisis in family, losses of different kinds like the death of a beloved person, unemployment, financial crisis – these are all examples of difficulties in life that can be a reality to many people, including those who have faith and follow God's paths. 'Why?' is the question that first comes to most people in such situations. And more: 'Why does God allow me to endure such problems when I am his son/daughter?' A frequent answer that may help is 'It is the will of God.' Certainly Jesus taught us to pray 'Your will be done' (Matthew 6:10), and he himself understood his suffering as the will of God (Luke 22:39–46). What does this really mean and how can we apply it in times of suffering? How should we react when suffering comes to us? The Bible readings for this week will help us to find at least the beginnings of an answer.

Notes based on the New King James Version by

Magali do Nascimento Cunha

Magali do Nascimento Cunha is a Brazilian Methodist, a journalist and an educator. She is a professor of Ecumenism and Church and Society at the Methodist School of Theology in Sao Paulo, Brazil. She has also been involved in several projects on Christian education, and on ecumenism in different communities.

Testing brings maturity

James 1:2–16

James writes to Christian communities facing trials. Persecution by the Roman Empire, and the experience of *Diaspora* that forced families to disperse to distant lands in order to preserve both their lives and their faith in Christ, were the cause of deep pain. James brings a new perspective to these Christians' suffering. Instead of explaining it as punishment or God's forgetfulness, the writer invites them to look at their situation with joy because good things may emerge from it.

First, suffering is seen as a test of patience that results in perseverance. Second, exercising perseverance promotes a search for wisdom based on faith, and the writer is in no doubt that God accompanies his children in the difficult moments (verse 5). Further, suffering is seen as a temptation, but never from God. The writer recognises that everyone is liable to temptations, but they are blessed who endure them: 'for when he/she has been approved, he/she will receive the crown of life which the Lord has promised to those who love Him' (verse 12, adapted). A similar message is written by John from prison to the churches under persecution (see Revelation 2:10).

What may we learn today from this experience and teachings? Patience and the search for wisdom are the source of joy in times of difficulties. Living like this, we may become blessed and mature Christians.

God, source of all mercy and strength, be our sustainer in times of suffering, pain and fear. In the name of Jesus, who endured temptations and kept firm in his commitment to the Father.

Who has never been submitted to injustice in life? Perversity, actions of violence and evil over those who do right are likely to be the experience of Christians at some stage of our lives. The most natural response to being wronged is revenge – retaliating with the same treatment that we have received. However, today's passage – addressed to Christians in the *Diaspora*, persecuted and displaced – is that this is not the true attitude of a disciple. On the contrary, the writer advocates those who experience such treatment to keep patience with no thought of revenge or violent action, 'for this is commendable, if because of conscience toward God one endures grief, suffering wrongfully' (verse 19).

Not returning abuse

1 Peter 2:18–25

The passage points to the example of Christ, whose steps his followers should follow. 'When he was reviled, he did not revile in return; when he suffered, he did not threaten, but committed himself to him who judges righteously' (verse 23). Jesus' actions in times of persecution and suffering were consistent with his teachings: love one's enemies, turn the other cheek when slapped, and so on (Mathew 5:39, 43).

No one is saying this is easy. However, can we be called Christians without following in the steps of our master? And the passage hints at how we may do this: 'For you were like sheep going astray, but have now returned to the Shepherd and Overseer of your souls' (verse 25).

Dear Lord, it is not easy to follow your steps, especially in times when we face sufferings. You, who faced death as part of your commitment, give us the opportunity to be your faithful disciples and good friends.

Leave vengeance to God

Romans 12:9–21

Yesterday, our reflection on the first letter of Peter led us to dwell on how to avoid returning abuse. Today, Paul keeps us on this track. He himself knew very well what it means to suffer: he was a prisoner because of the gospel when he wrote to the Romans (see Romans 1:1); had faced a strong and unjust conflict with the church leadership in Corinth (see 2 Corinthians); and we know that he had to live with suffering (a 'thorn in his flesh') despite his claims to relief from God (as in 2 Corinthians 12:7–10), among many other situations that he refers to in his writings.

In the letter to the Romans, Paul presents a list of attitudes that teach us how to behave as Christians. Paul teaches that Christians need to rejoice in hope, to be patient in tribulation, continue steadfastly in prayer; bless those who persecute them; bless and not curse; repay no one evil for evil; not to avenge themselves, but rather lay aside wrath; not to be overcome by evil, but overcome evil with good (verses 12, 14, 21). Paul insists: if a thought of revenge comes, leave it to God, it belongs to God (according to Deuteronomy 32:35, quoted by Paul). Congruence with Christ: this is what the apostles searched for in their teachings and attitudes. And this is also our goal.

Lord, make me an instrument of your peace;
where there is hatred, let me sow love;
where there is injury, pardon;
where there is doubt, faith;
where there is despair, hope;
where there is darkness, light;
and where there is sadness, joy.

from the Prayer of St Francis

'Do not be afraid' is a message that permeates the whole book of Revelation (see examples in 1:17 and 2:10). It is amazing that many people see in this book the precise opposite: the preparation of a future of God's vengeance and punishment. However, when we pay attention to the message of this letter, written in times when Christians were threatened by the Roman Empire, we see John's attempt to rekindle the flame of hope and courage in those who were perhaps frightened and overwhelmed. The message of John, who was in prison, is all the time encouraging patience and renewal of hope. Chapter 22 speaks to the communities in despair – and brings to us today – one of the most beautiful images of the book: the land irrigated by the river of life and nurtured by the tree of life, waters that bring relief and refreshment and leaves that are there to heal all suffering and pain.

What a wonderful word of hope! How can we be afraid and in despair when there is a promise like this spoken into our situation? Our God's eyes are not closed to our suffering; God's justice includes times for relief and healing, not only for individuals but also for nations.

The nations will be healed too

Revelation 22:1–7

Loving God, on this Holocaust Memorial Day, help us to renew our hope in your promise. Help us to know that you are ready to spread the leaves of your tree of life to heal the suffering of your children and all nations that suffer injustice in our world.

Attitudes to suffering   Magali do Nascimento Cunha

Love casts out fear

1 John 4:7–21

Yesterday, we reflected on the book of Revelation, recalling the difficulties that faced Christian communities, and which prompted the letter, also remembering that the author himself, John, was in prison. Those times were very hard for Christians: prohibition to express publicly their faith, persecution, prisons, displacement. It is perhaps difficult for us to imagine the situation they faced, but it is not difficult to imagine the fear they must have daily struggled with: the fear of being imprisoned, fear of death, fear of losing their homes and possessions, fear of losing family, and so on. And all this because of faith.

It is not difficult to understand why the writings of the earliest Christians insist time and time again on the overcoming of fear. How many passages in the Gospels can you recollect that show Jesus challenging the disciples to overcome fear? See, for example, Mark 4:35–40, Luke 1:29–30, John 20:19–23. In all the New Testament writings, fear is the opposite of faith and love. According to the first epistle of John, 'There is no fear in love. But perfect love drives out fear, because fear has to do with punishment. The one who fears is not made perfect in love' (1 John 4:18). Therefore, as John says, if we are in God, as God is love, we are in love too, overcoming all fear. Love is the way against all fear.

The Lord is my light and my salvation – whom shall I fear? The Lord is the stronghold of my life – of whom shall I be afraid?

Psalm 27:1

Magali do Nascimento Cunha   Attitudes to suffering

One of the most important attitudes to cultivate in our life of faith is the attitude of prayer. Prayer is the way of keeping communion with God and renewing God's presence in the whole of our life. Through prayer, we learn to understand the will of God in our lives and we express to God who we are and what are our dreams, fears and anxieties. In our communion with God, our hope is renewed and we find courage to live positively, despite all the obstacles we face.

Your will be done

Luke 22:39–46

It is wonderful to get a glimpse of the prayer-life of Jesus, through the testimony of the Gospels. When the disciples asked him to teach them how to pray (see Luke 11:1–4 and Matthew 6:9–13), Jesus gave them the Lord's Prayer. He taught them to think of God not as an exclusive God but as a father of all people, One who is worthy of exaltation, whose will is always good, even when we cannot understand it. Jesus not only spoke about this but also taught it through his own life.

Today's passage shows Jesus at perhaps the most difficult moment of his entire life: facing imprisonment, close to death, prayer was for him the support he drew on to confront that hard situation. So a prayer-life may be for us also the cultivation of the entering into the will of God, especially in times of doubt, suffering and despair. Through prayer we may learn to overcome the temptations of fear and capitulation.

Pray the Lord's Prayer, slowly and thoughtfully.

Readings in Galatians

1 One gospel for all God's people

Notes based on
the New Revised
Standard Version
by
**Erice
Fairbrother**

Erice Fairbrother is an
Anglican priest in
New Zealand and an
Associate of the Order
of the Holy Cross. She
is a reader and writer
in feminist theology,
poet and liturgist,
with work published
in New Zealand and
overseas. After being
a Missioner for five
years in a mission as
poor as the people it
served, Erice moved
to the Bay of Plenty,
where she is Vicar in
the parish of
Otumoetai.

Preparing for the week

Over the coming week, we follow Paul as he calls
the Galatians to remain faithful to their original
embrace of the gospel. This call comes out of a
context of debate and threats of division in the
Church of that time. The context has parallels in
our own time, where debates and threats of
division continue to confuse the true priority of the
good news. During the week we discover hints and
directions which help us rediscover that priority:
that the good news is not ours to cast in our own
image, but is always for the sake of the other – the
poor, the vulnerable, the least among us. At one
point Paul acknowledges that the request to
remember the poor is a priority he is 'eager to do'
(Galatians 2:10).

As Paul calls the Galatians, we too are called to
see, to notice, to remain faithful to the life we have
chosen, and to live it in such a way that it makes a
difference, a difference that will be found in our
freedom and unity.

In New Zealand there is a saying: if we want to move forward, we must first look back to see what we value from the past, in order to move into the future. We must pay attention to where we have come from, to carry into the future the ability to honour the revelation we first received, and the relationships which have helped us to live into that revelation.

In the world in which we live, everything is tested. Nothing can be taken for granted; ethics and values seem to be tied to current trends, to the situations we find ourselves in. Yet it is here that we can turn with confidence to the evidence of our past experiences, to the people who have been signposts on our journey thus far. As we look back at times of confusion, of uncertainty about the future, we can recall times when we had confidence and a sense of possibility in our relationship to Christ. To remember is to recognise that we have the capacity to be confident anew, to face challenges, to have vision and hope.

Knowing who we are, recalling whose we are, remembering those who have been with us on our journey, is a place of strength. From this place, we can become more completely who we are called to be.

Looking back, moving forward

Galatians 1:1–12

I long to become more fully who I was created to be; may I never forget the ground of my being, and be always thankful.

They glorified God because of me

Galatians 1:13–24

Our lives describe the journey we have been travelling since birth. It is in the very journey itself that the truth of who God is, in us, with us and for us, is revealed. Contexts and content will change, relationships can twist and turn, some may disappear from view. Yet there is a consistency at the heart of this living, patterns among the places and people, which earth us and keep us alive to ourselves and to others. In times of reflection, of pause and renewal, the eternal truth of our living comes into focus. In these moments, the truth of where God is, and indeed has always been, becomes undeniable.

Perhaps this is why we tell family stories, why lives of saints and sinners hold our attention and fascinate us. In the telling of their journey the light and shadowing of something greater than them alone emerges. Perhaps that is why our own journey begins to have meaning. Something greater than ourselves emerges. Something other than us is revealed.

Neither dogma nor creed will build faith. The building blocks of faith are earthed in the gift of our life and its living. When we see this life in someone else, we see God. As you and I live this life, God is seen in us.

May the journey of my life reveal the truth of God within me, so that others may see and come to know it in their own lives too.

The first time I met Tai he was waiting at the door of the Mission for the Food Bank to open. With tattoos that spoke of time in prison, Tai spoke quietly of his five children under 6, abandoned by their mother, and left with him. Tai had given up his job to care for them, and gone on a state benefit. From a life supported by mates and his gang, Tai was now alone at home, struggling to give the basic best to his children. Tai continued to come to the Mission for over a year, the food parcels becoming less important than the friendship and support he found in our community life.

True priority

Galatians 2:1–10

Tai's story is repeated in many places. It is the story of the poor, the unloved and the modern outcasts. They wait for us to see them. The Church in our time is racked with controversies that would seduce us away from the call to make the poor our priority. Our small Mission was often conflicted about what was right or wrong, but in the end our unity was always refound when we returned to prioritising the care of the poor. Paul found unity in such service. Following his concern about the controversy raging in Galatia, we find he responds without hesitation to the call to remember the poor. This is what ultimately matters. This is the priority that leads to peace and unity.

Teach me to remember the poor, to see and to serve.

The life within

Galatians 2:11–21

To visit a Marae, in New Zealand, is to enter into a different cultural world. It is a place where issues can be talked through, conflict opened up and discussed, agreements negotiated, and relationships restored. It all happens in the greetings, in meeting and in the sharing of food together. How different from the way it works in our wider society. We non-Maori have built a society filled with legal regulations, competitive and combative values, leaving little room for relational interaction and personal priorities.

The Christ story calls us to look to community life that is built on relational values. Paul describes this as the life of faith, as 'the Christ who lives in me' (verse 20). To seek life-giving relationships is to seek Christ. To commit to building life-giving communities is to choose relationship based on social values. The law can never replace the call on us, as Christians, to take responsibility for creating and maintaining a safe and sustainable society. Neither secular laws nor church laws can ever excuse us from the call to live the life that we find in Christ. It takes faith – faith in one another. It takes trust – trust in our neighbour. It takes love – love of the unloved and those who reject it.

May I seek to live a life that is not about doing the right thing because I should, but because of the love and faith and trust that lives in the deepest part of me.

Erice Fairbrother   Readings in Galatians

The Rule of St Benedict is full of exceptions. Over and over again, the Rule for community life is adjusted to become a source of freedom. The Abbot or Abbess is instructed to manage the monastic world in a way that sets everyone free to live the spiritual life, simply and with joy. Benedict's Rule, although part of an older Christian tradition, is still a source of freedom for those wanting to find new life in a world that tempts us to more and more cumbersome lifestyles. The Rule leads us to desire only that we have enough, not at the expense of one another, but so that all of us will be able to live in freedom.

Freedom in faith

Galatians 3:1–14

This is the radical edge of the spiritual life. It calls for self-giving, rather than self-enhancement. It keeps us conscious of our relationship to others. Our response to them justifies our right to claim to be of the tradition of life-givers, of a forgiving and reconciling faith. To live well but simply, to live well so all may be well, is to become a blessing. Faith born out of blessing is a faith that endures. It is a priceless gift. It comes without condition or condemnation. It is a faith that embodies the promise of new life. It comes with a call to be co-creators with God, building a new creation where freedom is the rule, not the exception.

Let my life be a blessing, my faith my freedom.

Readings in Galatians   Erice Fairbrother

Unity

Galatians 3:15–29

During summer in New Zealand, there are days when to look out to sea is to discover that the blue of sky and water have become one piece. The horizon, the point of difference, disappears, and the beach-gazer is enveloped in a moment of sheer beauty. There are days when at the top of a ridge after a long walk in the bush, all the varieties of tree and fern become a vision of green, in all its diversity, a single wash of colour, a unity glimpsed in a moment.

The desire for unity, for a peace created out of the beauty of our diversity and difference, is at the heart of social justice and love of neighbour. It is a unity that can catch the breath, something glimpsed in moments of clarity. To catch the view from afar, something that envelops us as we stop to reflect, is to be given a vision that continues within us like a prayer.

Paul takes us to a place where we can gaze into the sheer beauty of God's vision of unity. Here the things that so often divide us are named as the very things that are the source of our commonality. The diversity of culture and peoples, of issues, and of gender now becomes something whole and free and fulfilled. Paul gives a glimpse, a moment of possibility, a vision that, like a prayer, calls us to live it and so bring it to birth.

May the unity we long for be birthed in me.

Iain Roy   Readings in Galatians

Readings in Galatians

2 Freedom with the Holy Spirit

Preparing for the week

What does freedom mean for you? In prison, it's pretty obvious – it means 'getting out'. And likewise, perhaps, in a violent or abusive relationship. But in an oppressive state, or working under oppressive conditions, 'getting out' might mean freedom for you as an individual, but the real freedom will be overturning the tables of oppression for others. And, of course, there are less visible imprisonments – anxiety, fear and grief; addiction, loneliness. A healing freedom here will need time, and relationship, and growing trust.

'Freedom with the Spirit' must mean all of these, and even more: freedom *to do what the Spirit does* – to be able to 'love as naturally as I sneeze' (as one theology lecturer of mine once put it); freedom to be bearers of peace, justice and healing to our neighbours, our 'enemies', our world itself. Why, then, do we so often devalue freedom, imagining it little more than 'the space to do what I want'?

As Paul continues his letter to the Galatian Christians, he wrestles with those who demand conformity – to the 'old' practice of circumcision. But Paul's 'new' way is far from encouraging individualism. He invites his readers to a different kind of conformity – to the ways of the Spirit, ways which, we can be sure, exceed even Paul's imagination!

Notes based on the New Revised Standard Version by

Al Barrett

Al Barrett is a parish priest in Hodge Hill, Birmingham, in England. With his wife, Janey, they have a young son, Rafi. Alongside parish work, Al writes and teaches in the areas of child theology and liturgy.

'My little children . . .'

Galatians 4:1–20

I was as close as I could be to my wife as she laboured to bring our son, Rafi, to birth. It was a long, drawn-out process, with moments of considerable anxiety, and plenty of waiting, culminating in a climax of painful pushing, bloody mess and the tears of birth. And then, as the professionals left us to it, a growing sense of great responsibility, combined with an utter lack of expertise: 'What do we do now?!'

We've now had eighteen months of weaving, strand by strand, a web of love around Rafi, that enables him to trust, learn, take risks, grow. In friends who have fostered and adopted children, we've seen something even more painstaking: labouring with their children to dismantle walls of anxiety and mistrust, to allow rebuilding to begin.

Paul, too, knows something of the pain of childbirth and the perplexities of adoption. 'Until Christ is formed in you' (verse 19), he labours for the Galatians. There is much for them to *un*learn, and much to learn – in the intimate, 'gutsy', child-like sense of learning who, and how, to trust. Can they let go of their grasp on 'grown-up-ness', and dare to 'become like little children' (Matthew 18:3)? Dare they trust Paul to tell them the truth about themselves? Will they have the patience (with the messy, painful bits, and the sheer *time*) to let the Spirit unpick their unhealthy dependencies and instincts, and grow something new in them? Dare *we*?

Abba, Amma, you know me and love me.

Sometimes, we have to 'read against the text'. Here, the text reads against itself! 'Drive out the slave and her child,' echoes Paul, as if quoting words from God. But read the story in Genesis 21. The words, in fact, come from Sarah, Abraham's wife and Isaac's unlikely mother. And they are spoken out of insecurity, and quite possibly envy.

And just how did Ishmael, the son of Sarah's slave-girl Hagar, 'persecute' Isaac? Read the story. The worst crime he commits, it seems, is simply 'playing' with his half-brother. And what of God? Read the story. God journeys with Hagar and Ishmael through the wilderness, and blesses them with 'a nation' of descendants.

No doubt Paul's opponents claimed to be 'children of Abraham and Sarah'. So Paul, with emotive words and not entirely consistent logic, claims Sarah as his own, 'shoe-horns' her story to fit his own agenda, and insinuates to the Galatians: 'kick out those who threaten your security'.

It's a strategy we're not unfamiliar with. When we feel ourselves excluded, our sense of identity shaky, our boundaries blurred, it is tempting (and often, in the short term, quite effective) to draw the sharp contrasts, cling more tightly to our notions of 'us and them' (whoever 'they' might be), and retell old stories to serve our own ends and exclude others.

Dare Paul go a little deeper into his own 'there is no longer . . .' (Galatians 3:27) and embrace his enemies as brothers and sisters? Dare *we*?

Abba, Amma, teach me the love that crosses dividing lines.

Love slaves?

Galatians 5:2–15

Freedom means slavery. That is more than counter-cultural for us – it's counter-intuitive, almost nonsensical. And we might imagine Paul's first readers had a similar reaction. But this is where 'freedom' as we imagine it, and the 'freedom' that the Spirit stirs in us, turn out to be poles apart.

'Freedom as [the] opportunity for self-indulgence' (verse 13) could almost be a dictionary definition, in Western society. And its worst effects, as we know only too well, are that we end up 'biting and devouring one another' (verse 15). Freedom to consume leaves a trail of victims of consumption – not least the consumer her or himself. In contrast, Paul invites us to discover a freedom *from* such consumption – the freedom to love, through mutual service.

But be careful with such radical words. These are not commands to the already enslaved. They are not words of God to those living in violent, abusive or exploitative relationships. Here is an invitation to a community of people who are discovering what it means to honour one another as children of God. If it is 'slavery', then it is not slavery as we know it – entirely mutual, without hierarchy or inequality, and with the generous love of those who are coming into the inheritance of something vast, abundant, inexhaustible – and that needs no competing for.

'Through love become slaves to one another' (verse 13). Dare we experiment, in our communities, with something so dangerous? Dare we even imagine the possibility?

Abba, Amma, free me to love.

I'm a bit addicted to internet shopping. A click of the mouse, and I've got what I want . . . but then I want *more* . . . I'm fooled into imagining that things are running out fast (even time itself) – and that I need to get them before someone else does. Such 'works of the flesh' (verse 19), as Paul calls them, can tear at the fabric of relationships, of community.

'Tell me what you want, what you really, really want . . .'

Galatians 5:16–26

Last Lent in my church, one of our visiting speakers suggested that we, the church, often make the mistake of 'trying to offer people what the shops, cinemas, holidays offer them. But we're not in that game,' he said. 'There's something inevitably boring about the life of faith. Being bored is an important part of learning to be still enough to pray, to put up with people you really struggle to like, to learn stuff that doesn't make much sense when you're young, to sit with it even when you wonder what's the point and where's God?' (Gary Hall, 'Shopping Addiction and the Fantasy of Happiness', unpublished talk, 2009).

Dare we put a brake on our need for an instant 'buzz', and open ourselves to the 'long game' of the Christian life? Dare we put our pursuit of 'happiness' on hold – and pursue the 'fruit of the Spirit' (verse 22) instead? How might we draw others into wanting to nurture such things?

Abba, Amma, nurture in me love . . . joy . . . peace . . . patience . . . kindness . . . generosity . . . faithfulness . . . gentleness . . . self-control . . .

Imagine a community . . .

Galatians 6:1–10

Paul has spent long enough dismantling the edifice of 'rules'; surely he's not in the business of rebuilding it right here?! Over the years of the Christian Church, there have certainly been those who have seized on 'the law of Christ' as being just that. But rather than outlining a new set of rules to replace the old, Paul paints a picture of the 'character' of the Christian community.

Here, then, is a community where each member is encouraged to reflect critically on her own Christian practice, rather than measuring herself against others – but is alert, too, to the burdens others carry, and offers her shoulders to share them. Here is a community which longs for the restoration of those who go 'off the rails', but also pursues such restoration with gentleness above all. And here is a community which seeks the good of *all* God's creation, but will not let such a huge vision obscure the needs of the neighbour here, now.

Does that sound like your church? Yes? And No? It was just the same for Paul. If reality doesn't look completely like the picture he paints, then Paul here is trying to fire – and free – our imaginations for what *could* be. And when we dare to believe the impossible . . . we might just dare to try doing it!

Abba, Amma, fire our imaginations with your love, give us courage to experiment and gentleness when it goes wrong.

A friend of mine recently got a tattoo on her arm. The first and last verses of Psalm 139, in Hebrew. It's quite beautiful. And the process, my friend says, was both satisfying and cathartic. These marks of a particular moment are now engraved on her body for ever – but she feels different – freer, perhaps? – because of them.

Written on the body

Galatians 6:11–18

I don't think I've got the pain threshold – or perhaps the 'commitment threshold'? – to contemplate a tattoo, but I'm aware that my body carries its own markings: marks from growing up and growing older, from accidents and injuries, from encounters both welcome and unwelcome.

I'm aware, too, that many others in our world carry more profound and painful markings than me – and markings that, unlike my friend's tattoo, they have not chosen: marks from giving birth, from illness, from self-harm, or from the violence and abuse of others.

Circumcision was a particular kind of conformity – a marking out as 'one of God's people'. Paul points his readers towards a different kind of marking: the marks of the crucified and risen Jesus, wounds borne in love for a world captive to violence; wounds still engraved, but somehow transformed, in the one who returns to friends and enemies alike, bringing forgiveness and new life.

What might 'a new creation' mean for your marked body?

'Abba, Amma, you have searched me and known me . . .
See if there is any hurtful way in me, and lead me in the way everlasting.'

Psalm 139:1, 24

Marks of a successful church

Five marks of a successful church

Notes based on the Revised Standard Version and the Greek text by

Brenda Lealman

Brenda Lealman has been an RE adviser and school inspector, with a special interest in the place of spirituality in education. She is also a published poet and a former chair of the Creative Arts Retreat Movement (CARM). She has travelled widely including staying in ashrams in India and as guest lecturer at a theological college in the Canadian Arctic. She is retired and lives on the North York Moors, England.

Preparing for the week

What are the marks of a successful church?

Self-consciously worthy Pharisees and scribes, pretentious rulers and high priests live inside most of us and therefore in our churches. All religions and their institutions have their shadow sides. There are churches where, sadly, the shadow side takes over. What are some of the indicators of this? Controlling leadership that expects conformity and censures when questioned. Failure to affirm the gifts of others and the diversities of personal spiritual growing. Defensiveness; resistance to change; use of sabotage or gossip to undermine decisions. Emotional abuse that happens when members of a church, usually unconsciously, seek out an individual or group to scapegoat so that the dysfunction is projected and the victim(s) carries the blame and consequent guilt and rejection. Unsuccessful, unhealthy churches can make 'tears scald and start', can cause profound unhappiness and emotional diminishment of members. If you are suffering emotional abuse in your church you should not blame yourself; and you should talk to someone you trust.

We live in imperfection; we are imperfect; our churches are imperfect. Paradoxically, it seems to be when we admit imperfection, our inner beggar, our brokenness and powerlessness, when we touch the untouchable in us, that we rise and are given new life. 'This Jack, joke, poor potsherd, patch, matchwood, immortal diamond, / Is immortal diamond' (From 'That Nature Is a Heraclitean Fire' by Gerard Manley Hopkins). Really is! Are successful churches those that admit our Jacks and patches?

Palestine was occupied territory. Zacchaeus collects taxes for the occupying power, Rome; he's rich because the Romans allowed tax collectors to keep any money they could extort from people above a certain fixed amount. Zacchaeus: a little man with an ego inflated by his experience of success and wealth? An ordinary, hard-working man who has taken on his job in order to make a better life for his family? His behaviour is considered shocking by his fellow villagers: he's a sinner, 'dirty', an outcast, a man who breaks Jewish purity laws, and thrives through association with those regarded as enemies. Jesus' own behaviour, too, is shocking: he invites himself to stay with this worst of sinners, when there are so many respectable people who would give him a meal and a bed for the night.

But Zacchaeus is a hungry man – hungry for something more, for something that is missing in his life. He desperately wants to see and hear Jesus. He's willing to make a fool of himself by climbing into a tree – a sycamore tree at that, a scrubby tree that was made fun of in Palestine. Zacchaeus has dropped his outer defences of success and wealth, stops covering up what he's really like. He exposes to himself, to the people of his village, and to Jesus, the beggar inside him.

Pray for the perception and grace to face the truth about yourself; for the longing and courage, whatever the cost, to discover your inner depths.

A successful church lets go of defences and pretences

Luke 19:1–10

Marks of a successful church · Brenda Lealman

. . . means spontaneous generosity

Mark 12:38–44

A diatribe against the scribes. The scribes are the religious elite, and yet their religion is all pretence, skin deep. They dress finely, choose the best seats in the synagogue, seek human approval. That's as far as their spirituality goes: the desire to manipulate and impress. This is sham religion. They have a mission – that of self-aggrandisement.

The spirituality of the scribes is calculating, self-serving, leads to manipulative relationships. In contrast, the poor widow's generosity is uncalculating; although her gift is minute, she gives all that she has, freely, without weighing up the cost, the losses, or gains, to herself. There is no ulterior motive, no mission, just pure gift. Pure, spontaneous, joyful self-giving. This is genuine spirituality that comes from the heart, from inner depths. Mother Teresa of Calcutta told her religious sisters that they weren't there to lead those they served to Christ but, simply, to be Christ to them.

Reflect on some of the ways in which we and our churches can be undermined by skin-deep religion: by the desire to impress; by the need to be needed; by an intensity of mission to get 'numbers' in.

Brenda Lealman   Marks of a successful church

An uncomfortable dinner party! Jesus immediately breaks the rules by failing to wash his hands before eating. He then launches into a series of stinging indictments of his host, a Pharisee, and of the Jewish purity system. The Pharisees were among the unquestioned religious elite: guardians, together with the temple priesthood, of the Jewish purity system, obedience to which was the perceived benchmark of spirituality. Jesus' main criticism is that the Pharisees focus on outward show, ritual observance. They abuse their religious authority by insisting on rigid observance of objective standards, by defining 'the right way' to express spirituality. Jesus' final blow, perhaps delivered with some laughter (many of Jesus' words are full of humour): the Pharisees' outer cleanliness is meticulous and yet inside they are as unclean as tombs where unclean (according to Jewish law) corpses rot away. The irony is that the Pharisees campaigned for the extension of the purity laws.

Jesus is no polite, easy, compliant guest. His dinner-party conversation is biting, touching what must have been raw places of pride and authority; he takes enormous risks, questions what is usually unquestioned.

. . . inspires exploration, questioning, growing in faith

Luke 11:37–44

Are you open to surprises, willing to take risks, explore and ask questions about your faith journey? Can you share something of your spiritual journey in your church, or do you feel that your experiences and feelings must be repressed because you will be misunderstood or censured?

Marks of a successful church   Brenda Lealman

**. . . empowers
the powerless**

Acts 4:5–22

Peter and John have healed a lame man in the temple precincts. The healing was witnessed by a crowd of people and there is no denying that it happened (see Acts 3:9,10; 4:14,16, 22). Peter tells the crowd that this healing has come by faith through Jesus.

The authorities hold Peter and John in prison until the next day, when the temple authorities gather: the powerful, highly educated members of Jewish society, members of the high priestly families; formidable people who are used to intimidating people. It's an 'us' and 'them' situation: 'we', the powerful, perceive that Peter and John are 'them' from the powerless classes, 'uneducated, common men' (verse 13) – not necessarily illiterate but not well educated like the rulers: just 'ordinary' people.

Peter again asks: by what power was the lame man healed? The authorities had been mistaken in their estimate of Jesus: the healing power came through him. The word used for 'healed' is 'saved', in Greek. Despite his ordinariness, Peter speaks fluently, with 'frankness' or 'freedom' (a more accurate translation of the Greek than 'boldness' meaning physical courage). Peter and John are forbidden to speak or teach in the name of Jesus. Courageously they reply: We're bound to speak about what we've seen and heard (verse 20).

Find out about and pray for churches where 'ordinary' people (as judged by conventional social values) are being empowered and are taking great risks by, for example, fighting injustices, enduring persecution, supporting asylum seekers.

Brenda Lealman   Marks of a successful church

Sensation: Levi, a tax collector, an outcast of Jewish society, leaves everything to join the group of followers that Jesus is collecting around him. Another sensation: Jesus eats a festive meal with Levi and his tax collector friends. The Pharisees and their scribes ask Jesus why he mixes with the untouchables of Jewish society.

. . . pulls down barriers

Luke 5:27–32

Attitudes in the West to food and meals are often casual nowadays; meals at the time of Jesus still held religious and ritual significance. There were rules about the food that could be eaten, how it should be prepared, who could, and could not, share the meal together. Eating a meal with someone was a sign of mutual acceptance. Decent, law-abiding people would not eat with outcasts, the unclean. But Jesus deliberately breaks the purity laws and eats with the untouchables, tax collectors. Is this Jesus' radical vision of an alternative community: open, inclusive, motivated by compassion, not by keeping rules?

But why Jesus' particular concern for the untouchables, the imperfect? The Pharisees and scribes saw themselves as achieving perfection by doing and believing what is 'right'. But it is not this perceived perfection that interests Jesus: rather, it's the admitting of imperfection, of our inner poverty, that leads to transformation and possibility of wholeness.

Is your church – are you – grounded in believing and doing 'what is right', and as a result failing to live creatively?

Pray for your church to be an inclusive, open, compassionate community.

Marks of a successful church   Brenda Lealman

. . . lives poverty

1 Corinthians 1: 18–31

A challenging indictment of our social values and the values found in our churches. The church in Corinth is not entirely healthy. Its members are divided into factions, aligning themselves behind various controlling, probably eloquent, overbearing people. There's in-fighting among the factions: each perceives itself to be superior to the others. Paul hits out hard at this behaviour: it is undermining at a profound level Jesus' message and actions. The significance of those runs counter to values of power, pretentiousness, showy wisdom (rhetorical skill was a highly rated aspect of 'wisdom'). The cross signifies powerlessness, reverses accepted social values; indicates an alternative way of life.

Further, Paul says, the very lack of status of most members of the Corinthian church shows whom God is interested in: he chooses the 'low and despised'. The essence of God's creative power is in bringing something out of nothing, in the transforming of those who are nobodies. It is worth reading the moving opening verses of chapter 2: Paul pictures himself as an un-impressive, vulnerable person, not eloquent; indeed speaking in public makes him anxious and fearful. His bearing demonstrates need. Note, too, Paul's use of paradoxes: weakness as strength, foolishness as wisdom. Is living with paradox one of the experiences of a deepening spirituality? Is it by living poverty that we, and our churches, are led towards fullness?

The possibility and glory of being fully and deeply human in Christ: is a successful church one that keeps that vision constantly alive?

Pray for the sort of poverty that waits, trusts, receives.

Brenda Lealman   Marks of a successful church

Readings in Matthew 4–10

1 Proclaiming the kingdom

Preparing for the week

Jesus begins his ministry proclaiming the good news of the coming kingdom of God. The 'good news' is what Isaiah describes – 'How beautiful upon the mountains are the feet of the messenger who . . . brings good news' (Isaiah 52:7). It is the good news that God reigns. That means Caesar doesn't reign, nor Satan, neither does the marketplace, nor exploitation, nor violence reigns, nor any of the forces that break us down and undermine us.

This is an astounding proclamation, bewildering because it flies in the face of experience. To believe it, we learn in the readings for this week, we ourselves need to become part of the proclamation, as Jesus did. We, too, will become fisherfolk – reconciling, healing, gathering in those who are estranged and exiled. We whose spirits have been defeated, who mourn for what has been lost, who hunger for righteousness, are those God counts on to hope for something better. The kingdom of God is always coming, but only because those who believe in it have not lost this capacity to hope, to envision alternatives and to resist the present order. The German pastor Martin Niemöller, imprisoned by the Nazis during World War II, said, '*Die Herren dieser Welt kommen und gehen; unser Herr kommt,*' that is: 'The lords of this world come and go; our Lord comes.'

Notes based on the New Revised Standard Version by

Tom Arthur

Tom Arthur is a recently retired United Reformed Church minister living in Cardiff, Wales. He spends his days teaching (NT Greek and biblical studies), writing, painting and playing with his five grandchildren.

Choosing life

Matthew 4:1–11

Satan is like the consumer market designed to control the way we make decisions. Make bread of these stones, he says. Sounds good. But is consuming our final reality? Isn't life more complex than that? What happens when the urge to satisfy our own appetite comes up against the hard facts of life lived in community?

Throw yourself off this parapet, he says. Can we just do what thrills us without experiencing the consequences, getting blitzed on drugs and wasted on alcohol, fleeing from reality? Where does the idea of our own invincibility come from? What tempts us to act as if there were no consequences?

Worship me, he says, and he will put the world in our hands. Looks good. The kind of freedom Satan offers is to do what we want, without consequences.

Satan offers Jesus a world in which we never have to grow up, a world in which we have no worries as long as we do what everybody else is doing: consume, enjoy, grasp as if there were no tomorrow. It may feel like freedom but in reality it is a kind of East German Stasi police-state world that we come to love because the captains of marketing tell us that everything is designed for our pleasure, and we never have to think or take responsibility.

Against all this, Jesus asserts a greater freedom. The temptation is to accept one's prison and never have to choose.

God, give us the capacity to open our eyes and choose.

When John the Baptist is arrested, Jesus decides to return to Galilee for his own safety. These are forbidding times, like the time of exile when, in the words of Isaiah, people 'walked in darkness' (Isaiah 9:2). Here on the shore of Lake Galilee Jesus sees Simon Peter and Simon's brother Andrew fishing, casting a net into the sea. He sees James and John with their father Zebedee in a boat, mending nets. He calls them to follow him, and learn to fish not for fish but for people.

Gone fishing

Matthew 4:12–22

For readers familiar with scripture, the story vibrates with meaning. Jeremiah describes the people of God scattered in exile, and describes God appointing fishermen to gather them in, as if in nets, and bring them home. And you probably didn't know that the territory of Zebulum and Naphtali Matthew describes here didn't exist in his day. Here is another reference to the story of exile, when people 'lived in a land of deep darkness' (Isaiah 9:2).

It's a dark world today, too. Communities are as broken and scattered as ever. The promise is that the people who walk in darkness will see a great light. So Simon, Andrew, James and John are called not just to announce the good news but to be part of that good news, becoming what Paul calls ambassadors of reconciliation. That's what disciples do. We too. Immersing ourselves in God's work of reconciliation and liberation is what it means for us to be fisherfolk.

God, make me a welcomer.

Readings in Matthew   Tom Arthur

It's the law

Matthew 4:23 –
5:12

Good for those whose spirits have been crushed. Good for those who mourn. The beatitudes make no sense unless you know a thing or two about the difference between Roman law and Torah.

Roman law is like our church jumble sales. Once a year we prowl the neighbourhood for jumble. All the householders load their unwanted stuff into our vans, to be carted off to the church, and for about 24 hours the whole neighbourhood is tidy. Until Saturday's jumble sale, when people buy all the discarded stuff on display and clutter up their houses again. But for about 24 hours the neighbourhood is tidy. Keeping things tidy – by force – is what Roman law was all about. Cicero said the Empire extended wherever Roman law was enforced, wherever obedience and conformity were secured. When the Church adopted this idea, sin became disobedience.

Torah by contrast is liberation, an exodus journey from Egypt to the promised land in which the rules of mutual respect and concern for the least powerful become the measure of a free society. Free, but not often a very tidy society. Those whose spirits have been crushed are blessed because they know what it means to long for a better world. Their disobedient prayers become the seeds of liberation. They know something about hope that those of us who live more comfortably and in control need to hear, and provide the energy for a necessary resistance to our tidy agendas.

God, give me the spirit of disobedience.

Tom Arthur   Readings in Matthew

Light in darkness

Matthew 5:13–20

Jesus says you're the light of the world. Really? Sometimes it feels like someone down the hall has flicked your switch. We're all mature enough to know the pain that comes when things don't work out. The face we try to put on for the world when inside the nerves are tying the stomach in knots. The anxiety when you lost your job and couldn't face your wife. Maybe you have cancer, and you're alone with your own mortality. And suddenly you feel a part of that community of powerless people you've always thought of as 'other people', statistics. People who can only fall back on God. Who hasn't felt like that? I have. You have.

This is the point at which Jesus says 'You are the light of the world' (verse 14). Good for you, when you have kept the faith even when you are persecuted. You have remained faithful. In the darkness you have kept the light. Your witness is a light to the world.

Look at the crowd gathered on the mountain listening to Jesus. Who are they? The rich? The comfortable? Who from your community is there? Who *needs* to hear the encouragement that they are salt of the earth, the light of the world? To these, who from raw experience know how to hope more extravagantly, Jesus teaches what the law has always been about: compassion, reconciliation, equity for the despised, justice for the dispossessed.

God, make me shine like a beacon.

Habits of the heart

Matthew 5:21–37

You've heard the mouldy old joke about the young man, carrying a violin, lost in New York, who asks an elderly gentleman how to get to Carnegie Hall. 'Practise, my boy. Practise,' he says.

Practice is as important in faith as it is in music. In music, the passion doesn't often come until we have learned to play our scales through grim repetition, however mechanically, and then manage to stumble through a little Bach for the first time and experience how wonderful it is. It can be done! So we practise more and more until we really get it and can make the violin sing.

Similarly, we practise the Commandments as if we are learning ten easy pieces for a recital, or we repeat the Apostles' Creed until it becomes, as John Updike once said, 'like a path worn smooth over the rough terrain of our hearts'. When the Lord's Prayer and the Kyrie and the Bible itself become habits of the heart, we no longer stumble through them like children doing five-finger exercises. We discover their underlying mysteries; they become *us*.

Jesus unfolds the Torah to reveal its inner meaning in the same way a concert violinist interprets Bach. It's not just about murder; it's about anger. It's not just about adultery; it's about loyalty. The Commandments may feel like prohibitions to beginners. But to those who practise them they are the positive bricks for building the kingdom.

God, let your word light my path.

Tom Arthur   Readings in Matthew

Howard Zinn, an historian and anti-Vietnam War activist, was a hero of mine in my young adult years. He was once arrested for disturbing the peace. More accurately, he said, he was arrested for disturbing the war.

What do you know about the *Pax Romana* – the 'Roman Peace' in the time of Jesus? How would you contrast the peace of reconciliation with enemies that Jesus describes here with the work of 'pacification'? How is pacification achieved? Who benefits, primarily? Who does it oppress? Remember that the Gospel of Matthew was written some time after the brutal pacification of the Jews following the rebellion of 70 CE. The call for radical peace-making here is risky. It disturbs the war.

The kingdom of God, the content of our hope, is very different from the society we know too well. To catch what Jesus is saying here we need to go back to the Beatitudes, to 'the meek shall inherit the earth' (verse 5) – a quote from Psalm 37, where the meek are identified as the righteous and contrasted with the wicked. 'The Lord laughs at the wicked,' says the psalmist, 'for he knows their days are numbered' (Psalm 37:13). God's kingdom is all about the kind of society that listens to the voices of those who fall between the cracks. 'From oppression and violence he redeems their life' (Psalm 72:14). This is God's perfection, and we are called to be perfect, too.

God, make me a channel of your peace.

Blessed are the peacemakers

Matthew 5:38–48

Readings in Matthew 4–10

Notes based on *The New Testament 'Freshly Translated'* (by Nicholas King, Kevin Mayhew, 2004) by

Helen-Ann Hartley

The Revd Dr Helen-Ann Hartley is Tutor in New Testament at Ripon College Cuddesdon, and Associate Priest in the parish of Littlemore, Oxford. In addition to her college and parish duties, she is a frequent broadcaster for BBC Oxford.

2 Kingdom living

Preparing for the week

Christianity is not just about believing certain things, but also about *behaving* in ways that live out the gospel message. Concern for social justice and provision for those less fortunate than ourselves is deeply embedded in the Judaeo–Christian tradition. Many of the Hebrew prophets lamented the way in which God's people did not live up to their calling; the prophet Amos, for example, cried loudly for justice to the poor. This prophetic 'call to action' is inherent not just in the message of Jesus in the Gospels, but has inspired men and women down the ages, continuing to this day. Perhaps significantly for our reflections this week, Matthew presents Jesus' story from the perspective of Jewish Christianity. In other words, Matthew's own community is made up of a mixture of both Jewish and Gentile Christians, and Matthew is keen to incorporate traditions that his community would have recognised, presenting Jesus as the fulfilment of Jewish hopes. Matthew is most interested in emphasising the importance of keeping the Law, striving for ethical goodness, and relating well to those within the community (and ultimately to those outside). Chapters 6 and 7, the basis of our readings this week, come from Jesus' 'Sermon on the Mount', which combines many of these elements: keeping the law and ethical action (both as personal and corporate). It gives us an opportunity to consider our own behaviour, how we treat our own bodies, and how we relate to those around us.

For further thought

- What difference does your faith make to how you behave?
- What could you strive to improve?
- What is your prayer for the actions of the Christian churches as you begin this week?

What's your motivation?

Matthew 6:1–8

It's very common for church meetings to include lengthy discussions about finances. Money forms such a crucial part of our day-to-day existence; it's hard to ignore it. Many charitable organisations rely solely on the good will of people who donate time and money to their cause and who are willing to support and promote what the organisation stands for. Initiatives to raise money are many and varied; one local clergyman I know has gone to some extremes to raise funds for his church, including parachuting out of an aeroplane and, most recently, swimming with sharks! While this has gained him much publicity (the media seems to rather like 'whacky vicar' stories), one must never forget the folk who give to churches week by week, whatever they can afford, without pomp and ceremony. It is something they do because they know that the church is important in their local community and, without money, good work cannot be done.

The church is much more than a building of course, but the building stands as a visible place of Christ's presence in the midst of brokenness, a place of stillness where all are welcome. This is true of my own parish church in Littlemore, just outside Oxford. I am continually humbled by the many acts of kindness that I see – actions not done to attract attention, but done because that is what it means to 'live out the gospel'. This is what Jesus talks about in our reading today: he warns against practising religion in order to draw attention to oneself. In our 'it's all about me' culture, this can be a hard message to hear. But it is a vital one.

God who became one of us, vulnerable and yet full of strength, may we practise what we preach not because it makes us look good, but because it honours and glorifies your name.

Readings in Matthew   Helen-Ann Hartley

When you pray, say . . . !

Matthew 6:9–18

When I was at university, I went to a lecture given by a well-known theologian (not a Christian) who dismissed prayer as self-indulgent. Although I was firm in my faith, I came away from the lecture feeling very downbeat. I had always taken prayer for granted, and the lecturer's words had made me reflect. Prayer is partly about petition, asking for God's guidance and intervention in situations that seem beyond our control; but it is more than that, as our reading for today suggests. Matthew and Luke both record the tradition of the Lord's Prayer, the 'classic prayer' of Jesus that most people, even today, seem to know. It is easy to recite it without thinking about what it says, or to recognise that it is a prayer full of prophetic energy and challenge.

Jesus doesn't casually say 'when you pray you can try it like this . . .'; he uses a command: 'when you pray, say . . . !' Christian tradition has long interpreted this prayer as being about the meeting of basic needs, and indeed there is much in the prayer to indicate this: the request for bread, for God's presence in our lives, and for forgiveness and protection in our day-to-day doings. What is often overlooked is the eschatological framework within which this prayer is presented. There is urgency in how we approach God, and acknowledgement that everything is placed within a time frame that lies beyond our own lives.

Two verses on forgiveness follow the Lord's Prayer: prayer, it seems, cannot work unless the members of the community are reconciled to one another.

God, help us to pray in a way that is not self-indulgent, but that attends to the needs of those around us. Your presence calls us into action. Help us to respond where it is needed.

Helen-Ann Hartley   Readings in Matthew

Our lives are often full of 'to do' lists that seem endless. Diaries get filled up months, even years, in advance, and 'time off' seems an impossibility. Some of the most challenging yet valuable experiences I have had are the two retreats that preceded my ordination as deacon and then priest. I simply had to slow down, focus on the present moment and remember that my relationship with God was truly important. Sometimes, when we get caught up in the busyness of life, it's good to ask, 'where is God?' Our reading today is a call to remember the importance of seeking God where we are: in our work, in our rest, and yes, even in our play (to use the classic threefold advertising slogan of a well-known chocolate bar!).

Living in the present moment

Matthew 6:19–34

Christianity does not call us to abandon what lies around us, but rather to strive to bring God into situations that we find ourselves in, whether that be at work or in our homes and local communities. This is surely the point of the incarnation: God became one of us in order to experience our humanity, the good bits as well as the not so good. The message of this passage makes for un-comfortable reading: not storing up earthly treasures; being generous; serving God instead of Mammon; with not being anxious about food or clothing. How should we respond as Christians?

Lord, how can we live our lives without being caught up in the drive to commercial gain?

Readings in Matthew   Helen-Ann Hartley

Ask, search, knock . . .

Matthew 7:1–12

One of my favourite hymns is 'Seek ye first the kingdom of God . . .' which is based on verses from our reading today. The hymn may be sung as a round, with the chorus sung by one group while the verse is sung by another. This is a most effective representation of the gospel message: we do not strive alone, but with others. We might not always sing the same song at exactly the same time, but whatever we do, we should strive to do it in harmony with others. This lies at the heart of the famous 'Body of Christ' image used by Paul in 1 Corinthians 12. Each of us has a part to play, and without each person doing his or her bit, God's will on earth would not get done!

In today's reading, Matthew turns his attention from one social issue (what to do with and about earthly possessions) to another (how to treat one's neighbour). The passage is not just about ethical behaviour (do this, and don't do that), but is more about a desire for mercy, humility and tolerance (traits which lie at the heart of the prophetic tradition of the Hebrew scriptures). The so-called 'Golden Rule' (well known in pre-Christian Jewish tradition) brings to a climax this central section of the Sermon on the Mount. It is a radical call, that absolutely everything, without exception, which is required by love and the commandments of Jesus, we should do for other people.

Eternal God, help us to do unto others as we would have them do to us.

It is significant that the Sermon on the Mount ends with a series of warnings, all of which act as a balance to the series of blessings that began the Sermon. Whilst we might be blessed with our faith, we should not be complacent and we should never take our faith for granted. The reading for today recalls many of the important themes of 'kingdom living', and the urgency of paying attention to our own actions and the actions of those around us.

Verse 14 often causes some concern: it is not an assertion that most human beings will go to hell; biblical scholars reflect that it probably means that we should act as if only a very few will enter paradise. In other words, our faith should 'keep us on our toes'. How we behave really does matter, both in the here and now, and in the life to come beyond our earthly existence. These are challenging words indeed, but not impossible. Our faith opens to us a wealth of opportunity, the door is never closed to those who at least try. The identity of the false prophets in verses 15–23 is not known for sure. We can only say that they must have been Christians whom Matthew wished to attack (with good reason).

When is a good fruit not a good fruit?

Matthew 7:13–23

Lord, help us to strive to know you better, and to make you known in the lives of those with whom we come into contact. Help us to make your presence real in our world.

Readings in Matthew   Helen-Ann Hartley

Beware of dodgy building techniques!

Matthew 7:24–28

This memorable parable is one of my favourites, mainly because of the rather catchy song-version of it that I use with the pre-school group that I visit regularly in my parish's primary school. Building on a solid foundation makes excellent sense; building on sand seems ridiculous. Shades of grey really don't have a place in Matthew's world. There are two responses to Jesus' words: obedience and disobedience, and two human fates, salvation and destruction. This can serve as a useful check in our daily lives. What does our faith call us to do? How does our faith demand we respond to situations we face? Of course this will vary greatly depending on where we find ourselves at any given moment, but it is worth bearing in mind.

In Matthew's version of the parable (it can also be found in Luke 6), there is a contrast between hearing and doing. Matthew seems to be saying to his community that it is all very well to hear the message of the gospel, but unless actions follow, what is the point of professing faith in Jesus Christ? This is where the imagery of the foundation comes in; faith comes in many forms, but unless our foundation is solid, it cannot last.

Perhaps you can think of experiences you have had where your own faith has been challenged? What are the things that have enabled you to remain rooted when the going has got tough?

We pray that our faith may be built on solid rock, and not on sand, and that when we feel challenged by the stresses and strains of our lives, we may stand firm, with your help, God of strength and steadfast love.

Readings in Matthew 4–10

3 Healings

Preparing for the week

Phoebe, it's a long way from the village of Aberdaron in Wales to the town of Sepphoris, where you used to live, and a long time since you walked this earth towards the end of what we call the first century. I'm a 21st-century follower of the Way, captivated by Jesus. I send you my greetings in his name.

Iago, my greetings to you. Yes, I knew of Jesus, from Nazareth – a village but four miles from here. And I turned 80 earlier this year. I married at 15, about the time he died. I remember the way he 'lived on' in people's hearts and lives. Ever since, in this busy trading crossroads of a town, I've heard stories about him. And those scrolls my son collected! I've found a neighbour to read to me again from the scroll from Matthew's community – the part you're interested in.

Good. Let's start. Others will read what we've said, and make their contribution too . . .

Join in. It's in pondering, in the silences, in the opening of our hearts and minds, that we find ourselves thinking or saying something that has never occurred to us before. Is not this how the Spirit works with us in the very particular circumstances of our lives? So there are no set prayers this week – you will find your own as you join in.

Notes based on the Revised English Bible by
Jim Cotter

Jim Cotter is an ordained Anglican who ministers in the parish of Aberdaron in north-west Wales to householders and to visitors. He also writes, and publishes, in partnership with the Canterbury Press, as Cairns Publications. See www.cottercairns.co.uk.

A man with a skin disease, and a young servant

Matthew 8:1–13

Iago	Phoebe, here's a man with a skin disease, shunned and isolated.
Phoebe	Not because he was contagious but because his skin was blemished. So he was 'unclean' and could not be a full member of God's community. It wasn't the pain: it was the isolation that was awful. We live together so much that few of us can bear to be on our own for long.
Iago	So the man keeps his distance but makes an act of faith – or is it a desperate cry? And Jesus comes up to him – with the risk that someone will notice and declare him an outcast too – and touches him.
Phoebe	The first time in years, probably. And though the disease vanished, the real healing was that he could live in a household once more.
Iago	I get the impression of Jesus as being 'in touch' with himself first, serene at a deep level of his being, at one with the greater power we call God. His presence, his power, his compassion, his not minding what others might think.
Phoebe	And Jesus wasn't afraid of centurions either. We certainly were. We hardly liked the Romans. This time Jesus cured from a distance. Perhaps because the young servant was already well loved and had a secure place in the household.
You	Respond in your own words and ways . . .

Iago	Phoebe, how did families work in Sepphoris in your time?
Phoebe	A man brings his wife back to his father's household. If the husband dies, his widow goes to live with one of her sons. If she hasn't any, or if they have died, she usually returns to her own family.
Iago	So the fact that Peter's mother-in-law is living in his house means that she had no sons of her own, no other family to return to, and so came to live with her son-in-law?
Phoebe	Yes, she would be feeling insecure – and covered with shame. That would matter to her far more than any fever. But if she's sick, she can't fulfil even the simplest obligations of hospitality.
Iago	So to be cured would mean that she could hold her head high again in the family and the community.
Phoebe	Everyone gets sick. Most people die before they're thirty. We cope with that. But to be alone, with no meaning or purpose in your life: that is to lose all sense of dignity and worth. That's what Jesus restored.
Iago	Jesus goes on to say that he has nowhere to lay his head, no household to be part of (verse 20). Yet he had such a presence that others could, as it were, find their 'home' in him. Was he challenging us to find our true home in God, with others who had found the same, and then not worry about the rest?
You	Respond in your own words and ways . . .

A mother-in-law

Matthew 8:14–27

Two violent men	

Matthew 8:28 – 9:1

Iago	Phoebe, this is a puzzling story.
Phoebe	You mean the herd of pigs and the dramatic scene of two men in a burial place?
Iago	It sounds a bit like what we would call a 'horror story'. In my country a story of an exorcism doesn't seem real to most people, though in other parts of the world it is a common event. I can understand the inhabitants of the area not wanting Jesus to stay around. I think I'd have been terrified.
Phoebe	Leave the drama on one side for a minute. Surely you recognise that there's a constant struggle in human lives between a desire for evil and a desire for good, between that which destroys and that which creates, between that which disfigures and that which transfigures. And here we have another example of the commanding presence and power of Jesus. I know Matthew doesn't give us the picture at the end that we find in Mark's Gospel, but think of the contrast: two men whose behaviour is violent, destructive, wild, uncontrollable, and those same men sitting calm, clothed, and in their right minds.
Iago	It's quite a contrast to the other stories, which are so quiet and simple.
Phoebe	Perhaps you need to ask yourself whether you're rather afraid of powers within yourself that can still get out of hand. Are you sure you're always in your right mind?
You	Respond in your own words and ways . . .

Iago	Phoebe, we both have aches and pains that neither of us expects will get easier. Even miracles can't last for ever! We won't be running free in the wind any more!
Phoebe	Yes, I know how you feel. But I'm not as restless as I used to be, more at peace. I've learned to let go of resentments, to be free of my inner paralysis. My father was violent at times, and my mother and I suffered from his outbursts. It's been hard to forgive him.
Iago	Then you understand this story quite well.
Phoebe	I think so. A sudden cure is wonderful, of course. I've seen a few; but I've noticed that sometimes the person doesn't change. You can leap in the air all you like, but if you're carrying an inner burden, it'll wear you down bit by bit. You need to inhabit the world of forgiveness if you're to be healed and not merely cured.
Iago	And what do you make of 'the Son of Man' having authority to forgive (verse 6). Isn't that God's business?
Phoebe	'Son of Man' isn't a title of honour or power. It simply means, 'a human being', perhaps, 'a human being full of God', truly, completely, divinely human. What we thought was in God's hands is now shared with us. We can and we do forgive. Divine and human forgiveness are intertwined with each other. It's a long haul, though, clearing the inner clutter of resentment and bitterness.
You	Respond in your own words and ways . . .

A paralysed man

Matthew 9:2–17

A woman and a girl

Matthew 9:18–34

Phoebe   I hear this story and I shudder. My niece, when she was about nine or ten, was raped. She never completely got over it. When she was twelve, and her own monthly bleeding began, she was in shock. She wouldn't get out of bed, and she turned her face to the wall, refused all food and drink. We thought she was going to die. Gradually, my aunt's patience and care touched her enough so that she began to live again. She did eventually marry – that was a minor miracle, finding such an understanding man – but she never conceived.

Iago   Are you hinting that something similar may have happened to the girl in this story?

Phoebe   Yes – and who knows what injury had been sustained by the woman whose body had been leaking blood for twelve years. Scarred, removed from ordinary life. Knowing she was unclean.

Iago   And the power of Jesus?

Phoebe   When I first started to listen to these stories about him, I remember thinking, here's a man I could trust. I could have opened my heart to him, told him anything, let him touch me. I'd have known that he wasn't looking for anything for himself. So for the woman and the girl in this story: they could accept their own bodies at last, and were free to join in the everyday life of their households. Walking tall again . . . affirmed as a woman . . . healed. And that's what good fathers do for their daughters.

You   Respond in your own words and ways . . .

Jim Cotter   Readings in Matthew

Iago   Phoebe, during our conversation, have you been implying that it is those who have been healed who are the true healers, however skilled or clever doctors can be with their cures?

Phoebe   Yes. And it's a gift of God, who doesn't hoard power to himself. I remember when I was young that my father and mother gave hospitality to two of Jesus' disciples. We were used to giving travellers – traders, mostly – a meal and a pallet for the night. We were always eager to hear their news. I kept as still and quiet as I could, hoping nobody would notice I wasn't in bed.

Iago   I remember doing that too, creeping half-way down the stairs and listening to what was going on!

Phoebe   I knew we had a lot in common! Well, these two strangers came. They looked like beggars, but they weren't begging – they held their heads high. They weren't carrying a pack or purse, nor even a staff to ward off dogs and thieves. They were, simply, themselves. At the time my mother's sister had lines in her face from looking after her wounded daughter. But in the two visitors' presence, she relaxed and her face was beautiful again. They were themselves, but more than themselves. Well, we plied them with questions, well into the night . . . I probably dropped off to sleep in the middle of a story.

Iago   In the middle of the story . . . Yes . . .

You   Respond in your own words and ways . . .

IBRA International Appeal

Imagine the only book you have to help you read the Bible is in French (or if you're a French speaker, try Tagalog!). Maybe you can understand bits of it, but imagine your joy when you discover someone has translated it into English for you!

Hundreds of thousands of people around the world experience similar joy when they discover the IBRA books and readings lists have been translated into their language. And this is all through the generosity of IBRA readers.

Each year, the IBRA International Fund provides funds for local groups to translate, print and distribute IBRA Bible notes and reading lists. Last year more than 68 000 people in eleven different countries received copies of the IBRA books which had been translated, printed and distributed by IBRA partners. The reading list was also translated into French, Spanish, Telugu (India), Tokelau (Samaoa) and several Congolese languages, enabling 250 000 people to receive them in a language useful to them.

The funds are given exclusively by IBRA readers like you, who give generously towards the fund, raising over £20 000 each year. With your gift, more people will be able to experience the joy of reading the Bible using notes or a list of readings in a familiar language.

Please consider either giving for the first time, or increasing your donation this year. You can donate using the envelope which is part of the leaflet insert that came with this book, or add your donation to your order for next year's books.

Thank you!

International Bible Reading Association
1020 Bristol Road
Selly Oak
Birmingham
B29 6LB
Tel. 0121 472 4242

Mercy for sinners

1 God wants sinners to come to him

Notes based on the New Revised Standard Version by

Lori Sbordone Rizzo

Lori Sbordone Rizzo is a native New Yorker who works with disconnected youth in Brooklyn to help them pass their high-school equivalency (GED) test. By the grace of God, she earned an M.Div. in 1998 and still hopes to be ordained; until then she preaches the gospel in these meditations and by showing up to work every day.

Preparing for the week

Great news! God welcomes sinners. Forgiveness for our ugliest deeds offered freely. We need not fear their hold on us another moment. All we have to do is raise our hand and admit that we need it.

Ah! I knew there was a catch.

People who believe they have life under control do not do well in the Gospels. In the first reading, Jesus is at dinner with a Pharisee named Simon when a woman arrives whom everyone somehow knows to be a terrible sinner. The religious men are all scandalised. Jesus responds with a parable about two debtors. The lesson for Simon and his friends is clear: you do not feel that your debt to God is as great as this woman's. Fine. We can address your arrogance later. But at least admit that you have some debt. At least concede that she is not the only one in the room who stands in need of forgiveness.

Once, I ran into some evangelists shouting, 'Jesus died for you,' from a street corner. I shouted back sarcastically, 'Who asked him to?' At some point, though, we all must take a frank self-assessment and realise that we have no other choice but to ask God to send Jesus, because if he doesn't die on that cross, there is no escape. When I look at the cross, I know two things: I am responsible for this, and God did this because God loves me. Those are two mighty truths.

Scandal

Luke 7:36–50

The woman came in with the rabble. It was customary for people throwing big banquets to allow the poor to pick through the leftovers, simultaneously praising the host's generosity to the invited guests. Somehow, this woman had heard that Jesus was extending God's forgiveness to people who had previously been considered beyond reach. Suddenly, there was a way back into that blessed community. Overwhelmed by gratitude, she rents conventions asunder and offers herself, body and soul, to the Master. Simon thinks he has caught Jesus in his trap: if this so-called prophet can't see that this woman is filth, how can he be trusted to discern the holy? Jesus snaps, 'You brought me into your house and totally disrespected me, Simon. What's going on?'

No one denies that the woman is a sinner. Jesus doesn't sit her down and say, 'Listen girlfriend, I know how hard it is to be a woman alone in this city. You are entitled to a little indiscretion.' By his very presence, Jesus makes her feel the burden of her sin; and then he demolishes it. Forgiveness is meaningful when it comes from one offended. Jesus has never met this woman; she has not directly wronged him. But as all sin is an offence against God, when Jesus forgives her, he is saying, 'If you offended any of these you have offended me.' His forgiveness is the true scandal.

Dear God, allow us to see how much we have been forgiven, so that we may come to love you more.

Mercy for sinners   Lori Sbordone

Busted

Luke 18:9–14

Two men travel to the temple for the atonement sacrifice. During the incense offering, people gather in the court for private prayers. The Pharisee believes that he needs no help in his relationship with God. He sees himself as one whom God would seek out for company, as if they were cut of the same cloth. The tax collector harbours no such delusions. Tax collectors were the worst element; they were crooks and collaborators who ran a state-sponsored extortion racket against their own people. They could wring the last penny from a starving widow without losing sleep. He would have hardened himself against people's cries for mercy; otherwise, he would not have lasted in that job. Now, he stands before the Holy One, and he is busted.

The priest offers the atonement sacrifice, but the tax collector doesn't join the congregation. He yearns for the benefits of the sacrifice, but knows himself too well to see how he can ever be included. Until perhaps he remembers a time when the cries of a widow got to him, when he refrained from extorting the tax because someone's pleas for mercy pierced his heart. If *he* could be turned from extracting the penalty, why not God? So he beats his breast to show that he understands the gravity of his actions, and implores God to 'make the sacrifice for me'. God will answer this prayer.

Look with mercy on me today, O God. Find a way to bring me to you.

Lost sheep

Luke 15:1–10

Eva came into our programme last year. In my many years of teaching I have never met anyone so angry. I weathered her hatred by reminding myself that none of it was personal. Eva is broken, God knows how. The details I learned from her social worker were more than sufficient to explain why she acted as she did. Our ministry to her would be to endure her anger; take it in and snuff it out. Mid-term, her teacher quit. I introduced her to the new guy as 'very intelligent, but doubtfully teachable'. He tried; he gave her too many chances, but inevitably he had to concede that she was damaging the classroom. I remember counselling him, 'Ramon, you are not the good shepherd. You cannot leave the ninety-nine to save the one.' It hurt to speak those words. Before we cut her loose, I secured her a seat for the exam. She passed everything but maths.

It is not uncommon that I run into former students. If I find Eva one day to be a journalist or lawyer, I will not be surprised. I am no hater, like the Pharisees to whom Jesus preached these parables. I am not the best shepherd; I've lost more than a few along the way, but I do try to rejoice when God brings them home.

Loving God, help me to rejoice in all that you are doing amongst us.

Mercy for sinners   Lori Sbordone Rizzo

Assessment

Romans 3:21–26

The burning question on our students' minds is, 'How long will it take for me to get my pass?' We administer a three-hour test, collect some homework, and then we give them the results. The news is rarely good. They might have some self-awareness of their issues with maths, but they are never prepared to hear that their reading level is low: 'Miss, I can read.' 'I know you can, but not well enough to pass the test.'

Paul argues through the first chapters of Romans that we have all been assessed by the law, and the news is not good. We yearn to be with God, yet we are totally unequipped. No doubt, we are aware that we have issues, but most of us figure that we have enough altruistic qualities to balance them out. Paul gives us no comfort; 'All have sinned' (verse 23). All, from the Virgin Mary to Mother Teresa, without exception.

We show our new students classrooms where others such as themselves have accepted their assessment and are moving forward. You don't have to be good to join, but you must be merciful – to yourselves and to your classmates. If God enables us to join God in eternity, we all will need serious remedial work. Practise mercy now, by remembering that, but for the gift of God in Christ, we all fall short.

Give us patience God, to know that you are not done with any of us yet.

Lori Sbordone Rizzo

Mercy for sinners

Jesus comes home from the crowds he has encountered along the road, but the house is mobbed with people hungry for a word. He starts to preach, but the roof opens and a paralysed man is lowered into the classroom. Rabbi Jesus turns the distraction into a teachable moment. 'Son,' he says to the paralysed man, 'your sins are forgiven' (verse 5). Huh? 'Only God can forgive sins (verse 7). Who does this guy think he is?' He returns their question with one of his own: 'Which is more difficult – the healing of this man's body, or the restoration of his soul?' Healings, like flowers, fade; the paralytic's body will inevitably fail in death, but the restoration of our souls – this is eternal work. If Jesus is who he claims to be, miracles are no stretch. Forgiveness will require a sacrifice.

Trick question

Mark 2:1–17

In terms of physical healing, only the paralytic needed it; everyone else was presumed healthy. Once Jesus shifts the conversation to sin, this presumption of health gets shaky. 'Those who are well have no need of a physician' (verse 11), says Jesus; when you get this, you'll be tearing up the roof for yourself.

We are not as unlike the Pharisees as we'd like to think. We expect affirmation of how righteous we have become, when the truth is that we cannot go a day without falling short of God's best. Tear up the roof. Get to Jesus any way you can.

Lord, we are sin sick. Have mercy and heal us.

Mercy for sinners   Lori Sbordone Rizzo

Surely

Romans 8:31–39

I once met a man who cultivated trees. He could take a tree that was sick and save it by grafting it onto a healthy one. First he would examine the tree, looking for a branch that was free from disease. When he found something good, he cut it off and stripped the open end. Then he would find a strong tree and drive a spike into its trunk in a process he called 'wounding'. Finally he'd twist the oozing end of the grafted branch into the open gash of the healthy tree, making a 'wound-to-wound connection'. All that was left to do was hope that the branch would abide in the wound of the tree.

There is a chorus in part two of Handel's *Messiah*: 'Surely he hath borne our griefs and carried our sorrows' (Isaiah 53:4). In the months before I came back to faith, I must have listened to that chorus a hundred times a day. Two melody lines are set against each other – one sounds a rescue; the other a beat-down. You can almost hear the hammer rise and fall. When I understood that Jesus agreed to this beating so that his life could flow through me, I understood how much God loves me. Jesus didn't walk with confusion to his fate; he wasn't drunk or demented. He walked surely. He thought it through, calculated the cost and did it anyway.

James Huntington observed, 'Love must act, as light must shine and fire must burn.'

Love act, fire burn, light shine.

Mercy for sinners

2 God's forgiveness is for everyone

Preparing for the week

As I have been writing, my beloved cat is dying. She is taking full advantage of my sympathy, curling up alongside me and nudging my arm to stroke her. Her name is Menow – after the Greek verb 'abide'. I was in my second year of seminary when she came into my life. I was writing a paper on Paul's prayer for the Ephesians to know the love of God (3:13–21) when a friend from class called and asked if I wanted a kitten. That was before I came out as a lesbian. I couldn't dare speak that truth, not even to myself. I am sure that Menow knew. She knows all my secrets; they don't seem to faze her. When my seminary community found out, they ripped me from their fellowship like a loose thread from a garment, but Menow abides. She might not like all my choices. When we get to heaven and can speak with each other, I may find that she disapproved of many things; still she abides besides me, purring.

The love of God abides through all our changes. It is merciless in pursuit of our self-deceptions, but merciful in faith that our true selves will gloriously emerge. The love of God is not diminished in showing mercy: rather it is enlarged, strengthened. Not one thing in heaven or earth can separate us from it.

For further thought

• What stories can you tell of the power of the love of God?
• Tell these stories to yourself this week, and be prepared to share them with others.

Notes based on the New Revised Standard Version by

Lori Sbordone Rizzo

For Lori's biography, see p. 74.

Woman

John 8:2–11

I am a woman no man has loved. No one has ever thought me beautiful. I have never been special to anyone. Even the women won't come near me. I'm trash, so I trash myself. Everyone's got to be good at something – well, I'll be good at filth. Now, I am very popular! I can't tell you how many men I have. They like me because I'll do anything. I used to enjoy it, but lately their groans are like sledgehammers on my brain. I feel like my soul is shattering to bits. Soon there will be nothing left but dust.

I was dragged from my house by the very men I had degraded myself with. They were going to use me to trap Jesus. They'd used me every other way they could think of, hadn't they? 'Master, this woman was caught in the very act of adultery. The law says to stone her. What do you say (verses 4a–5)? He sat down in the dirty street and began to write in the dust. I thought I saw my name, and I wept – not from fear of what was about to happen, but from gratitude that someone would remember my name. He asked them to consider their own sin, and suddenly they were all as dirty as I was. Then Jesus called me and said, 'Go and sin no more' (verse 11).

I'm not garbage. I'm beloved. I close my eyes. I see his face; and I am clean.

Lord Jesus, give me grace to be the person I am in your eyes.

Lori Sbordone Rizzo   Mercy for sinners

Face-off

Romans 5:6–21

I was a kid during the Vietnam War. I asked the adults I knew why our young men had to go to war against their will. If the presidents wanted war, let them fight it – Lyndon B. Johnson versus Ho Chi Minh in a winner-takes-all match! They'd laugh, then send us to church to learn about David and Goliath. In this story, Israel is at war with the Philistines, and Goliath offers Israel a challenge: 'rather than both armies going to battle, send your best soldier against me.' All of Philistine would be in Goliath; all of Israel would be in its champion. The winner takes the field. Not one in Israel has faith enough to face Goliath, save David who takes the giant down with one smooth stone.

This idea of a representative champion is behind Paul's teaching. Adam was bested by Satan in a sneak-attack in the garden. As a result, we all became subjects of Satan's rule. God supplies a new champion for us in Jesus. Right at the moment when evil seems to have won, God flips the script by raising Jesus from death and revealing him as Messiah. In Jesus' victory, all humanity is freed from the eternal hold of sin and death. When we join with all of creation in acknowledging that Jesus is Lord, we proclaim that by his victory we live in a new dominion of grace and peace.

Thank you, Lord Jesus, for your victory. Grant that I might always live within your dominion.

Mercy for sinners   Lori Sbordone Rizzo

Windows on the world

Revelation 7:9–17

I don't know what I'm doing here. I'm no hero. I was just a dishwasher in the restaurant on the 102nd floor. I didn't even see the plane crash. There was a sudden explosion, unbearable heat; then Jesus showed up and simply walked us into this place. He is awesome – beyond anything I ever imagined, and this place is so bright you feel as if it's shining right through you. The thing is, I was never the shiny type, and there are legitimate saints here – firemen and rescue-workers. What did I ever do to rate such fine robes?

Friends and family stapled flyers with my photo along Broadway, hoping to find me alive. The pictures served as points of contact, and I watched as people rushed to the rescue, then braced for the reality. I feel such love for them, such as I have never felt for anyone. Love comes easy here, as easy as breathing. I can see it in their faces; they are trying to 'deal with it'. We are New Yorkers; we pride ourselves on being able to take whatever is thrown at us. I want to scream, 'Yo! Take a minute. Let God clothe you with strength for the next fifty things you need to do.' I want them to know that they don't need to carry this burden on their own. We are close. Ask for help.

Thank you, God, for the fellowship of saints and angels.
Give me faith to open my hands today to receive their gifts.

Lori Sbordone Rizzo   Mercy for sinners

John Newton followed his father into the slave trade. He loaded human souls onto his ship as easily as bales of cotton. Apparently his wretchedness exceeded his profession as, on one voyage, his crew bound him and traded him to an African queen, whom he was forced to serve for several years before a family friend redeemed him. The experience did not make him rethink his position on slavery. Several years later, during a storm that nearly capsized his ship, he cried out to God for mercy. Upon their safe return, he devoted himself to prayer and studying scripture, and although he tried to be a 'more humane slave-trader', he did not quit until paralysis left him physically incapable of continuing.

This could have been the end of Newton's story, except that in pushing deeper into God, he experienced a 'second conversion', where he felt the weight of misery he had perpetrated, and repented. His pamphlet describing conditions on slave ships during the infamous 'middle passage' from Africa to market was instrumental in turning public opinion against the trade. However, he is most famous for composing 'Amazing Grace', a hymn that is beloved of many because it rings true to our experience as wretched souls navigating blindly through 'dangers, toils and snares', yet confidently testifies, ''twas grace that brought me safe thus far, and grace will lead me home.' God's grace, offered freely to a slave trader. What do you say but, 'Amazing!'

Amazing

Ephesians 2:1–18

Jesus, you are my saviour. May my life sing your praises.

Mercy for sinners   Lori Sbordone Rizzo

Lamp unto my feet

1 Timothy 1:1–17

Saul loved the scriptures, and the scripture was clear: anyone who hangs from the tree is cursed (Deuteronomy 21:23). The true horror of crucifixion wasn't the nails, but that God's face was turned away from the unfortunate victim, and God would never do this to the Messiah. Jesus smashed all Saul's certainties when he revealed himself on the Damascus Road, striking Saul blind as a metaphor for the uselessness of his own reasoning. Humbled and renamed, Paul disappears into the desert, to learn more about Jesus and make sense of what happened.

Here's why I love Paul – that he loves the scripture, and cannot accept that there could be an untruth in it. 'Your word is a lamp to my feet' (Psalm 119:105), therefore it cannot contain a false clue about the Messiah. He grabs hold of the resurrection and Deuteronomy, refusing to let either drop, until it all becomes clear. The one on the tree was cursed; Jesus took the curse off all the children of Adam by choosing to die on the cross, and with the resurrection, God reveals him as Messiah – the one who came to save us. From this labour, the doctrine of redemption is conceived, or as Paul calls it, 'the glorious gospel of the blessed God, which he entrusted to me' (verse 11).

Almighty God, your word is beautiful. Grant me strength to shape my life in accordance with its marvellous design.

Lori Sbordone Rizzo   Mercy for sinners

I am a thief. My neighbourhood was an armed camp. The religious people told me to wait for the Messiah, but I couldn't stand the suffering another moment. I learned to hate all Romans. It's them or us. My assignment was to hide along the road and lay siege to any Roman dog that passed us. We were to descend upon them like a sudden storm, steal anything worth selling, and if necessary, kill them. They look upon me as if I was some sort of beast. I want not to care about this, but I do. I am told I will get over this in time, but when? Then one day, they catch us. Suddenly the reality of the game I have been playing slaps me across the face like a soldier's whip. Now they will make an example of me by nailing me to a cross and leaving me to die along the side of the road. Why not? Haven't I done the same to others? I deserve everything that's coming.

But there is a man beside me who is beautiful. He seems to love everyone, even the soldiers who drive nails through his hands. Yet, they ridicule him. They seem to go out of their way to abuse him because he claims to be our king. If we did have a king, I would want him to be just like this man. He is good, not like us. I look in his eyes, and I see how things could be.

Thief

Luke 23:32–43

Jesus, remember me.

Mercy for sinners   Lori Sbordone Rizzo

Conversion and change

1 Power to change

Notes based on the New International Reader's Version by

Sibyl Ruth

Sibyl Ruth is a Quaker living in Birmingham, UK. Her mother is from a Jewish background and her father was a Baptist. She is a freelance writer.

Preparing for the week

As a teenager my favourite song contained the line, 'Lord help me, I can't change.' It was Lynyrd Skynyrd's *Free Bird*. This line is repeated slowly – and then the melody quickens, lifts, flies . . .

Words and stories do change us. For me books – though not always the Good Book – have been a major influence. As I read I understand myself, and others, in a better light. I grew up in a house where a lot was left unsaid, where it was thought that a single wrong word could do real harm. Books cast a more benevolent spell.

Quakers – also known as Friends – are less scripturally based than many churches. Stress is laid on personal experience of the Divine. An early Friend, Isaac Pennington, wrote that true religion lay in 'feeling the power of endless life, receiving the power and being changed into power' (*On Justification*, 1658).

We might think our personal narratives lack significance. Yet each existence holds life-changing moments. If we are mindful, we'll be aware when these moments arrive. We can listen to whatever is guiding us. We'll know how to speak and act.

I believe this more than ever, as I approach a set of events known as 'the change'. A time for me to read old stories and find new meanings.

We like the *idea* of being helped out of difficulty. But we're hindered by our views about how aid should arrive. Naaman strikes me as the kind who'd be hard to help. As a commander he'd be more used to sorting others' problems, liaising with the rich and powerful. He only stooped to take advice from a slave because he was desperate.

From this point on, the story gets farcical. Naaman's like some man who is sent on a hostelling trip – but who checks in at the 5-star hotel down the road. He's got suitcases and an American Express card – but no walking boots. Naaman does have the wit to visit Elisha once he gets the prophet's message, but he's still not happy. Naaman knows what 'proper' healing is. Why should a big shot like him listen to an underling? And why should he keep jumping into some stupid river?

Once again it's the servants whose advice is worth listening to. The turning point is reached when Naaman does exactly what the man of God told him to do.

Faith itself can be a hindrance, if we are too attached to our notions of who God is and how s/he will be revealed. Sometimes help comes in ways that we'd never expect. At these times the cleverest – and stroppiest – among us may be saved by doing exactly what we're told.

Whose advice will we take today?

Taking advice

2 Kings 5:1–14

Changing – and staying the same

2 Kings 5:15–19

Fairytales are full of examples of people having their wishes granted, only to find this creates fresh trouble. In real life we can waste ages dreaming about transformation. TV makeover shows offer a secular version of this fantasy. Others of us think that if God would intervene in our lives – just once – then we'd live happily every after.

But divine intervention may be like biting off more than we can chew. However hard we try to deal with the experience of being changed, we'll carry on getting things wrong. Because part of us is still the same muddled self. Yes, we have had some earth-shattering experience. We are full of zeal, resolved to do better. Yet we're still rooted in our culture and history, in a web of old relationships. How can we reconcile our future with our past?

Extraordinary things happen. But we respond in ordinary ways. So we'll use money to try and purchase the moment. Or we'll hang on to some object to keep the experience alive. And suppose others won't accept that we've changed? Maybe it's okay if – just outwardly – we behave like the people we used to be . . .

The great thing about this story is it's a comedy. For all his power and status, Naaman's a bumbling hero. Yet ultimately his good intentions, his true gratitude for what he's received, turn out to be enough. And that's something for which we can all be grateful.

What changes are we struggling to deal with?

To be honest I don't connect with Naaman, beyond a faint pleasure in seeing a guy who thinks he knows it all getting it wrong. I identify more with servants, the people who cleverly manage the moods of their employer. But Rahab – now there's a woman I would like to meet!

Then, as now, when government agents knock on the door, the safest thing would be to give them everything they want. Only Rahab doesn't take the safe path. She's a smooth operator. A fast talker. Someone who knows how to hide spies, and broker a deal. Perhaps her work has given her useful practice in dissembling? Rahab knows she has to keep in with the current king of Jericho, *and* with his successor. She's aware of having a business to run and a family to look after. (I suppose you could say it was about life/work balance.) But despite these real concerns, what she is clearest about is God's will.

Rahab says that everyone in Jericho feels weak. But she comes across as strong. Nothing fazes her. Nor is she neurotically fussed about staying squeaky clean. (Funny isn't it – the way the men in power are allowed to make all sorts of mistakes, yet a woman is supposed to be perfect?)

I was glad to learn that Joshua's spies kept their side of the bargain. They had promised to be kind and faithful. Probably Rahab wasn't shown kindness or faithfulness that often.

Keep a promise. Take a risk . . .

A tart with a heart

Joshua 2:1–14

Conversion and change

Sibyl Ruth

Going home

Ruth 1:1–16

I was called after my father's mother, Annie Ruth. She came from a line of Welsh Nonconformists, so it's likely that a biblical name was chosen deliberately. As a girl I was proud of my inheritance. I knew it was rare for women to get a whole book to themselves. But the details of Ruth's tale didn't mean much to me.

Twenty years later the narrative acquired new meaning. Like biblical Ruth, I'd formed a strong bond with an older woman. And I was aware that, while society only sanctifies certain relationships, love crosses generations and breaks rules about gender.

These days I'm more interested in Naomi. I look back on my father's life. Annie Ruth suffered a fatal cerebral haemorrhage when my father was 18 months old. Her death meant that he moved not from Judah to Moab – but from Brecon to Dowlais.

In Dowlais then, as now, there was real deprivation. In the twentieth and twenty-first centuries the Lord's work must be done via government-funded regeneration, through multinational companies.

As an adult my father moved again – to England, where there were more opportunities. But despite having a good career, a wife and family, he was often disappointed. I can hear something of him in Naomi's cry: 'My life is more bitter than yours. The Lord's powerful hand has been against me!' Naomi wanted to go home. My father's ashes are buried by his parents' grave, in Brecon.

Blessed are they that mourn . . .

Sibyl Ruth · Conversion and change

Sometimes I could believe the Hebrew scriptures were a new work. At other times they are a dusty ragbag holding some nasty bits of history. How are we to make use of these scraps?

It is useful to consider spiritual leadership. Is it about sticking to long-established rules? Does it also encompass an unfolding relationship with the Divine? Most churches want the best of both worlds. Quakers seek to weigh tradition against a continuing effort to 'heed the promptings of love and truth which we trust as the leadings of God' (*Quaker Faith and Practice*, chapter 29).

Hezekiah's efforts to re-impose the law make him seem a stickler for tradition. To modern readers, who want to live peaceably in a multi-faith world, his zeal is problematic. But Hezekiah's relationship with God was also a dynamic one. We're told, 'The Lord was with Hezekiah' (verse 7).

I have struggled to reply when asked if the Lord was with me. Ten years back, my partner and I met Elders from my local meeting to discuss our wedding. One of them turned to me saying, 'And where does God come into this?' Eventually I said I couldn't imagine being married without some sort of access to goodness.

Hezekiah had access to goodness. And wouldn't all of us who struggle to do the right thing, to lead by example, like this sort of epitaph: 'There was no one like him among all of the kings of Judah. There was no king like him either before him or after him' (verse 5)?

What might being guided by love – and truth – involve?

Leadings

2 Kings 18:1–12

Conversion and change   Sibyl Ruth

Keeping hope alive

2 Kings 19:14–20, 32–37

It was as the number of survivors dwindled that Holocaust Memorial Day came to be officially marked. I used to organise educational events for young people about the *Shoah* (often called the Holocaust or Nazi holocaust). Historical events hold a message for later generations.

I think of the Holocaust when I consider Hezekiah's words to God. Sometimes prayer is an act of defiance. A person may assert the existence of a power for goodness, even as their own world is being destroyed.

And I think of my Jewish great-aunt, Rose Scooler. During 1944–5 she was a slave-labourer in the concentration camp at Theresienstadt. I don't know if she prayed, but she did make up defiant poems. In these she mocked her captors, lifting the spirits of fellow prisoners. Her verses remind me of Isaiah's message that states – twice – that Sennacherib 'will not enter this city'. In the most appalling conditions, my great-aunt would not allow despair to enter her heart. She wrote:

> *Here I've met a host of men and women*
> *who, living through a season of emergency,*
> *lost what made them more than animal*
> *– their basic human decency.*
> *Yet I found others who'd persevere*
> *in acts of saving grace . . .*

The word *Liebestat* is used in the original German text of this poem. Literally this means 'actions that spring from love'. This enduring faith must have helped her to carry on. Although many, many people in the camp perished, Rose Scooler – like Hezekiah – survived.

What values do we need to keep going?

Sibyl Ruth   Conversion and change

Conversion and change

2 Life transformed

Preparing for the week

It is commonly held that the Bible is a compilation of inspired words that provide answers to the real-life questions of believers both in the past and now. Such answers and explanations are to enlighten questioning minds, and result in inspired decisions within particular situations. Inspired decisions are needed to bring about change or renewal in individuals and in societies. As the catalyst for such inspired decisions, the Bible is a living medium for God's active presence in the world today.

This week's reflections took shape as I placed the biblical passages alongside the experiences of the struggling poor and of church people in the Philippines. Conversion and change as actions of God provide the focus of the notes. I hope that my reflections on the change that can take place in individuals, social groups and nations may contribute something significant to contemporary believers in similar situations throughout the world. I invite you to bring your own situations and questions to interact with my thoughts and reflections, so that the scriptures may inspire your decisions and be the catalyst for action for change in your setting.

Notes based on the New International Version by

Jonash Joyohoy

The Revd Jonash Joyohoy is a priest of 17 years in the Philippine Independent Church, a catholic church that more than a century ago developed out of the Filipinos' continuing struggle against foreign domination. At present he is serving as parish priest of the La Purisima Concepcion Parish in Malabon City, Metro Manila, and at the same time as Executive Director of the Bishop Ramento Project for Rights Defenders, based in Manila, Philippines.

God transforms situations

Psalm 126

This short psalm shows Israel's acknowledgement of God as the one who brought them back to their homeland from captivity. They believed that the events and conditions leading to their return were God's actions to transform situations. Yet they also acknowledged that restoration of their lives and fortunes depended on their own work, as they sang of sowing and reaping (verse 6). The psalm asserts that God brought about freedom for the people, but the rebuilding of the nation relies on their own labour and initiative.

Most people believed that the 1986 people-power revolution in the Philippines, which toppled Marcos, was God's action in history. Images of nuns and clergy carrying religious images and flowers to confront military tanks and personnel sent shivers through the Christian world. Christians and freedom-loving people all over the world responded with monetary assistance, hoping that the people released from dictatorship might rebuild their nation fast.

Yet a quarter of a century later, the Philippines and its people continue to languish in a pit of worsening poverty. The bright prospects promised by the 'bloodless revolution' are now almost forgotten. It seems that God started the transformation of the nation but the people failed to take their future into their own hands. Those in situations of political and economic captivity – Filipinos and others – may have plenty to learn from Psalm 126.

Incarnate God, enable us to acknowledge your presence in us as individuals and with each other, so that we may be able to do our share in your mission.

Jonash Joyohoy   Conversion and change

Simeon prophesies the change that the infant Jesus will bring about in apparently straightforward political terms: 'This child is destined to cause the falling and rising of many in Israel, and to be a sign that will be spoken against' (verse 34). As we read Simeon's prophecy from the hindsight of 2000 years of history, perhaps we can see in it foreknowledge of the bloodshed and violence that was to mark so much of that history. (Think of the crusades, or the persecution of Jews and witches, for instance.)

Jesus – the promise of change

Luke 2:25–35

Certainly the Gospels are no strangers to political opposition, though they do not endorse violence. Originating from a working-class family and representing the underside of society, Jesus certainly roused a good deal of opposition, not least from those in positions of power.

The promise of 'change' in Simeon's prophecy offers an image of 'the rising and falling of many'. In our time, perhaps we may read this as a call to people on the margins of society – whatever that might mean – to rise up against oppression. Jesus, the one in whom the promise of change is given, is able to identify with all people who know themselves to be marginalised – regardless of race, gender or nation. These are the ones we are also called to work change with and for – not using violence, but using the peaceable political means at our disposal.

Dear God, allow in us true appreciation of your actions in history and draw us closer to your side.

Conversion and change   Jonash Joyohoy

The change to Zaccheus

Luke 19:1–10

People like Zacchaeus – wealthy, well-connected types – appear to be increasing in number in our world. They can be seen going to church every Sunday, often donating huge sums of money towards the work of the church. When they speak about Christian values, they sound very convincing, and they are often regarded as good examples for the faithful. Yet few of them are to be seen doing what Zacchaeus did. They are rarely seen talking face to face with the likes of Jesus and his followers: fisherfolk and ordinary workers – the common accusers of the rich and powerful. Not many rich Christians welcome poor and ordinary women and men into their homes in the way Zacchaeus did.

Yet we should not despair of such things happening in our world. Though rare, they are not unknown. Our story manifests the limitless possibilities brought about when an individual truly allows Christ to change them. Conversion may take place within the echelons of power and corruption, since grace is for all without preference or discrimination. Genuine change for the rich may be as difficult as it is for a camel to go through a needle's eye, but still, 'What is impossible with men is possible with God' (Luke 18:27).

How does Jesus' promise of change need to work itself out in practical terms for those of us who are rich in the world's goods?

Through your infinite power, dear God, give us the grace of courage and humility so that by accepting your will we may gain your favour.

Jonash Joyohoy   Conversion and change

Change and conversion may happen not only to sinners but even to oppressors and enemies of the gospel. The case of Saul is a clear example.

Saul's blindness and healing, which are dramatic features of the story, may have a wider symbolic significance when we think of what happens in situations of persecution and oppression in our world today. Those who persecute and violate the innocent, whether because of differences in belief or through obedience to superiors, often demonstrate a loss of sound judgement and an arrogant self-confidence that allows them to act in oppressive and destructive ways. This experience may be comparable to a kind of moral blindness needing healing (although blind theologian John Hull cautions against speaking of blindness in this way).

The opening of Paul's eyes led to a complete change of direction, from being a prosecutor of the faith to becoming the chief defender and follower of Jesus Christ. When seen from my own context of the Philippines, conversions like this may not be so very unusual. There, it is not unusual to hear of conservative or anti-activist clergy and layfolk turning into active participants in people's struggles.

Loving God, with you nothing is impossible. Give us the power to bring about change in ourselves even when it seems impossible.

Saul encounters Jesus

Acts 9:1–16

Conversion and change   Jonash Joyohoy

Saul begins to preach

Acts 9:17–30

Immediately after recovering his sight, Paul began preaching the gospel boldly and fearlessly, in Damascus and Jerusalem. In both places plots were hatched against his life.

Today's activist clergy in the Philippines often started out as innocent postulants aspiring to become faithful clergy in the traditional mould. Few dreamed of becoming modern-day prophets, marching on the streets alongside the struggling poor, accused of being communists by the authorities or by church members. Many started as critics of such church involvement in politics.

What changed them? Their contact with the reality of the situations of the poor. Seeing the suffering of those on the margins, getting to know their daily struggles, sharing in their efforts to escape poverty – it is this which has been their Damascus Road encounter, opening their eyes and changing them. For them theology has become an active pursuit of justice which emanates from solidarity with the suffering and the poor. Boldness and fearlessness in both word and deed characterise their ministry, and a number of them have even paid the ultimate price of their faith, being among the thousand victims of extra-judicial killings which have taken place in the Philippines. Such faith, whilst costly, has the power to inspire and attract many, by its integrity and courage.

Where might your faith be demanding you to become actively involved?

Loving God, give us wisdom to see your will and courage to preach your word even in difficult situations.

Followers of Christ must face and withstand many misleading influences in the world, aside from threats to life. In this passage, Christians are cautioned against being carried away by the schemes of false teachers and by 'myths' which take us away from the truth (verses 3–4). In today's context, I suggest that we need to beware of those in global corporations who, for the sake of their corporate interests, use huge resources to subvert the Christian message. The greed of huge businesses can all too easily turn society as well as individuals aside from truth to falsity, from reality to alienation. They operate according to a law based on patronage, deception and fear, rather than one based on justice, mercy and compassion.

In the midst of worldly enticements and threats, the writer exhorts: 'keep your head in all situations, endure hardship, do the work of an evangelist, discharge all the duties of your ministry' (verse 5). This charge reminds us that followers of Christ do not belong to the world but God's kingdom. Evangelists must not lose their sense of calling as Christ's loyal agents, and must keep their focus on the discharge of their duties. But they do not do this in their own strength. The Counsellor whom Jesus promised (John 14:15) is active in them, keeping their vocation alive and encouraging them to stand firm.

Where do you see false myths, and how do you resist them?

Help us to stand firm upon your promise, O God, so that we may see the way you see, and remain faithful to our calling.

Readings from Colossians

1 Christ in you, the hope of glory

Notes based on the New Revised Standard Version by

Brian Haymes

Brian Haymes is a Baptist minister who has served in several pastorates and taught in two English Baptist Colleges. He is a former President of the Baptist Union. He is married to Jenny, and they have two daughters and two grandchildren.

Preparing for the week

Paul did not found the church at Colossae but, from prison, he writes a letter of encouragement and affirmation. He is aware that the congregation faces temptations from their surrounding culture. These are ways of thinking that seem attractive to contemporaries but, perhaps without their realising it, compromise or diminish the significance of Jesus Christ. As such they mislead and deny disciples the full glory of Christian experience. So Paul writes a pastoral letter, with some strong and vivid teaching about the significance of what God was doing in Jesus.

We can prepare ourselves for the reading of this letter by first noting any aspects of our society where people seek other claims to know God, where the Church is tempted to add other insights to Christ as the way to being happy and fulfilled. Take note of the assumptions behind the main news items or advertisements. In what way are they presenting the 'real world'? Are there ways in which we are being controlled or our liberty curtailed by assumptions rarely questioned by the media? Reading the letter will help us ask 'what is the good news of Jesus?' and 'are there ways we currently dilute the gift of God?' Let us ask God for discernment as we read, think and act.

What an affirmative beginning this is! Paul writes to 'the saints', which means, as it always does in the New Testament, members of the church, baptised into Christ Jesus. The community, however mixed it is in its membership, belongs to God by grace and that is what makes them 'holy'. It is a very positive, graceful view of the church.

To the saints!

Paul thanks God for three aspects of the life of this local church. First, they are faithful to Christ as his followers. Second, that faithfulness shows itself in love – this inclusive congregation is self-aware of its calling in Christ. And third, the hope they have in Christ shows itself in graceful living, bearing fruit. The hope they have came to them through the good news about life, death and new life in Jesus.

Colossians 1:1–8

So the saints are sharing the life and love of God, and inevitably they share the mission of God as the gospel bears fruit in all the world. Paul knows of this because of the testimony of his colleague Epaphras, who has witnessed the Colossians' love, a gift of the Holy Spirit. Do you think this can be said of the congregation to which you belong?

Gracious God, thank you for the saints with whom we worship. Help us to be faithful to our calling, so that in hope, faith and love our lives bear the fruit of the gospel of Christ.

Readings from Colossians   Brian Haymes

What do you pray for your church?

Colossians 1:9–14

When you pray for the church what do you ask for? Are your hopes and requests consistent with the gospel of Jesus? Here is a brief insight into what Paul consistently prays for the Colossians.

He prays for their continued spiritual growth. The focus is on the members being filled with the knowledge of God, with wisdom and understanding. This knowledge is more than intellectual – something going on in the mind – although it does involve knowing what God has done in Jesus. It is also a matter of experience, a deep knowing in the heart and emotions. And it also involves practice, living in a way that pleases God and reflects God's nature. It is not a matter of being clever so much as being godly, living lives that bear fruit in many ways.

Christians will need to be strong to live this way because the temptations to do otherwise are very real and intense. So Paul asks for the strength God gives to those who need it. Notice how patience and joy characterise this kind of living. And thankfulness, because of what God has done. Paul reminds the church of its rescue, liberation and forgiveness. What do you think that means?

God of our journey, help us to grow in knowledge, wisdom and practical understanding.

These words ask to be sung. In fact, they may well come from an early Christian hymn that Paul is quoting. No one has ever seen God but, if God were to be visible, God would be like Christ. In him the invisible is visible. Christ is the first-born of all that is. Everything that is, is his work – all creation, all the powers that shape and rule human living, all came to be through Christ and for Christ. All things have their meaning, their coherence, in him, the risen head of the church. In Christ is the fullness of God and through him is the reconciling work of God.

This is no little Christ of the inner life of religious experience and feelings. Here is the cosmic Christ in and through whose life we share the life and purposes of God. For Paul, this might be a big claim, but it is nothing less than the truth. For the Colossians, tempted and concerned by all manner of hidden teachings and claims to secret knowledge, Christ is good news. Christ is every-thing that God is.

Nothing therefore can be compared to Christ; human cleverness, political influence, military might, chance and fate, disease and death, all are subject to the Christ of God who gave his life for us.

All praise be to God, the Christ-like God, source of our hope and freedom.

A glorious Christian hymn

Colossians 1: 15–23

Serving for your sake

Colossians 1:24 – 2:5

Paul may not have founded this church but he knows that in Christ he is called to care for and serve the members. He does this gladly, though in prison, understanding that he shares in the work of Christ.

Christian service begins in gratitude. We are called to the privilege of sharing Christ's life and work. At the heart of that work is making Christ known. It has nothing to do with self-promotion, but all to do with grace. That fundamental mystery beyond human understanding, the mystery at the heart of all that is, God has made known in Christ. Making him known comes as a gift, and not a matter of human achievement, and so is nothing but privilege.

As a servant of Christ, Paul gives himself for the church, even for those he has never met. He will not keep his life in Christ to himself. He wants to share the treasure. To present everyone mature in Christ is the goal of Paul's ministry. Ministry is a life of gratitude to God, lived and offered for others, through Christ and for Christ. The apostle's interest and longing is not just for the churches he has planted but for all people in Christ. A cosmic Christ means a cosmic mission into which Christians can throw themselves.

Lord of the church, bless your servants with hope and large-heartedness.

Brian Haymes   Readings from Colossians

Big baptism!

Colossians 2:6–15

A number of teachers think that behind these chapters of Colossians lies the idea of baptism. Here it is specifically mentioned. Baptism is being buried and raised with Christ, the cosmic Christ. It is being made alive by the power of God, coming to share the life of God. It inevitably means living differently under the rule of this great Christ.

This is such a huge claim that we might be tempted to compromise it a little, by adding our own insights or those of our contemporaries, to Christ. Often we are persuaded by these other approaches because we think they are in fashion, or more accurately define the real world. But for Paul, nothing can be added to Christ. Indeed, he knows that all these good ideas that tempt us can take on a life of their own – approaches to life like consumerism, nationalism, the deals the advertisers sell us as the way to happiness and fulfilment. These modern expressions of the powers do not bring life. At their worst, they mean death. But the cosmic Christ has put them in their place, which is as his servants. In baptism we name the one supreme liberator. So, Paul urges, live your lives in him, follow him.

Living Christ, you have set us free from the powers that would enslave us and mislead us. May we so trust you that we live your life and reflect your glory.

The cosmic Christ in Holy Week

Colossians 2: 16–19

It is depressing but understandable when people of faith major on incidental matters and miss the big idea. We can make a huge case over a detail, turning small matters of opinion and personal judgement into issues of principle. So we distort faith into a culturally conditioned way of life. We can do this very religiously, as if these observances are the heart of the matter. We do it in the name of God. But God in Christ has set us free from that kind of self-imposition. Paul wants his readers to focus on Christ.

It's not that what we eat, or the special festival days we keep, are of no value. It's that these can become seriously demanding and unsatisfyingly insubstantial. We become busy about religious ideas and duties which may impress others but leave us empty. We sense again Paul's pastoral love for the church members whose enthusiasms can run away with them. If the diets and days, the visions and angels, do not point to Christ – then put them aside. Paul longs for Christians to grow in faith, hope and love. For that we must focus on Christ and so allow the life God gives to grow in us. It's not for us to desire the active life that others admire, but rather that the beauty and goodness of the life of Jesus be in us.

Gracious God, through the passionate love of Jesus, draw us deeper into your life and work.

Readings from Colossians

2 Do everything in the name of the Lord Jesus

Notes based on the New Revised Standard Version by

Brian Haymes

For Brian's biography see p. 102.

Preparing for the week

We move into Holy Week. We shall hear again the extraordinary story which leads to the cross of Jesus. And as this goes on we shall read further into Colossians, as Paul helps us explore the new life in Christ. We shall remember in this week the powers, military, political and religious, which lead to death. We shall tell the amazing story of suffering love that in all the chaos is the one matter still standing. How shall we do everything in the name of this Lord Jesus?

You might like to keep a diary of your reflections this week, as you hear the story of Holy Week and read the words of Paul. Look for moments when the two interact in your mind and experience. Notice when the assumptions behind the news seem to reflect a way of describing the world which is very different from one where the cosmic Christ reigns. And when and where in the politics and news of this week do you hear the call of the cosmic Christ? Where do the claims of the media and those of Christ collide today?

On taking religion too seriously

Colossians 2: 20–23

It is a sad matter of fact that, in all religions, people can make mountains out of molehills. Someone has an idea, which was helpful at the time. As the years go on we forget quite why we do something, but it becomes all the more important. We say it is essential for our identity and so it becomes an imposition, a burden more than a blessing. The rules of religion become essential, and so faith is distorted. The practices once were helpful but become deadly when we forget their meaning and simply impose them. When that happens, temples need to be cleansed.

Is it possible that 'human commands and teachings' (verse 22) are shaping our lives too much? They can sound so right, even good and holy. A key question is, of course, for whom are we doing these things? For ourselves? Or for God? Paul senses that some religious practices are simply a matter of self-indulgence. We like it that way. It makes us feel good. By concentrating on such things we avoid the real claims of God and refuse the life which is in Christ. So the good becomes the enemy of the best, and liberty is reduced to a new slavery.

Open our eyes, loving God, that we may see ourselves and our practices for what they are. Set us free from loyalties that prevent us from sharing your life.

Early forms of baptism were vivid expressions of being buried with Christ and being raised to his new life. Candidates would come from the water wearing new clothes. Paul speaks, more than once, of putting on Christ, laying aside an old self in the tomb but now being clothed in a new, forgiven life according to the image of its creator.

Live out your baptism

Colossians 3:1–11

This new life is no theoretical matter, neither is it simply an inward experience. It finds expression in the way we live together as the church, the company of those who share the life in Christ. Paul expects Christians to live differently because they are in Christ.

Some of the sins to be avoided, as listed by Paul, sound predictable. Others, more social than individually personal, are telling: malice, slander, abusive language. Sadly such things are not unknown in congregations. And Christians are not immune from telling stories that grow in the telling and lose touch with the truth. And note the inclusiveness of this new community gathered in Christ. The usual distinctions between races, nationalities or social classes have no place in Christ's company.

On the basis of these verses, does your congregation look baptised?

Thank you for the fellowship of your church, those people among whom you found us, and in whose friendship you help us. May we live as the community of new life.

More on the life of the baptised

Colossians 3: 12–17

If yesterday we seemed to focus on what behaviour does not fit with life in Christ, today Paul offers us something more positive. He calls church members 'God's chosen ones', which echoes the biblical language of covenant. Here the primary choice is God's. We assume it is ours, a matter of human rights! But before we have any choice to make, God has chosen to be for us in Christ, for all of us! Being part of the church, therefore, is not simply our decision. It is a response to God. We have answered a call and are holy and beloved because, by grace, we belong to God.

Now we have a guide for our relationships and life. We are to clothe ourselves with the virtues of Christ, practices we learn together in his company. We forgive one another, because we are forgiven. Love and peace are God's gifts which we share. And worship becomes so important in shaping this community. We listen together to the scriptures and let them form our common life. We have every reason to praise and thank God, so we sing for God. And we do all this for Jesus. All our living is in him and for him. The community of the chosen lives eucharistically, in thankfulness to God. Now again, on this basis, does your congregation look baptised?

Thank you that you chose to be for us in Christ. Thank you for our place in your church.

How we respond to this passage will reveal something of how we treat the Bible. Are these words of Paul to be taken, once and for all, as the way Christians should relate at home and at work? Should we continue the hierarchical patterns set out here, where the duties of the weaker are discussed (wife, child and slave) and then those of stronger superior persons (husband, parent and master)? Or should we recognise that Paul is writing out of a context which is not ours?

If we take the words as a new law we distort Paul's approach to faithful discipleship. As a matter of fact, his words here are a real advance on the more rigid practices of that day. But most of us will find this a very conservative approach in its context. Has Paul faced the full implications of his teaching about a new humanity in Christ where there is no longer slave or free, male or female? Have we?

What comes as a challenge here is the way the apostle is working out the implications of the rule of the cosmic Christ, especially in the home and at work. That abides as a vital task for serious Christians. Do our relationships reflect the new life in Christ, or the old ways of a society not yet living out the redemption of God in Christ?

Divine parent, help us to live as sisters and brothers in your family.

The church at home

Colossians 3:18 – 4:1

Good Friday

Colossians 4:2–6

This day for Christians is dominated by the story of the cross of Christ Jesus. We watch, hardly knowing what to say, as human cruelty, human systems of force and power, meet with the divine love for the whole world. Paul has urged the Colossians to avoid becoming entangled with social, political and philosophical theories about the world. Here we see some of the most persistently powerful of them doing their worst. The cross stands in contradiction to these ways of ruling the world.

Here Paul urges us to live prayerfully, in gratitude. We are bidden to pray for those who suffer today for the cause of Christ. Paul cherishes the hope that he and doubtless other faithful ones will be able to tell of the fundamental mystery of God revealed in the cross. There is a sharing in the cross for those who share the life of God.

There is a graciousness which belongs to gospel speech. The message is not one with which to threaten others, to beat them into submission, to spread fear and oppression. May our language of the cross be winsome and loving, such as God uses to bless even enemies.

Before the cross we bow, with Paul and all the saints and angels. Your death appals and yet captivates us. Did ever such love and sorrow meet? We worship you in awesome wonder, with gratitude we cannot put into words. You are loving us into life.

Christ lies in the tomb on Saturday. Meanwhile life of a sort goes on and Paul concludes his letter with greetings and instructions to get on with the tasks of discipleship. We note how personal this is. Look at how Tychicus is described, a wonderful commendation from Paul. Among those mentioned is Onesimus, runaway slave of Philemon, now a Christian brother and church member.

Waiting the coming day

Colossians 4:7–18

The cosmic Christ is no general theory but the active personal love and life of God, stronger than death and sin, making a difference to slaves, owners, and all of us. But it is clear that Paul expects some definite response to God's grace in Christ. So Archippus needs to get on with what he is charged to do. While it is true that, crucially, there are things that God must do for us that we cannot do for ourselves – like forgiving our sins and raising Jesus from the dead – Christian living is always distorted when we neglect our responsibilities in God's service. It's not that we add to our salvation but that, by our lives, we witness to it.

Paul's final greeting in his own hand reminds us of a paradox. He is in prison but he knows a freedom in Christ that his gaolers do not know. He is free to be a servant and to find in the service of Christ a perfect freedom.

Gracious God, we wait a glorious day. Today seems sombre and dark. It is as if creation scarcely dares to draw breath. Help us to realise in deeper measure what Christ has done for us already as we wait and worship.

Brian Haymes

Living with Easter

1 Christ is risen

Notes based on
the New Revised
Standard Version
by
**Omana
Mathew**

Omana Mathew
belongs to the Mar
Thoma Church in
India. She holds a
Master of Theology in
Women's Studies. She
has worked among
women who have
been victims of
domestic violence
and is currently
involved in
programmes working
for women's rights.

Preparing for the week

'Death is not extinguishing the light. It is only putting out the lamp because the dawn has come'

Rabindranath Tagore

The Easter season is a season of celebration of life. Easter denotes the resurrection of Christ – a divine act that brings immense hope in the midst of uncertainty and death. We are called to be witnesses of the risen Lord: to proclaim our love for God and others through obedience to Christ's teachings, knowing that by so doing we shall find the fullness of life promised in and by Jesus.

Resurrection in itself has little meaning without the cross. Every resurrection has a cross behind it. Jesus taught the paradoxical way that only by death comes life, only by spending our life do we retain it, and only by sacrificial service do we exhibit true greatness. Nevertheless, this does not imply some kind of miserable, joyless life. On the contrary, resurrection calls us to choose life and give life. So our faith in the risen Lord should enable us to be channels of God's saving grace in this world.

May the 'shalom' of the risen Lord reign among us and strengthen us to discern the signs of our times and act accordingly.

The risen Christ is the main theme in St Paul's writings. Belief in the risen Christ is the strongest foundation of Christian faith. Jesus' life and ministry demonstrate a constant fight against the forces of death and reveal God's authority over worldly powers and principalities. The resurrection event is a triumph over evil forces and death. This truth was first revealed to the apostles, later to hundreds of believers, and then to Paul himself. These testimonies are also an answer to those who had no faith in resurrection.

Christian faith is rooted in God's transforming grace and power, which was manifested through the risen Christ and needs to be reflected in our beliefs and deeds. Victory over the forces of death and the transforming grace of God give new meaning to our Christian witness.

Are we able to uphold our faith in the risen Christ in a context where the forces of death are operating? Can we make resurrection a reality when hundreds of people are dying due to poverty, war, deadly diseases and other human-made calamities?

Risen Lord, help us to live in that power of resurrection through which you attained victory over death. Grant us the grace that our faith in the risen Lord may be manifested in our lives and deeds. May we become channels of your transforming grace in our struggle against evil forces and structures.

Resurrection – the foundation of Christian belief

1 Corinthians 15: 3–11

Faith in the risen Christ – an affirmation of life

1 Corinthians 15: 12–26

Paul recapitulates the good news of the risen Christ in this text, proclaiming that denial of the resurrection of the body is denial of the resurrection of Christ. Such a denial empties the Christian message of truth and the possibility of eternal life. Faith in the risen Christ is the strongest biblical and theological basis for affirming the body, proclaiming it as divinely designed and part of the body of Christ. Jesus' body was not left to perish, but God raised him to eternity.

In a world where human bodies, especially women's bodies, are commodified, denigrated, destroyed and attacked, this is an affirmation we desperately need to uphold. I have become passionately convinced of this through my work with women who have experienced shocking domestic violence. The resurrected body of Christ conveys powerfully the idea that the human body needs to be safeguarded from all violence and commodification.

We are called in our different contexts to recognise human bodies as temples of the living God and channels for the fulfilment of God's purposes. We also need to affirm the significance of protecting and preserving the body of the earth as we affirm that Christ's death and resurrection was not just for human beings but for the whole universe.

Thanks be to you, loving God, for the joy of Easter, in which we see all pain and suffering swallowed up in Christ's victory. Risen Christ, give us the grace to value and affirm life wherever it is denied.

Omana Mathew   Living with Easter

All four Gospels agree on one significant fact – that on Easter morning when it was still dark, women disciples went to Jesus' tomb. The women's vigil at the crucifixion and their witness of the risen Christ are essential parts of the Easter story. Today's text gives us the most detailed account of Mary Magdalene's encounter with the risen Lord and her commissioning by him to proclaim the good news to the faith community. Her faith, deep devotion, boldness and willingness to transcend the patriarchal norms of her time, drove her to the tomb and led her to encounter the risen Lord.

Women – the first witnesses of the risen Lord

John 20:1–18

The empty tomb depicts transformed and renewed life: life that partakes of the very life of God – eternal life. Eternal life is not some otherworldly life, but beckons us to a radically new way of life here and now. It is a new perspective upholding the values of the reign of God which become effective in our fellowship with the risen Lord.

The women who went to the tomb continue to inspire us today in our faith journey. As we keep vigil with them, we look to encounter Christ in the realities of our time and place. Let us pray that we will be as quick and enthusiastic in our response to the life-enhancing mission of Jesus as they were.

Almighty God, give us the grace to encounter Christ in the realities of this world. Grant us the courage to resist the forces that constrict life, so that we may become channels of abundant life.

Omana Mathew

Risen Christ – hope of a new social order

Acts 10:34–43

During a recent visit to one of our rural parishes, I observed that the villagers all sat and ate together, irrespective of caste, when they were assembled in the church for worship. Yet once these same folk were back in their day-to-day home and work settings, they reverted to the rigid discriminatory practices of the caste system which continues to exist in India.

Understanding the message of the risen Christ in a context where discrimination, division and dehumanisation exist is a great challenge. Christ offers us the vision of a community which goes against the common bonds and separations that mark our ordinary human communities. The Church as the body of Christ should enable untouchable bodies to become divine agents of social transformation.

Christ's crucified body cries out to us to resist every dehumanising act inflicted on another body, whilst his risen body speaks of a victory over life-defying forces that we see everywhere around us. As we meditate on the glorious risen body of our Lord, are we not challenged to identify forces in the world such as casteism, poverty and patriarchy, as profound sins against God? Faith in the risen Lord invites us to create a just community where people experience right relationship in the body of Christ in the midst of continuing social differences and imbalances of power.

Living God, help us to envisage a new social order where the abused, misused and untouchable bodies of our society experience that they are part of the holy body of Christ.

Omana Mathew

Living with Easter

In this passage we are given two key titles for the risen Christ. First, Jesus is the faithful witness to the truth of God. In and through Jesus, God reveals the divine love and shows a new possibility in this world of sin: that one can live in love and overcome evil through loving deeds. Second, Jesus is the first-born from the dead. He lived in loving obedience to God, which meant opposing the forces that dehumanise and enslave human lives. He never allowed sin to have power over him. He pardoned his enemies and prayed for God's forgiveness, even on the cross. God raised him from death and thus Jesus is the first-born from the dead, 'the way, the truth and the life' (John 14:6).

How can we witness to the risen Christ in our own culture, especially for the marginalised, the displaced and the dispossessed? The message of the risen Christ should enable them to reap hope and receive life even in the midst of despair and agony, but for this to be a reality, we need to be living as well as preaching the transformed life that Christ offers.

Risen Christ – the way, the truth and the life

Revelation 1:4–18

Gracious Lord, we want to follow your way, seek your truth and live by the example of the abundant life manifested in Christ Jesus. Strengthen us so that we may not falter, but truly fulfil your divine purpose in this world.

Living with Easter   Omana Mathew

121

Total obedience as the new commandment of love

John 14:18–24

This passage exhorts us to keep God's commandments as an expression of true love for Christ. The risen Christ gives an assurance of God's abiding presence, saying: 'because I live, you also will live' (verse 18). The promise of not being left alone is certain.

Created in the image of God, human beings have been given an immense ability to love. It was through obedience to God that Jesus manifested his love and he expects the same from his disciples. Love for Christ involves an intense relationship not only with God, but also with human beings and the whole created order. This is a relationship that involves risk and sacrifice as well as genuine commitment.

We live in a world where broken relationships are on the increase, be it marital, familial or cosmic. Those who claim that they love their spouses or family members often bring pain and heartbreak through the failure of their commitments. Nature is being plundered and destroyed because of human greed.

Christian love is not just an emotional feeling but a costly love lived out in daily life. Though our calling to obey Christ's command of love is a hard task, God takes the initiative through the Holy Spirit, our helper and comforter.

Merciful God, we have proclaimed our love for you with our lips, but have failed to express it by keeping your commandments. Cleanse us and reinstate us so that we may truly demonstrate your costly love in the situations in which we live and work.

Omana Mathew   Living with Easter

Living with Easter

2 Christ is with his people

Preparing for the week

Among the many distinctive elements of the Christian faith, perhaps the most remarkable is the belief that Jesus, who is the Christ, was raised from the dead on the third day. The unique claim of Christianity is that by faith we can encounter the living Christ, the one who continues to meet people in the immediacy of their everyday lives and contexts.

The great African-American woman freedom-fighter Sojourner Truth's famed dictum for her preaching ministry was that she had only one text from which to preach: namely, 'When I found Jesus'. The readings in this coming week focus on how the encounter with Christ Jesus should lead us into demonstrably different forms of action that seek to bring God's justice and peace into the world. We should be God's good news in the world. The following reflections do not attempt to 'explain' the meaning of the appointed readings. Rather, the approach I have taken is one that reflects on the consequences of the passage for fruitful Christian living.

Living and loving God, help us this week to discover you afresh in the presence of the risen Christ who continues to meet with us at all times and in all places, whether we are expecting him or not. Help us to be alert to his presence and to rejoice in this fresh encounter each time we meet it in our daily lives.

Notes based on the New Revised Standard Version by

Anthony G Reddie

Anthony Reddie is a research fellow and Consultant in Black Theological Studies for the British Methodist Church and the Queen's Foundation for Ecumenical Theological Education, in Birmingham, UK. He is the author of numerous books, in the areas of Black Theology and Christian Education. He is also the editor of *Black Theology: An International Journal.*

Why me?

Acts 22:1–11

Voice 1	So tell me what happened again? It still doesn't make any sense.
Voice 2	What do you want me to say? I've told you what happened. Jesus came to me and spoke to me. Now I see everything differently. What more do you want me to say?
Voice 1	But you've got to admit that this is crazy. Why would Jesus Christ come to you? You've been persecuting vulnerable people for years. Asylum-seekers and refugees. The social outcasts and the socially marginalised!
Voice 2	You think I don't know that? You think the irony isn't lost on me as well? I know what I've done to his people. I am embarrassed about it. But it was my job to do that.
Voice 1	And yet Jesus Christ still comes to you and says he wants you to do his work?
Voice 2	You're not helping me to be honest.
Voice 1	Is that my fault? It just sounds crazy. I know Jesus says he loves all people and came for all people, but I really did think there were limits.
Voice 2	Well obviously, you were wrong. We both were. God's love in Christ seems to have no limits. Christ loves even me!.

Living God, we give you thanks that through your son, Jesus, you love all humankind, no matter what we have done. Help us to be mindful of this every day

Anthony Reddie   Living with Easter

Voice 1	I can't believe it, I really can't.
Voice 2	Well, it is amazing. You remember what I used to be like?
Voice 1	Remember? I've got the metaphorical bruises to show for it. You had a vicious tongue in the old days.
Voice 2	Especially against Black and Asian people. It was the culture in which I was brought up.
Voice 1	And now?
Voice 2	I just want to love everyone.
Voice 1	And what about 'those kinds of people'?
Voice 2	The ones I used to hate? They are beautiful human beings like me and you.
Voice 1	Unbelievable. If I hadn't seen it, I wouldn't believe it.
Voice 2	It's like the old me just packed his bags and left. And where there was the space for hatred and anger, now there is just the presence of Christ.
Voice 1	I hope the old guy never comes back.
Voice 2	I don't think he will. The new me just sees everything so much differently now. It's like something of the old has died and gone away.
Voice 1	And what we are left with is the new you.
Voice 2	Who is alive in Christ and Christ is alive in him.

The new me

Romans 6:1–11

Gracious God, we give you thanks that by the power of Christ's resurrection, we can experience a new life in you. Help us to walk in the joy of this new life every day.

Living with Easter   Anthony Reddie

Giving it all up

Philippians 3:7–14

Voice 1	You've lost nearly everything.
Voice 2	And I'm the better for it.
Voice 1	How can you be so sure? But everything!
Voice 2	And I am contented.
Voice 1	So let me get this right. In following Christ you have lost all the financial perks you used to get?
Voice 2	I'm now responsible in how I deal with all my clients. I don't bend the rules any more.
Voice 1	So now you do what exactly?
Voice 2	I let the spirit of Christ guide me in my dealings with the poor and excluded.
Voice 1	But that can't make you popular with your employers?
Voice 2	Like I said, I have other goals now.
Voice 1	And what about promotion and climbing the corporate ladder?
Voice 2	Climbing the ladder of faith towards Christ is now my only goal.
Voice 1	But you know there will come a time when you won't be able to hold the two things together?
Voice 2	I'll cross that bridge when it comes. Till then, I am content to do what I believe is right and is not ethically dubious.
Voice 1	And your faith demands all that?
Voice 2	Nothing less.

Loving God, help us through the inspiration of Christ Jesus to forsake all temptations, in order that we can be ruled by the only 'Lord' and the one 'Master'.

Anthony Reddie   Living with Easter

Voice 1	I am really grateful.
Voice 2	It was a pleasure.
Voice 1	But what you did has changed everything.
Voice 2	I am doing what God has gifted me to do.
Voice 1	I could never have completed that form all by myself. And the way in which you spoke up for me as well at the tribunal.
Voice 2	Look, it's no big deal. I have the skills to do that sort of thing. It's a shame that people like me are needed to defend the rights of people like you.
Voice 1	But all the same, I bet there are not many like you who would help someone like me and not ask to get paid for it.
Voice 2	It's my Christian duty. God in Christ has given me certain gifts for the benefit of all people.
Voice 1	Your presence made such a difference.
Voice 2	Just trying to do the right thing, and use my gifts, in order that someone who needs the love of God can get justice for themselves and their family.
Voice 1	I will never judge Christians in the same way again.
Voice 2	That alone is my reward!

All together now

Ephesians 4:7–16

God of justice and love, help us to be the living presence of Christ in our dealings with others this day. Help us to use the gifts you have given us for the benefit of all those we meet.

Living with Easter

Anthony Reddie

Loving our enemies

Acts 7:54–60

Voice 1	OK, let's go kick some butt.
Voice 2	I'm not going.
Voice 1	Look, that person slandered you. We've got to give them a good sorting.
Voice 2	And what good would that do?
Voice 1	But they are saying you are not up to the job, just because you're Black and a woman.
Voice 2	I know.
Voice 1	You must challenge them! You can't do nothing!
Voice 2	Those who want to believe it will continue to do so, no matter what I say.
Voice 1	But how are you going to defend yourself?
Voice 2	By simply being me.
Voice 1	And that is?
Voice 2	The person Christ Jesus wants me to be.
Voice 1	But you can't let those words stand undefended.
Voice 2	But my character and integrity will defend me.
Voice 1	What are you talking about?
Voice 2	Those who don't like me will always believe the worst, and those who do won't believe it anyway.
Voice 1	I will never understand this Christian faith of yours. It makes no sense.
Voice 2	It never will if you try to judge it by the usual standards of human society.

God, our mother and father, help us to live through those trying times when all around us are seemingly persecuting us for who we are and what we stand for. May the love of Christ empower us.

Anthony Reddie   Living with Easter

Voice 1	I want to thank you for everything you've done.
Voice 2	You need to learn to act differently in the future.
Voice 1	I was only defending myself.
Voice 2	The world is not fair. That's why you need to learn how to curb that temper of yours.
Voice 1	But I'm not like you. I don't mean to behave badly, but when the red mist descends, it all kicks off.
Voice 2	I was once like you. But Jesus Christ found me and having him in my life and trying to love him and live like him has made all the difference.
Voice 1	So you want me to be like you?
Voice 2	No. Jesus wants you to be like him.
Voice 1	How do I know that this Jesus is any good?
Voice 2	I've just told you what he did for me.
Voice 1	But how do I know that what you are telling me is the truth?
Voice 2	You saw what I did to help you? Why do you think I stood up for you in front of the authorities? Because Jesus loves you, I must also love and help you.
Voice 1	Is that it?
Voice 2	It's the start.

Saving others

Matthew 28: 16–20

God of all, help me to live in such a way that others may see Christ Jesus alive and reigning in my life, to the glory of your name.

Questions Jesus asked

1 Questions Jesus asked in Mark

Notes based on the New Revised Standard Version by

Geoffrey Herbert

For Geoffrey's biography see p. 16.

Preparing for the week

This Sunday starts Christian Aid Week, one aspect of Christians living in the way of Christ. Mark's Gospel starts with the verse: 'The beginning of the good news of Jesus Christ, the Son of God.' Every event and every question after that is asking, 'Who is this man?' At Caesarea Philippi, almost exactly half-way through the Gospel, Jesus asks his friends, 'But who do you say that I am?', and Peter answers 'the Christ' (8:29). Jesus immediately starts to talk about his death. Implicit in the question 'Who is this man?' is 'What does it mean to follow him?' – what is the quality and cost of living life his way? These questions are behind every question this week. Have we realised who Jesus is, and are we following in his footsteps? Big! But Mark's little book is big.

A prayer for this week:

Lord Jesus, show me more and more who you really are. Fill my life and shape it.

People listening to Jesus	Hey, what's this? We thought the Law was absolutely clear. It's right to save life on the sabbath, but wrong to do healing, because it's work. That's hard if someone close to us is ill, but we have to be obedient to God or everything will fall to pieces.
Jesus	My father cares about this man who was reduced to poverty because of that withered hand, and he hasn't rested even on his sabbath: he has healed him. That's saving a life.
Religious high-ups	Terrible! This Galilean upstart is playing God. Who does he think he is? People have been stoned to death for less than that.
Us	It's Christian Aid Week: we'll give a good bit.
Jesus	That's a beginning, but how about caring enough to get alongside my poor and suffering people in the world? How about working for them in the campaigns, or getting to know one or two and actually working with them? That would be more like my father's love, which is my love. Healing that man was my way of living it. How about you, Geoffrey?
Me	I'm one of those who dips into my bank account for Christian Aid, but that's more or less all.

'Is it lawful to do good . . . on the sabbath?'

Mark 3:1–6

For our prayer today let's keep silent, relax and think about nothing except making a space for Jesus in a new part of our life.

'Who are my mother and my brothers?'

Mark 3:31–35

Yesterday it was the members of Jesus' own faith who misunderstood, and implicitly rejected, his work. Today it's his family.

Mark's Gospel shows Jesus becoming relentlessly more and more isolated. He seems to provoke this as if he wants it, but (more deeply) he is opening himself to an enormous sisterhood and brotherhood – all the needy and forgotten people, and anyone who really wants to discover and do God's will. Potentially this also re-includes the very ones who reject him.

In Western culture family loyalties, though still there, are not as strong as in more traditional societies. We have lost something while at the same time becoming freer of the traps and binds of families. This in no way means that we are nearer the freedom of Jesus. He would challenge us too to rediscover more of the good foundation that family life gives, and also to use that together with our freedom in order to find new families based on 'the will of God'.

What is this 'will of God'? Yesterday I went to sit with a Muslim neighbour whose much-longed-for baby daughter has just been found to have a rare and terrible epileptic syndrome. I went just from duty, but in struggling alongside him until he spoke what prayer he could pray ('Show me your mercy in whatever happens') I found we were for a moment brothers.

Show me my brothers and sisters.

Geoffrey Herbert   Questions Jesus asked

James	A little seed? Yes, I can see the kingdom is starting small: that's us, just a little handful of seeds.
John	Mmmm, he's got big plans for us, though – this idea of the seed growing into a big bush and producing a lot more mustard seeds. He doesn't seem to think much of smallness.
James	Oh, but I think he likes small things too. They're precious, like jewels; seeds are sort of living jewels. And that's us!
John	Wow! Yes! Have you noticed how he leaves the crowds with his parables and no explanations? I reckon we're his special group – in on the secrets.
James	Perhaps, but have you noticed that we always get talking like we are now, and then asking him more questions?
John	Yes. He certainly gets us going, and doing the hard work. I hope some of the crowds get going like that: perhaps a bit of struggling with it will do them no harm, and make some more real followers.
James	And having all the answers given them wouldn't let them feel they have a real part. Jesus never does that with us: he always gets the answers out of us in the end, with just a bit of help. It can take a long time, but it's better that way.

Two disciples listening

Mark 4:30–34

For your prayer, keep silence and let the seed grow in you.

Questions Jesus asked   Geoffrey Herbert

'Do you still not perceive or understand?'

Mark 8:14–21

James	I thought we were really getting somewhere. Now he's telling us we're just useless.
John	Well, I was very hungry, and that made me forget everything else. I'm only human.
James	He's losing his cool because of all the trouble – endless rows with all those educated rabbis, then John the Baptiser executed by Herod. Jesus and John were very close, and I think Jesus is wondering whether he'll be next.
John	Yes, and he's taken us on this long trek away from all that, into Gentile lands, and that woman really had a go at him about not even giving her sick daughter a crumb from under our table. He was shaken by that, and I've noticed he has a new attitude to Gentiles: look how he did that feeding miracle for 4000 and some were Gentiles!
James	I noticed that too. It's a pity we forgot all that. We're just dim, like he says.

Jesus' angry reaction to his friends is completely human and also aims to jolt them into readiness for the Caesarea Philippi questions (Mark 8:27, 29) about who he is, which he may have been pondering more lately. Who is Jesus for you? Listen to the answers you've read or heard, but then rely on your own experience.

Take time to know him and tell him. I did that only after 38 years from first meeting him when I was 16. How dim!

Geoffrey Herbert   Questions Jesus asked

They are on the long, terrifying road to the cross. Jesus has told them that being the Christ means this, and that his followers must take up their own crosses (8:34).

Now their dimness again: they start arguing about status. Part of my 38-year dimness was just that – a desire to excel, to achieve. I was already on the road with Jesus, and then in a way he showed me a child, or rather a new awareness of my own children, by then young adults, to shake me, to take me apart and show me how my ambition had sacrificed them.

In Western culture children are sometimes neglected by selfish parents, sometimes indulged or made the means of glory for them. I didn't do any of that: I just centred on my own career. Fortunately there was some foundation of relationship, so the future could be rescued; we could become friends, and I could show that I really cared.

In the Lord's time children had very low status. Jesus treats a child as treasured, and tells his followers to become their servants ('slaves' in the Greek). In other words status is irrelevant. What really matters is loving and costly service. Jesus also tells them that in doing this they will be caring for him. We are back to Monday's reading: Jesus' utter identification with the lowly and dis-possessed.

Use the beggar's prayer of silence and neediness before God. We have nothing to offer.

'What are you arguing about?'

Mark 9:33–37

What can Jesus do for us?

Mark 10:35–40

James	The kingdom is great, and we're in on it! I really want to be part of it, one of the leaders.
John	So do I: I wonder who'll get the top job? I feel ready.
James	Shut up – he can hear us.
Jesus	What is it you want me to do for you?

Like the previous passage, this one is preceded by prophecy of the Lord's suffering and death (10:32–34). In the light of that, today's question is poignantly ironic: what Jesus will do for his friends is to die for them.

This time James and John say they are prepared to drink the cup and undergo the baptism of suffering – although perhaps with a kind of bravado like Peter's in the Last Supper. In the event, James did pay that price.

Mark's readers were perhaps facing dreadful persecution. In some parts of the world disciples still know that cost and fear.

For all of us there's the call to take our lesser crosses. A true cross is an imposed one, but we are called to take it willingly. You have yours. One of mine is a growing severe deafness: often I am angry, but sometimes I manage to carry it with grace.

Finally, a place in heaven is not for Jesus to give (verse 40). He is the Father's servant, and leaves to him the final outcome, relinquishing control.

Jesus, give me my cross. Father, I depend on you for grace.

Geoffrey Herbert

Questions Jesus asked

Questions Jesus asked

2 Questions Jesus asked in Luke

Notes based on the *Good As New* version by

John Henson

For John's biography see p. 1.

Preparing for the week

Jesus was a great teacher, an expert in every kind of teaching technique – gripping story-telling, visual aids, lessons geared to the ability and life-experience of the hearer. Here we explore more of Jesus' use of the question and answer technique. Like the best teacher, Jesus does not directly shoot the truth at his hearers, but invites them into the learning process. This involves questioning, playing with ideas, challenging even what seems most obvious. Jesus also invited questions and was not afraid of them. Often he did not give a straight answer, that way encouraging each to come up with the answer themselves. Thus the truth that begins to grow in the mind and heart of the questioner will not be abstract truth, but their truth, rooted in their own understanding of what makes sense. This has to happen over and over again in every new age.

For Jesus, the quest for truth was everybody's privilege, not just those with 'authority'. Sometimes the questions Jesus asked or sent back to a questioner called them to re-examine what they regarded as fundamental, and coaxed them to wade further into the depths of faith. As you read again these well-known incidents, try to explore new lines of thought yourself. Don't just rely on the lines this commentator presents!

Questions to aid reflection as you meditate on each passage:

- What precisely provoked Jesus' question?
- How did the question challenge their perception of reality?
- Did the question do its work?
- How would you respond if Jesus asked the question of you?

Questions Jesus asked   John Henson

Why were you searching for me?

Luke 2:41–51

He was in the worship centre, sitting among the teachers, listening and asking questions. Everybody who heard him was impressed by his grasp of the arguments and his intelligent comments. When Mary and Joseph saw him, they couldn't believe their eyes. Mary said, 'This is not the way to treat your parents! We've been worried stiff!' Jesus said, 'Why the problem finding me? This is my home; there are things I have to do here.' They didn't have a clue what he meant.

Good as New, p. 186.

There are so many ways of looking at this story. Today someone might have asked social workers to investigate a case of child neglect. On the other hand, Mary and Joseph may have been the sort of parents who realised that children need to have the freedom that involves some degree of risk if they are to be properly prepared for this uncertain world. Jesus' question, however, has a tinge of rebuke. Not only was he safe, but as a child on the border of his teens (technically an adult according to Jewish custom), he had the right to a share in adult responsibility and decision-making. Many Christians today are trying (a bit late) to be 'inclusive'. Jesus set a child in the centre – the place of authority. Do we welcome the child's contribution or are we still patronising?

Loving God, teach us to give children the affectionate care they need and the equality which is their right.

I'd rather you didn't try to flatter me with respectful titles like 'Reverend' and 'Sir', if you've no intention of doing what I ask you. I tell you, anyone who comes to me for advice, and acts on it, is like a builder who digs down deeply and sets the foundations for a house on solid rock.

Good as New, p. 195.

'Why do you call me "Lord, Lord,"?'

Luke 6:46–49

Jesus is not impressed by the use of flattering titles. Usually the word 'kurios' is translated in *Good as New* as 'Leader' not 'Lord'. *Good as New* aims to make the Christian message under-standable to those who live and wish to live in the twenty-first century. 'Lord' has the subliminal meanings, 'House of Lords', 'War Lord', 'Landlord' – not very good background noises for Jesus! For times when Jesus was less than pleased with the use of the title see Luke 9:51 and Acts 1:6.

A lot of Christian worship seems to be based on the desire to flatter Jesus. Many 'worship songs' are heavily loaded with words like 'majesty', 'dominion', 'power' and 'authority', with pictures of a crown and a throne. Not only are these concepts outdated in democracies, but also Jesus did not like them in his day. He told Pilate he was not after earthly rule. It was not the way he thought of his place in God's New World. There the first place would be accorded to the humblest.

Jesus, help me to be as uninterested in titles as you are.

Questions Jesus asked
John Henson

Where is your trust?

Luke 8:22–25

'Boss, wake up, we're sinking!' Jesus woke up and stood firm against the wind and the rough water. There was a sudden change in the weather, and everything went calm. Jesus said, 'Where's your trust?' The friends were frightened and didn't know what to think. They said, 'Who is this? He even has the weather under control!'

Good as New, p. 200.

Good as New translates 'faith' as 'trust'. The word does not mean having a religion or reciting a creed. It means relating to a person. What sort of trust in Jesus did his friends have on that windy day? Their words seem such an effective climax to the story – 'He even has the weather under control!' But Jesus' question is about the trust they had when he was asleep in the back of the boat. Easy enough to trust him when, as they saw it, he had just performed a miracle. What if the weather had not changed and they had had to swim for shore? Would they have trusted him then? Jesus was contemptuous of those whose trust depended on 'signs and wonders'. The fact that the boss was on board plus their practised skills should have been enough for them to have managed their craft in the wildest of weathers on their little lake.

Some Christians today like lots of supernatural action. Trust in the presence of Jesus is not enough. Where's *your* trust?

Jesus, God's true likeness, help me to put my trust in you.

Stop worrying about things of no importance. What does it matter what you eat or drink or whether your clothes are in fashion? A good life doesn't depend on going to posh restaurants or having the right wardrobe. Take a tip from the crows. They don't go to work every day, or put their money in a bank when they get paid, but God makes sure they have something to eat. . . Be like the wild flowers. They don't earn their living, yet they're better dressed than Solomon with all his beads and bangles! . . . It's time to stop vexing yourselves with questions like, 'Where shall we eat tonight?' or 'Have we ordered the right wine to go with the meal?' You'll make yourselves ill, having to make so many decisions!

Good as New, pp. 211–12.

Why do you worry?

Luke 12:22–31

Jesus announced good news for the poor. Here he addresses those above the poverty-line: people with money who can make choices. Two dangers here – anxiety, fear of losing and joining the poor; lack of trust, our bank balance our assurance, not God. As I write, the world is in recession. Will it be temporary or preface a continued decline in living standards? By the time you read this we may have a better idea. Our wealth has not been good for us. It is based on injustice, has corrupted us, and brought stress. So if we find ourselves with fewer things and less choice, shouldn't we give thanks?

Take my silver and my gold . . .

Is it with a kiss you betray the Son of Man?

Luke 22:47–53

As Jesus said this, a group appeared led by Judas, one of the twelve closest companions of Jesus. He tried to kiss Jesus, but Jesus said, 'Judas, do you mean to trap me with a kiss?'

Good as New, p. 234.

I am old enough to remember the song, 'Whenever we kiss, I worry and wonder – your lips may be near, but where is your heart?' Today young people assess their potential partners by whether they are good kissers. I often receive unexpected kisses, without a by-your-leave, sometimes in church. I don't mind, but I was brought up with the idea that kissing was for close family and friends, those to whom you have a degree of commitment and loyalty. As a fan of the TV series *Torchwood*, it was good to see Captain Jack and his boyfriend having the sort of kiss that showed they meant it, and I hope our society one day becomes civilised enough to enable men to greet one another with a kiss without anyone batting an eyelid.

We assume that the kiss between Jesus and Judas was a formal greeting with no deep emotional overtones. But the horror with which the Gospel writers record the incident suggests otherwise. It was a sign of love that was debased by its falseness. Followers of Jesus are reminded that the joy of kissing is one of God's gifts, but should be genuine, not a 'trap' or a game with another's affections.

Jesus, help me to show affection and to mean it.

The same day, two friends of Jesus were on their way to a village called Emmaus, a few miles from Jerusalem. They were discussing the events of the weekend. As they were talking, Jesus met up with them, going the same way. They didn't recognise him in the failing light. Jesus said, 'You were deep in conversation as you were walking along. What were you talking about?' They hesitated for a moment and their faces were sad. Then one of them called Clover said, 'You must be the only visitor to Jerusalem who doesn't know what's been happening the past few days.'

Good as New, p. 238.

What are you discussing with each other?

Luke 24:13–27

All our readings this week have drawn attention to a question of Jesus that contained a criticism. Today's example is different. Clover and his companion (his wife Miriam or his partner Basil?) meet a stranger who turns their sorrow into joy by chatting to them. The ability to cheer is a great gift of the Spirit. For some years I suffered from depression. I had a colleague who only had to hear that I was 'down' to be on the phone. He had me chuckling in no time.

Jesus spoke good news and was good news. The Church comes over to many as bad news, and while it does that it will continue to be marginalised. Christians are needed who will get alongside people where they are and help them to feel good about themselves and about life.

Help me to cheer someone up today.

Questions Jesus asked

3 Questions Jesus asked in John

Notes based on the Contemporary English Version by
Dafne Sabanes Plou

Dafne Sabanes Plou is a freelance journalist from Argentina and a member of the Methodist Church, who collaborates with women's groups in the area of Christian education and evangelisation. She is also a member of her church's Communications Committee.

Preparing for the week

Jesus' questions are not easy questions. Most of us wouldn't feel comfortable answering his questions. They go straight to the heart of the matter. He doesn't go around things or sound ambiguous or try to be politically correct. His questions demand honest answers. His followers or those who happen to be addressed by his questions do not always capture their searching depth.

Sometimes, when asking, Jesus sounds surprised or disturbed by the fact that those who are with him seem not to understand him fully. Are we ready to be questioned by Jesus? Are we ready to answer his questions? As contemporary men and women, perhaps we have become too individual-istic, too self-assured. In order to be able to reply to Jesus' questions, we need to leave aside the images we have built of ourselves, and humbly accept that there's still much to be learned from a God who decided to become a human being just like us – yet is very different from us.

It was late at night. The park was empty except for the street children, who lived under the bushes in summertime, and the TV crew led by one of the star young journalists broadcasting their 'real life' stories, making viewers believe that one had to be brave to venture into such a place to approach its nocturnal inhabitants. At first, it was hard to make the children talk. They seemed to fear the cameras and did not trust the journalist. But little by little, some confidence was gained and one of the children, about 12 or 13 years old, told his story. There was enough violence, sadness and despair in it to make it work, and the TV crew seemed satisfied.

But the journalist decided to end his interview with a clever question. 'What would you do if you saw Jesus walking down the park? What would you ask him for? What is your wish? What do you want?' The child just looked straight at the camera. 'I want a happy family,' he said with a shy smile. There was a long silence. The journalist and those behind the cameras found there were tears in their eyes.

What do you want?

John 1:35–42

Thank you, dear Jesus, for challenging us to become like children. Help us to put into action our justice, care, love and compassion in order to overcome the exclusion that keeps others out of your fellowship.

Questions Jesus asked   Dafne Sabanes Plou

Do you want to be healed?

John 5:2–9

She was a newcomer to the women's guild's weekly meetings. She spoke very little. Everybody in the neighbourhood knew that her eldest son had left home without a trace long ago. That afternoon she looked a bit anxious. When we sat in a circle for intercessory prayers, she timidly took a letter from her pocket. 'May I read it, pastor?' Her voice trembled – with anger or despair, it was difficult to say. 'Mother, I'm in prison. I'll be here for the next nine years at least. Please, come to see me.' Nine years? That meant her son was a violent juvenile delinquent, no doubt.

'I feel like hating him, I can't stand this any more!' she cried out. 'This is so painful. I feel so ashamed. My wound is so deep . . . ' We all surrounded her, some embraced her, someone held her hand. 'Do you want to be healed?' asked the pastor. Intercessory prayers became a powerful healing tool in that women's group. Every day, at a set time, the women prayed for their neighbour and her son, for their spiritual healing, for the healing of their broken relations, for strength to face the challenges posed by the new situation. 'I gave him a New Testament,' she told us when she came back from her first visit to the prison. 'I feel he has to get to know this Jesus!'

Dear Jesus, we know that your healing power can sustain a mother in her grief and a son who has gone astray. Teach us to be part of your sustaining love through the prayers and actions of a caring community.

He wondered what Bill and his two children would do for Christmas. Bill's wife had left him a few weeks before and he couldn't imagine Bill preparing any special celebration for his family. So he decided to invite them home for Christmas dinner. But Bill's daughter made him feel uneasy. She was born disabled and had never walked. When she was a little girl, it was moving to see her in her wheelchair. Everybody was nice to her. But now she was a young teen and her growing body showed bluntly the extent of its deformity. To think of her at his family's Christmas table was disturbing. 'Does this bother you?' he asked himself. It did. But would he be true to Jesus' teachings if he left Bill and his children on their own, just because of his prejudices?

When Bill and his children got to his home on Christmas Day, they were soon plunged into the family's activities: men around the fire looking after the barbecue; young people chatting and listening to their music; women setting the tables, dressing salads and decorating desserts. Even in her wheelchair, the young girl helped a lot. She could carry the china, the wineglasses and the flowers. She looked happy. He stopped worrying.

Next Sunday, during thanksgiving prayers, Bill gave thanks for a lovely Christmas dinner. 'My family and I felt we were included as equals,' he said.

Does this bother you?

John 6:52–65

O God, help us to understand that only your 'true food' and 'true drink' of justice and integrity will nourish our bodies and souls.

Why won't you have faith in me?

John 8:42–47

In the 90s, Argentinians had a president whose favourite slogan was: 'Follow me, I won't let you down.' Neo-liberalism was at the height of its wave and people believed the country would become part of the prosperous First World in no time at all. Burgeoning consumerism, investments in giant projects, the dollar replacing national currency, discourses about quick growth and making money promptly: all shiny wrappings covering – nothing. Most people did not want to see the reality. They thought themselves im-pregnable and bought the dream of becoming a 'developed country' in just a decade.

There were those who resisted and spoke out, including churches, human rights organisations and social movements. Among them was a rock group. In one of their songs, that became very popular, they identified the core problem: *'What do you see when lies become the truth?'* they sang. But until the 2001 economic disaster befell the country, people did not want to hear the truth about the sham.

'Why won't you have faith in me? After all, I'm telling you the truth,' says Jesus. Why is it that we would often rather follow 'the father of all lies', even if our own lives and safety are at stake? If we refuse to listen, it is because we'd rather not belong to God.

Holy Spirit, give us the strength to stand for the truth when lies are plenty and seem to triumph.

Dafne Sabanes Plou   Questions Jesus asked

Why is it that people seem so tough nowadays? Is it individualism? Is it self-sufficiency? Is it the idea that it is better to act and think for oneself? There seem to be many who think they don't need anybody's help or care. In a way, it looks good that people want to be independent and not bother others unnecessarily. But this is not a positive attitude if it hides pride and an overlarge ego.

Do you understand what I have done?

John 13:1–12

And then, if we are so self-sufficient, are we ready to understand the extent of love? Today's reading tells us that Jesus was well aware of his destiny, that his time was coming to an end. He was also clear about the love he had for his followers in this world. And he could feel 'he loved them to the very end' (verse 1). Washing his disciples' feet was a way to show his abundant love for them. Did Peter reject this action because he was too proud? Or because he couldn't sense what Jesus was going through? Or a combination of both? Pride usually makes us blind to other people's feelings and doesn't let us see what is really going on.

Jesus' question shows us that he doubted his disciples fully understood him. He had to explain the reasons behind what he had done. After so much time together, he still had to explain things. But he did it, and there was love in this, too. Are we ready to understand him?

Our Father, let us leave our pride and self-sufficiency aside so that we can serve our neighbours with open hands and allow others to show their care and good will for us.

Questions Jesus asked   Dafne Sabanes Plou

How can you ask me to show you the Father?

John 14:1–14

A woman in her 40s approached her. 'Are you the pastor's wife? I'm Tessie. I used to live in the church across the railway station. You and your congregation helped us to get a house in the new development.' She did remember her. The woman and her three children had lived in the church premises for some years, but the time had come for them to go. The congregation needed more space for their activities and the family had to understand that it would be better for them to live on their own. It was a hard decision. The place was far away. The pastor's wife still remembers helping them to move. When the truck left with their belongings, she felt their sorrow. Would there be resentment in their lives because of this?

'Tell the congregation my three children have finished their secondary school. Two of them already have a job and the youngest one wants to study to become a teacher,' she said with pride. 'Tell them, too, that we have kept our faith. It was hard to adapt to the new place. There was almost nothing there, just muddy streets and a few houses – but in one of them, a group of believers met to sing and pray almost daily. We joined them because we also wanted to show God's love to others.'

Jesus, guide us to give witness to the Father's love and care with our daily deeds and actions.

Imagination and creativity

1 Imaging the divine and the human

Preparing for the week

The imagination dreams, broods, astonishes us with new possibilities, urges us to try out fresh ways of communicating what it means to be human. The creative artistic imagination delights in the material world, uses stone, paint, wood, sounds and words to draw out new life. The biblical writers use not stone but poetic language, images and metaphors to make visible the invisible: a sort of unveiling of what is hidden in human experiences, in the depths of God's creation. Jesus was a great creative artist: he uses poetry, images, metaphors, riddles, stories, wit and humour to disturb, to startle with the challenge and joy of new insights. Perhaps the anxieties some Christians have about artistic expression come partly from a barely conscious fear of the terrifying fire of creativity and the consequences it can have.

We should be grateful to those biblical writers who, through their divinely inspired creativity and exercise of imagination, share with us stories of faith and faithfulness. These stories come alive in us, unleash our own imaginations, enlarge, deepen and illuminate our faith journeys; we're led to where we haven't been before. Such creativity dares us to suppose that 'the fictions of God are truer than the facts of men'.

Notes based on the Revised Standard Version and the Hebrew and Greek texts by
Brenda Lealman

For Brenda's biography see p. 44.

Imaging creation

Genesis 1:1 – 2:3

From two to three thousand years ago, out of someone's bafflement and dreaming, come these haunting images: breath, wind, spirit (Hebrew, *ruach*) hovering over formless void (*tohu wabohu*), darkness, watery waste (*tehom*). Out of this chaos, God brings what is new. Creates. Separates. Makes earth, the region of differences, of particularities; and heaven, the region of wholeness and oneness which God is.

After the creation of plant and animal species, God creates humankind in his own image. Note that both male and female are in God's image; God isn't masculine. Two Hebrew words for image are used in verses 26 and 27: *selem* translated 'image', and *demut* translated 'likeness', which also means 'model' or 'pattern'. *Selem* has the meaning, too, of 'shadow' or 'shadowy'. Are human beings seen as shadowy reflectors of God? Are we being challenged to play a part in the work of creation?

When the artist makes the final brushstroke on a painting, the work is still incomplete. The artist must let go of her work so that it continues to grow through others' responses to it. And so the creator God hands over creation to human beings to be its stewards. More: God withdraws to rest, *shabat*. He creates space for further possibilities to emerge, for creation to continue.

Reflect on images that a modern story of creation might include. Pray with one of these images.

Moses: wanted for murdering an Egyptian. Who betrayed him? Only the Hebrew he saved was present. Terrified; perhaps, above all, crushed by disappointment with his own people, Moses flees, conceals himself and his Hebrew identity in the desert. Life becomes comfortable: he is given shelter by a desert priest; marries; has a family. Why bother about the plight of the Hebrews? They show no signs of resisting their lot, anyway. But then . . . in the immensity of the desert, out of its silence, a thorn bush spiking with flames; the overwhelming sense of the living, flaming presence of the Holy; fire inside Moses; burning sand; sandals removed; the insistent voice. The urgency, the awe-ful power of the transcendent. Moses turned away, and turned again, says a poem by Norman Nicholson, 'And faced the fire and knew it for his God', the God he'd left behind (he didn't even circumcise his son), the God of his own people, the Hebrews.

Creativity releases potential

Exodus 3:1–6

The authenticity of a religious experience is usually indicated by its outcome. Faced with transcendence, Moses feels unworthy, but in spite of himself, his experience leads to action. With what reluctance, though, he takes on what was required of him. Read on to discover with what ingenious excuses Moses resists the call to return to Egypt.

A life turned round. But it isn't always comfortable to be offered the release of one's potential.

Give thanks for a particular turning point in your life that, though painful, turned out to be life-giving.

Imagination and creativity   Brenda Lealman

Creativity surprise

2 Corinthians 3:18 – 4:7

The creative imagination loves to play with images. Images (poetry is full of them) leave things unsaid, allow space for dreaming, hint. Central to this passage is the image of fragile clay pots that contain hidden treasure. The context is Paul's defence of his ministry by showing how different he is from the rival apostles. They make out that they are superior to Paul; God is on their side, the side of strength and power. This is not Paul's experience of God in Christ; rather his experience is of the paradox that out of suffering and vulnerability, God empowers and raises up, draws treasure out of crumbling pots. Paul comes as a servant or a slave, he doesn't seek recognition and power. Rather, he debases himself to meet the poor and undervalued. He is absolutely honourable in his dealings with the church: open, straightforward; not manipulative nor underhand.

Another key image is veil, *kalumma* in Greek. Jewish legalism led to the veiling of glory, to the diminishing of people; Christ gives freedom, life, glory (verse 18). Those in Christ have no veils on their faces but reflect the glory of the Lord; they are being re-created in God's likeness, are growing from glory to glory, into deepening awareness of God's presence. Paul gives us the challenging image of the Christian life as a dynamic, creative, transforming journey.

Reflect on key experiences in your faith journey. Pray that God will lead you more deeply into his presence.

Today, the Feast of the Ascension, Christian churches celebrate the dignity, the glory of human nature: human nature that has been created by God and re-created, transformed, in Christ. At vespers today, the Eastern Orthodox Church puts it like this: 'Jesus . . . today . . . you were taken up in glory; in compassion you exalted our fallen nature, and seated us on God's own throne.'

Imaging fullness of life

Romans 12:1–21

A key image in this passage is 'body', in Greek, *soma*. *Soma* signifies the entire person: our entire selves, not just body or soul; our entire human nature. It is our entire human nature that is to be opened and offered to God for transformation. So, we have to expect to live an alternative way of life. We must be modest, realistic about our gifts but affirming of them. We shouldn't take revenge; our actions must not be determined by the actions of others. Love must be genuine: in verse 9, *anupokritos* in the Greek means 'without hypocrisy'.

We grow in community (developed elsewhere by Paul in his metaphor of the Body of Christ) by sharing our gifts and using them to affirm each other, and to increase the human dignity of all members of the community.

Irenaeus, an early church father, sums up what both this passage and the Feast of the Ascension point to: 'The glory of God is a person fully alive.'

Reflect on what you like about yourself.

Imagination and creativity   Brenda Lealman

Suffering can be creative

Philippians 2:1–11

This letter was written when Paul was in prison either in the mid-50s or -60s. It is a response to pastoral need, perhaps the result of disunity in the church in Philippi. Being part of a community, *koinonia* in the Greek, is central to being a follower of Christ. Community involves gut-felt compassion (*splagchna*, bowels); and compassion means humility and mutual respect. Paul goes on to hold up Christ's life as the pattern for Christians.

In verses 5–11, Paul celebrates Christ's story – sings it almost – in stunning, poetic language. Imagine verses 6–8 like the downward sweep of a great church arch, then verses 9–11 soaring upwards like ribs of vaulting. Christ did not grasp at his equality with God; he yielded to God's will. The image here is of pouring out, being emptied (*ekenose*). Christ became a servant (echoes of Isaiah's picture of the Suffering Servant here – see Isaiah 52:14; 53:2, 12). He resisted the human compulsion to seek power and recognition even though this led to suffering and a shameful death.

Then, the upward soaring: Christ exalted, named Lord, all 'to the glory of God the Father'. The poetry of the passage compels and inspires, resounds with Paul's message: be faithful to the values and vision Christ gave us; you might be suffering now but you'll be led to glory.

Reflect on this:

'Don't grieve. Anything we lose / comes round in another form.'

Rumi

Imaging the divine

Mark 12:27–31

Jewish rabbis wrestled with the question: is there a basic commandment from which the rest of the law can be deduced? For example, one rabbi, Hillel, suggested: do not do to others what you would not want done to you. Jesus replies to the question asked by an unusually friendly scribe by putting together two love commands of the Hebrew scriptures: love God (Deuteronomy 6:5) and love your neighbour (Leviticus 19:18). Combining these two commandments required a high degree of imaginative thinking (although a case can be made out that Jesus wasn't the first to do so). Jesus prefaces the first commandment with the *Shema*, the Jewish confession of faith that God is one, unique (Deuteronomy 6:4).

Jesus removes rigid legalism from the heart of spirituality. In its place he puts love, *agape*. This sort of love is caring, vital, generous, isn't self-seeking, gives priority to relationships and community. Such love is creative and dynamic. Is that how we image the Divine? It seems paradoxical that God, who is one and sovereign, asks for our flawed love; that God, who is transcendent, is right here, inseparable from the dynamism of human loving.

Reflect on the images of the Divine you carry with you. Do they liberate both you and the Divine?

Be silent and still; let the prayer utter itself.

Imagination and creativity   Brenda Lealman

Imagination and creativity

2 With the eyes of the heart

Notes based on the Lutheran Bible by
Margarete Pauschert

Margarete Pauschert is a retired Lutheran minister who has served in two parishes of Berlin-Kreuzberg and Berlin-Moabit, Germany. She was responsible for the religious welfare of women and for the teaching of women ministers. She has been a regular broadcaster on the radio. At present, together with a friend, she runs a centre for adult education in a village by the Elbe River.

Preparing for the week

'It is only with the heart that one can see rightly.'
Saint-Exupéry, *Le Petit Prince*

New things have not yet developed, but new things are in the making. New things that are to be are God's work in the making. Already we see a great light – yet we are still unenlightened. We move between these poles, still in the dark. Faith has a vision of the morning light and the gradual crescendo of the chirping of birds – sounds like one of God's promises. Our eyes have already seen – but we haven't yet understood – as our consciousness has not yet integrated the new things.

Faith often knows more than reason. It keeps up the living memory of salutary experiences that linger in our hearts. With our stream-of-consciousness progression, we project our ideas onto God and the way we understand his work, and we try to talk about God in images. We use everyday events so that those who read and listen feel touched by God's new creation which is coming towards us.

In the end everything will be perfect and we will be the creations that we were meant to be.

'I create new things, I create a pathway in the sea and a road in roaring waters' (verse 16); such is Isaiah's message to his fellow prisoners in Babylon, but – 'neither is there a footpath through water nor does a road lead through the waters', they say. The resigned Israelites hung their 'harps up on the willows' (Psalm 132:2), they do not sing any more. War is necessary so that possibly – some day – peace will be possible – says the 2009 Nobel Peace Prize laureate, Barak Obama.

| God's new path – right through the waters |
| Isaiah 43:14–21 |

Practical constraints dominate our everyday lives; change is dubious, cannot be successful. There is no time for thought, we make breathless reactions instead of praying and doing. Violence against violence marks the international fight about the resources of oil, gas and water. Acting without violence, communicating without violence – is that only for dreamers?

But then, one day, things cannot go on as they always have; one day the banished people get hold of their harps again and their children wonder. The humiliated slaves, the apparently undignified people, start singing – of their coming home. Imagination lights up, peace is possible. And it was only one single voice that had kept saying: 'God shows his way, perhaps right through the waters.'

Help us, God, that we might be able to believe and that our heart may become strong so that we open our eyes and see your new creation. Do not let us sink into the water of melancholy, lead us on your way, even right through the waters.

Imagination and creativity   Margarete Pauschert

As in heaven, so on earth

Revelation 21:1–5

What is the new heaven going to be like? A heaven full of singing, music, dancing and palatial joys for everybody – or pure, ascetic, spiritual, without bodily joys and pleasures? Is earth going to be like heaven: just distribution of resources, peace and non-violence for everybody? In spite of all the promises made at the grave, suffering, disease and pain do not end with death; they are often passed on to the deceased person's relatives, friends or neighbours. The heavenly images are perishable like beautiful cloud formations that we can watch in the morning or evening sky. They follow one another like the pleasant earthly ideas of the good life that we hope for.

Such ideas or visions of the good life, even if they remain unachievable, have always inspired people. The notion that we may get rid of all pain and fear and only experience life's pleasures is a powerful one. And, we perceive vaguely, it does not matter how we go about it, but we know that we want it with all our strength and conviction. And this can be the beginning of change. 'Write it down – these words are reliable and true' (verse 5). We do not know what things are going to be like, but we realise we are experiencing a new heaven and a new earth.

God, you change conditions including us. Give us the faith so that we can change.

Margarete Pauschert   Imagination and creativity

1 Peter 2:2–10

Belonging – don't we all want that for ourselves? Did we not – as children standing in one corner of the school yard – longingly watch those who were always surrounded by others? Finding my place in a school class, finding peers and being liked by others; being really at home in my family; finding a lively group of persons that share my interests – these are common hopes.

Staying lonely means staying small, having little influence. Together we are strong – we feel that when we participate in a group we are empowered. In today's text, a living stone forms the middle of the new community – something equally offensive and holy. God has the power to transform people into living stones and together they will build the eternal house. This new building is for people such as us, who long with all our senses to find meaning in our lifetime. We long for the home where, in darkened times, we can stumble through our days and, in bright times, we can celebrate our successes.

The eternal house, built by the living, has no rigid rituals; in it our hunger and thirst for life and justice are satisfied. With every holy communion we are invited to enter this house, our home, when we hear the welcome: 'Eat and see how friendly God is' (Psalm 34:8).

You hold me by my right hand and already now lead me into your eternal home.

Psalm 73:23

Imagination and creativity   Margarete Pauschert

Don't be afraid, I am with you

Exodus 14:5–29

At the moment of greatest danger there is only a way through the waters for Israel – straits as narrow as the situation. It's not the exodus of a remnant any more, but a whole people are fleeing. Exhausted, completely frightened, they shout at Moses: 'It's your fault, there are only graves in the desert awaiting us' (verse 11). 'We did not ask for deliverance from the flesh pots of Egypt' (Exodus 16:3).

To stay or to leave? To choose captivity or a start in an uncertain future? Twenty years after the fall of the Berlin Wall there are still people who want the German Democratic Republic back. Complete support by the state – that is their recollection of the past, which makes them feel comfortable. 'It has always been like that, it must stay like that,' some people in my village say, but our children build biogas systems that will change our lives. 'We invested so much money in atomic research, we cannot withdraw now,' our politicians say – and protest has been varied and effective for 30 years.

Continuity in the trodden paths or do we dare something new? At a word, people may leave their families, give up relationships and move to a different country. The question has to be answered whether customary ways are more important than a form of freedom that we are not yet familiar with. Staying or leaving – we must make up our own minds without other people's help.

God's word is with us: I don't let go of you when the water comes up to your neck, and I hold your hand when you walk through fire. Say only one word – and dare to be free.

Margarete Pauschert   Imagination and creativity

In the beginning we dream that true love never ends. My love will not end, it is my truth; it cannot be destroyed by time. But then the forebodings of unhappiness come – unkindness, negligence towards the loved one, and separation can already be anticipated. It all started with jubilant happiness; it ends in lamentation and misery. Perhaps we cherished the idea we had formed of that person, but did not perceive the loved individual as a person in their own right. And if it is our heart that reads the loved one's features, we have not seen deeply enough perhaps –'we see the outside, God sees the heart' (1 Samuel 16:7).

Our heart. Doesn't it resemble an image in a dark mirror, always longing for love, always trying to find the God who protects our love and keeps us from separation and loss? Then we come to a far less noble end, and we are left with the debris of a marriage, or alone with our tormenting thoughts of a deadly disease or a broken friendship. Where is God then? Was my faith only piecemeal and my hope without reason? Were my hope and faith not plentiful enough? In the end, was my love lacking? These can be hard lessons to learn, when we have to dig and discover deeper love – not only for God and for the human other, but for ourselves in all our woundedness and frailty.

Love never gives up

1 Corinthians 13: 1–13

Give me understanding of how strong your love is, and then help me believe that I can practise love – however badly I have got it wrong in the past.

Imagination and creativity — Margarete Pauschert

Blessed eyes, blessed ears

Matthew 13: 10–17

'Didn't you notice that your Jewish neighbours, your customers, your patients, your colleagues "disappeared"?' we asked our parents. 'You must have noticed that they did not appear at their workplace any more, you must have passed their sealed apartment doors. They were rushed to the train station or pushed into lorries – didn't you see them?' How can it be possible, we say, that a child dies in the apartment right next door, and it was such a pleasant family? We see and yet we don't see, we dare not apprehend what we see. Our heart does not want to know what our eyes see. Seeing and looking away at the same time – that is like hearing but not understanding.

To look away, not to listen, is an all too human response. There are too many problems – I cannot take care of everything that is happening in the world – I am busy with my own problems. And our days are passing away, full of sorrow and grief.

And then, later – didn't our heart burn? There was a soft touch – no more than a breath of air. A song could be heard and we answered with our own melody. Only one word was spoken – a voice called out our names. We came to a halt, saw our responsibilities in life and acknowledged them. Our lives were full of joy and again we found in our hearts an answer to the question of what life is all about.

Blessed are our eyes when they see and our ears when they hear. Open up my heart so that I can hear your voice and see which path you are walking with me.

Imagination and creativity

3 Imagining differently

Notes based on the New Revised Standard Version by
Helen Richmond

Preparing for the week

In the face of unprecedented challenges, global warming, environmental degradation, economic inequality, movements of people, and ethnic and religious divisions we need to reimagine relationships within the global family. The gifts of imagination and creativity come from the Divine Creator and Lover, who is constantly seeking ways to enable us to release the potential of that which we have been created to be and to become. Imagination and creativity are paths that lead us closer to God and the spiritual journey may be more about what we learn on the way as much as where we arrive.

The readings this week invite us to look at the world through kingdom eyes as we are asked to imagine the world differently. This week we are invited to:

- Make a crossing journey through stormy weather
- Set out on a mission with no possessions
- Learn what is a true neighbour
- Allow Jesus to wash our feet
- Discover forgiveness at a beach barbeque
- Let concern for the poor be central to our Christian life.

It is impossible to read the pages of the biblical narratives that follow without recognising many amazing images and metaphors that point to the creativity of God, and the surprising grace which endlessly inspires faith and faithfulness and new dreams and visions.

Helen Richmond is a minister in the Uniting Church in Australia. She currently teaches theology and cross-cultural awareness at Nungalinya College in Darwin, the national indigenous training college of the Catholic, Anglican and Uniting Churches. Helen is co-editor of *Crossing Borders: Shaping Faith, Ministry and Identity in Multicultural Australia* (UCA Assembly, 2006). She is married to Ben Suherman and they have two sons.

Journeying to the other side

Luke 8:22–25

Crossing Lake Galilee in stormy weather became a life-threatening journey. Even hardened sailors and experienced fishermen became terrified, but Jesus calms the waves and urges his disciples to trust him. Jesus does not say, 'Let's go back,' but instead they cross to the other side and arrive in Gerasenes – Gentile territory, foreign land. Here the faith of the disciples would again be tested as they confront everything that represented what was 'unclean' and alien. Seen in this context, the gospel reading represents a crossing between two deeply divided worlds.

Crossing journeys test our imagination, faith and courage. When we move in new directions there will be risks but also amazing opportunities. Then and now, Jesus calls his disciples to get into the boat and 'cross over to the other side'. Increasingly our communities and churches are made up of people from diverse backgrounds; and we face the challenge of developing cross-cultural skills for building just and inclusive communities.

Jesus asks us to trust him enough and to have the imagination and courage to cross over to those who are different from ourselves. In the process, we are changed and the liberating power of the gospel is released. Who are the people God is asking you to cross over to?

'Crossing-over God', thank you for all the experiences you give that expand our understanding of you and one another. Help us to hear your call to 'cross over to the other side'. Calm our fears and give us imagination and courage for the crossing journeys that lie ahead.

Helen Richmond   Imagination and creativity

'Take nothing for your journey. No staff, nor bag, nor bread, nor money – not even an extra tunic.'

(verse 3)

Sent out empty-handed

Luke 9:1–9

We might imagine a conversation between Jesus and reluctant disciples: 'Are you sure it's meant to be like this, Jesus? You're expecting us to do what you do but we aren't ready. We have this list of things we need to take and lots of things we need to do first.' Jesus responds, 'No, that's not necessary.' He sends the disciples out in risky poverty to rely on the generosity of others. In an astonishing way power comes, people in many villages hear the good news, and their diseases are cured.

Sent out empty-handed the disciples had to learn a spirituality of trust and boldly imagine that God would provide for their needs. They might not always get a good reception, but they would find generosity and hospitality.

Jesus entrusted his message to his disciples and believed in the power of God to draw forth a response of welcome to the good news. As contemporary witness-bearers to the kingdom, how open are we to receive the gifts God gives us through others? What 'excess baggage' are we carrying? In what ways do our churches need to learn a 'spirituality of trust'?

O God, help us to believe that the gospel has the power to bring forth a generosity of spirit in ourselves and in others, a joy in giving, and a delight in offering hospitality and knowing that this is how your kingdom comes near!

Imagination and creativity   Helen Richmond

Imagining our neighbour differently

Luke 10:25–37

Jews and Samaritans had deep hostility for one another. Samaritans were considered 'unclean' because of their mixed heritage. Their ancestors had intermarried with the conquering forces. The rift between them widened after the Samaritan offer of assistance to rebuild the temple was refused. They later built their own rival temple at Mount Gerizim.

In response to a question posed to Jesus, 'Who is my neighbour?' (Luke 9:29) Jesus told a parable that would have deeply challenged, shocked and probably outraged his Jewish listeners. It was a despised Samaritan who stopped and rendered assistance to a person who had been robbed, beaten up and left to die by the roadside. This 'outsider' and heretic, rather than one of their religious leaders, demonstrated fulfilment of the law to 'love your neighbour as you love yourself' (verse 28).

We do not expect kindness and goodness from those whom we have been taught to fear or despise. In telling the parable, Jesus was inviting his listeners to imagine their neighbour differently. As we recall the deep tensions in our world, the fractures along ethnic and religious fault-lines, and the ongoing presence of prejudice and fear, the challenges are as real for us today as in first-century Palestine. Who are the people Jesus is inviting you to 'imagine differently'?

Loving God, forgive us for the times we withhold compassion from others. Expand our capacity to see in the face of a stranger, or even an enemy, our brother or sister.

Helen Richmond   Imagination and creativity

How could Jesus adopt the position of a humble servant to wash and dry his disciples' feet? When Jesus took up the basin and towel, Peter at first protested. Only later did he begin to understand the significance of Jesus' actions. In an acted parable, Jesus had demonstrated his love for his disciples. If Jesus, their teacher and Lord, had washed their feet, they too must wash each other's feet, and the feet of others.

The actions of Jesus on the night of his betrayal would be imprinted on the memory of his companions, those he called 'friends'. The events of that last night helped the disciples envisage relationships based not on power over others but on a radical sharing of power. Jesus imagined shared leadership in which each served the other – expressed in the washing of each other's feet. He showed that true greatness is not measured by the way the world conceives success, but by costly sacrifice and deep and loving friendship. It is signified by the basin and towel. It is leadership that is interwoven with servanthood, expressed in reciprocity and love in action.

Loving God, in an increasingly unpredictable global context we see the consequences of human greed and misuse of power. Keep alive in us Jesus' vision of a radically different way of sharing power and resources.

Loving and serving with a difference

John 13:1–17

Imagination and creativity · Helen Richmond

Reimagining ourselves through the power of forgiveness

John 21:1–14

A whole night of fishing and nothing to show for it. As the dawn approaches a voice calls, 'What have you caught? Cast your net to the other side'. Weary, and bleary-eyed, the disciples do as the stranger suggests. In amazement they watch as their nets fill with fish. Recognition finally dawns, and ever impulsive, Simon Peter jumps into the water, leaving the others to haul in the nets. On the shore Jesus is cooking breakfast. The charcoal fire may have reminded Simon Peter of that other fire where he had warmed himself while his Lord was interrogated. Jesus takes Simon Peter aside and three times asks him: 'Do you love me more than these?' To Peter's threefold confession of love, Jesus issues a threefold charge, 'Feed my sheep'.

Jesus gave Peter the opportunity to reimagine himself. Peter's identity was not going to be defined by his mistakes and betrayals, but by the faithfulness and the transforming power of the risen Lord. His new identity is centred on a new vision of serving God's people.

How is the risen Christ asking us to imagine ourselves differently and image a different future?

Risen Lord, you restore what we have lost. You take our empty nets, our disappointed hopes and broken promises, and offer grace in abundance. With Simon Peter, may we respond, 'Yes Lord, we love you.'

Helen Richmond   Imagination and creativity

The man had diligently applied himself to keeping the law, but had overlooked one vital ingredient: compassion for the poor. He lacked one thing, so Jesus said, 'Go, sell what you own, and give the money to the poor, and you will have treasure in heaven; then come, follow me' (verse 21). We are told the man walked away sorrowful, for he had many possessions. The gift of eternal life was within his reach but he was not able embrace it. His riches were an encumbrance that stopped him from being a follower of Jesus.

Reimagining the world

Mark 10:17–31

Preoccupied with many things, we too can lack the creative will to reimagine ourselves, and reimagine differently our relationships with one another. Like the rich man we can be reticent to step outside our comfort zone.

The sobering words of Jesus are a reminder that God asks us to risk giving up who we are and what we have achieved, to believe in the world as it could be. Compassion and practical care are central to this vision of a world transformed. Such a transformation seems impossible, but through kingdom eyes we are invited to imagine the world differently, and to see a world where life could be lived in abundance for all God's children.

Jesus, friend of the poor, set us free from attachments that hold us back from embracing the world that you intend to bring into being. May practical deeds of justice, kindness and compassion be evident in how we live out our faith.

Imagination and creativity   Helen Richmond

Readings in Matthew 13–19

Parables of the kingdom

Notes based on the New Revised Standard Version by

Sam Peedikayil Mathew

Dr Sam Peedikayil Mathew has been a teacher of the New Testament for 22 years. He serves as Professor and Head of the Department of New Testament at Gurukul Lutheran Theological College and Research Institute, Chennai, India. He has authored several books and articles. He has a keen interest in contextual biblical interpretation.

Preparing for the week

Words of wisdom came from Jesus, the artisan peasant who became a wandering preacher in Jewish Palestine. No wonder the religious and social leaders of his time took offence at him. They rejected his teaching not only because his wisdom was incompatible with his social status and family background but also due to the content of his teaching. He taught about a new society that overturns the accepted social and religious norms and practices of his day. Jesus presented before them a new community which is radically different in its nature and function.

The parables that Jesus used highlight some important aspects of this counter-cultural community, which he called 'the kingdom of God' or 'kingdom of heaven'. This new community of God has come into being in and through the life and practice of Jesus. It appears to be tiny and insignificant, yet it is universal and inclusive in its character and will be very effective in its role of comforting and transforming society. This new community of God is growing in the present and will reach its consummation in the future. In this week's readings, based on the Gospel of Matthew, chapter 13, we will consider some of these characteristics of the new community of God.

The parable of the Sower explains the various responses to the preaching of the kingdom of God, which is the new community of God. Since it was the ancient Palestinian practice to till the soil *after* sowing the seeds, some seeds often fell on rocky ground, or among the thorns or on the wayside. The seeds that fell on the rocky ground and wayside represent those who responded negatively to the gospel preaching. The seeds that fell among the thorns are those who initially listened to the gospel but could not grow properly due to the lure of the world and its riches. Those seeds that fell on the good ground stand for those who responded positively to the preaching about the new community and produced fruit.

Responses to the kingdom

Matthew 13:1–9

This parable teaches that not all people respond to the message of the new community in the same manner. People need to prepare themselves to receive the message of the new community. They need to have receptive hearts that may enable them to be part of this new community. Rocky and thorny ground needs to be converted to good ground to receive the gospel. Those who receive the gospel are required to resist the evil one who promotes the values that are opposed to the new community. The word of God must be received and allowed to take root in a conducive atmosphere in order to bear fruit.

How do people from your locality respond to the message of Jesus?

Gracious Lord, grant us discernment and willingness to respond properly to your new community.

Readings in Matthew   Sam Peedikayil Mathew

Reasons for negative responses

Matthew 13: 10–17

Hardness of the heart or dullness of heart is mentioned as the main reason for the negative response of some people to preaching about the new community. In the Bible 'hardness of heart' is used for the deliberate turning away from God. When it is said, 'God hardened the heart of people', it must be understood within the Old Testament background. In the Exodus event it is repeatedly said that Pharaoh hardened his heart. It is only when Pharaoh refused to listen to the repeated pleas of Moses on behalf of God that it is said, 'God hardened the heart of Pharaoh' (see Exodus 10:1, for example). When people harden their hearts to the point of no return, it can be said that God hardened their hearts. Thus people respond negatively to the preaching of the new community basically because they deliberately refuse to accept the values of the new community that are against their selfish interests and motives.

Through his life and teaching Jesus challenged people to be part of the new community of sharing, love, peace and harmony, by turning away from sin and turning to God. The message of the new community is open and clear to those who are willing to accept the values of the new community, but it is hidden to those who are closed and refuse to accept it.

How do you respond to those who respond negatively to the gospel?

Loving God, help us to be patient in the midst of negative responses to the values of your new community.

The interpretation of the parable of the Sower in this passage emphasises that the preacher is not responsible for the way people respond to the message. The role of the preacher is to sow the seed, that is, to preach the word of God. Various people respond to it according to the level of receptivity they have and their openness to the message of the new community. Just as the farmer is expected to sow the seed, the preachers of the new community are expected to proclaim the message of the new community. They are required to preach the word to all people without taking into consideration the kind of response they get. All kinds of people must listen to the proclamation of the coming of the new community inaugurated by Jesus through his life and practice. The preachers are exhorted not to be worried about the way people respond.

This parable of the Sower was really comforting to some early Christian preachers, who could not find much fruit from their labour. Through another parable in the Gospel of Mark (4:26–29) Jesus made it clear that the growing of the seed and the fruit bearing are the activity of the creation and not the farmer's.

In what ways are the values of the followers of Christ different from that of others? What do you think are the hindrances for practising those values in your present context?

Lord, give us the humility to remember that the growth of the new community is your activity, not ours.

The role of the preacher

Matthew 13: 18–23

Sam Peedikayil Mathew

Paradoxes of the new community

Matthew 13: 24–35

One of the questions that puzzled the early Christians was, 'Why do good and evil people exist together in the new community?' Jesus answers this question through the parable of the Wheat and the Weeds. Just as weeds and wheat grow together in the field, evil and good people co-exist in the new community from the very beginning. Until they bear fruit one cannot distinguish them. At the time of harvest they will be identified, separated and dealt with. Therefore, one need not worry about the visible presence of evil people in the new community. The parable calls for patience to put up with evil people in the present time.

Yet another paradox is the nature of the new community. Like the mustard seed, the new community appears to be quantitatively small and insignificant now, but it will become big and significant in the future. This happens by becoming a source of shelter and care for everyone, especially those in dire need of help. The parable of the Leaven drives home the point that though the new community looks tiny and invisible now, it has the power to transform a much larger community. Thus the new community now appears to be powerless, ineffective and insignificant, but its strength and power to bring about solace and transformation in society will be revealed in future.

Who do you think are the good and the evil ones in this world? How would you identify them?

Gracious Lord, give us wisdom to understand the paradoxes of your new community.

Sam Peedikayil Mathew   Readings in Matthew

The interpretation given to the parable of the Weeds and Wheat in today's passage reiterates the reality of coming judgement. At present weeds and wheat are found to be growing together in the field. But in future when they bear fruit their real identity will be revealed. The farmer will separate the weeds from the wheat after the harvest and the weeds will be collected together and burnt. Likewise, good and evil exist together in the new community now, but their works will reveal their true nature.

Based on their works, everyone will be judged, as is made clear in Matthew 25:40ff. Jesus declared that those who will be accepted by him are not those who call him 'Lord, Lord', but those who do the will of God, that is, those who follow his teaching. St Paul also reiterated this when he said that God would repay everyone according to their works (Romans 2:6). All people, irrespective of caste, creed, religion or nationality will have to stand before the judgement seat of God. All those who were willing to lend a helping hand to the hungry, sick, stranger and the needy will be accepted by God. Those who opted to live selfish lives, neglecting the poor, the needy and the underprivileged, will be rejected and condemned by God.

What do you see as the various responses to diversity within the Christian church? What are the different ways in which your local community/church can be made more inclusive?

Lord, enable us to understand others and help us to give up judgemental attitudes to others.

Future judgement

Matthew 13: 36–43

Readings in Matthew   Sam Peedikayil Mathew

The value of the new community

Matthew 13: 44–58

The new community that Jesus brought about through his life and teaching is compared to a hidden treasure, a pearl of great price and a net. Although the new community is hidden from many, it is visible to all those who have faith. For them, it is great treasure, more valuable and precious than any other treasure in the world. It is worthwhile to sacrifice everything to get this treasure. The new community is more beautiful and precious than pearls in this world. The values that are exhibited by the members of the new community shine like pearls and attract others to it.

Like the net that draws all kinds of fish, the new community is diverse in nature. This new community consists of people from different nations, religions, languages and social status. Thus the new community is marked by diversity and universality. Jesus taught that people will come from all corners of the earth to the kingdom of God: 'I tell you, many will come from east and west and will eat with Abraham and Isaac and Jacob in the kingdom of heaven' (Matthew 8:11).

The new community transcends all barriers of caste, creed, religion and nationality and is open to all to come in and be part of it. The new community preached by Jesus is inclusive in its nature.

What do you plan to do so that your community or church exhibits these characteristics?

Lord, grant us courage to promote the values of your new community and to be more inclusive and universal in the midst of diversity.

Readings in Matthew 13–19

Signs of the kingdom

Notes based on the New Revised Standard Version by

Susan Hibbins

Susan Hibbins is an Anglican, a freelance writer and editor. She is especially interested in choral music, and in her spare time is secretary of a local community choir of fifty people.

Preparing for the week

Imagine yourself as one of Jesus' disciples, sitting together some years after Jesus' earthly life and ministry had ended. As with any group of people who have been though much for many years, conversation turns to 'Remember when . . . ?' Maybe this group's memories would be very different from most others'. They would 'remember when' Jesus used what little food they had to feed thousands of people (Matthew 14:13–21); or the time when Jesus talked with a distracted father and then healed his child (Matthew 17:14–21). Three of those present might fall silent, still unable adequately to put into words the glory of the Transfiguration. One person might remember an impulsive leap from a fishing boat into the water and his terror when he started to sink, until Jesus put out a hand to save him.

With such hindsight they would see clearly what they could not grasp at the time: signs of the kingdom. Jesus was showing them through his life and his actions the way in which their own lives were to be lived. It was not easy for the disciples, when they were in the middle of such tumultuous events, to understand the significance of what was happening. Nor is it easy for us. Where do we see signs of the kingdom in our own lives?

More than enough

Matthew 14: 13–21

How do we feel today about miracles? Do we take the miracles of Jesus at face value and believe, as this passage describes, that more than five thousand people were fed from five loaves and two fish? Apart from the story, is there more we can learn about Jesus and about ourselves?

The disciples had no idea how to go about feeding so many people, thinking only in terms of what it would cost in order to buy enough food for them all. What they could rustle up was ludicrously small in the face of such need. In John's account (John 6:5–13), the food belonged to a boy, who gladly shared what he had. When Jesus took and blessed the food, was the miracle that others in the crowd also began to share their food with those who had nothing, instead of keeping it for themselves, so that everyone was blessed?

There is no right or wrong way to interpret this action of Jesus. There is no doubt, however, that Jesus took something very small and used it to bless many. We may think sometimes that we have very little to offer to God in terms of time or gifts. We may feel we have to 'buy' resources first: a theological degree, a training course, years of experience. Yet when we offer whatever we can, in God's hands it can become more than enough.

Dear Lord, please take the little I can give, bless it and use it for your glory.

There are times in all our lives when we feel, like the disciples, that we are about to be overwhelmed. We may not be physically threatened by storm or flood, but experiences we do not seek – sorrow, loss, disappointment or hurt – can and do make us doubt our ability to cope, and we fear that we shall go under. In such times it is heartening to remember that Jesus himself is near to us, as he was for the disciples: 'Take heart, it is I; be not afraid.' How Jesus steps out from the pages of scripture into the daily lives we all lead!

It is even more reassuring to grasp that Jesus understands how frail is our faith. Peter, sure that he can walk over the water when Jesus calls him, steps out of the boat, but when he is buffeted by wind and wave, he begins immediately to sink. How often do we feel the same? We experience Jesus' enabling power, only to feel overcome by the problems we still face. Like Peter we cry out to Jesus to save us; and always he is there to lift us up, calm the storm that threatens us, and restore our faith in him. Can we still doubt that he is with us?

What difficulty are you experiencing at the moment? Have you looked to see Jesus waiting to calm the storm and raise you from doubt to faith in him?

'Take heart; it is I'

Matthew 14: 22–38

Readings in Matthew

Susan Hibbins

Into all the world

Matthew 15: 21–31

Jesus has moved away from familiar territory in this passage, the only time he is recorded as doing so. His deeds have gone before him, however, and quickly he is confronted with a Canaanite woman who begs him to heal her daughter. Jesus' initial hesitation may puzzle us, when he insists that he has been sent 'only to the lost sheep of Israel' (verse 24). Was he thinking that he needed to prepare his own people first, so that they could then take his message further? But the woman is not easily dissuaded; with perseverance and her own quick wit, she shows a touching faith in Jesus that results in her daughter's healing, and later the healing of many others.

When John Wesley, the founder of Methodism, began his career as an Anglican clergyman, he preached within his own church to Anglicans. It only dawned on him gradually that he needed to take the message of salvation out to the lost and suffering, to whom God was unknown. When he did so, thousands flocked to hear him and were rescued from despair and unbelief. It may be harder for us to take God's love to a largely indifferent society, but we can all, by our actions and the way we respond to others' needs, show the God 'of Israel' to all we meet.

Lord, help me to remember that everyone I meet today is precious to you. May I show them the love you have shown to me.

Once again, Jesus and the disciples are faced with a large crowd of people who are without food. Some commentators have suggested that this is another version of the feeding of the five thousand story, although there are significant differences, not least that Jesus appears to be still with the people of Tyre and Sidon, who have come in their thousands to listen to and be healed by him.

For me, this is another example of Jesus' compassion for the people he is with. All through these stories of his ministry, his concern for people outweighs his own need. Several times in these readings we see that Jesus is trying to get away: to pray, to find some time apart for the disciples and for himself. He rarely gets it. Instead he finds the sick, feverish and fretful, he finds the noise and the heat, he finds people who cannot provide for themselves. And always he is patient, and always he listens and responds. His example is not an easy one to follow. We can find people's needs overwhelming, and we can become tired and distracted by too many claims on our time and energy. Yet Jesus understands our needs too. We too can find in him the sustenance and healing that helps us continue to serve.

Are you in need of renewal? If possible, arrange a short retreat or quiet day.

Compassion and caring

Matthew 15: 32–39

From glory to glory

Matthew 17:1–13

At last Jesus and three of his disciples are able to have some time away from the busyness and the hectic pace of the life they are living. In a complete contrast to the noise and demands on them below, on the mountain they are given an experience of the sheer glory of God, which they find hard to take in, and will surely never forget. Shot through this scene is light and wonder: Jesus' face shines 'like the sun'; his clothes are 'dazzling white' (verse 2). The disciples, afraid and uncomprehending – as surely we would be – see Jesus in a different dimension, out of time and normal experience. Perhaps, when they were faced with Jesus' shameful crucifixion and death, the three disciples would remember this moment, and cling to the thought that something greater lay beyond the seeming end of all their hopes.

We will never, in our earthly lives, have the same experience as these three disciples. Yet there are some moments when our lives are turned around – perhaps by a birth, perhaps by the death of someone we love – and we are given a glimpse of the light of heaven. It may only be fleeting, but we know the truth of it and where it has come from. And we can be reassured that the glory of the Lord is, indeed, all around us.

Help us to be aware of your glory, O Lord, shining into our lives. Illumine our darkness with your light, that we may see you as never before.

Susan Hibbins   Readings in Matthew

Morning worship at the cathedral was especially uplifting. The music soared, the sermon inspired, the Holy Communion was celebrated in an atmosphere of solemn dedication. Afterwards, in the precincts, we lingered, reluctant to leave.

Back to the world

Matthew 17: 14–21

Finally, we walked through the quiet cathedral grounds into the hub of a busy city that was noisy, littered and crowded with shoppers. The contrast was stark, jarring and unwelcome. It would have been easy to turn around and go back into that tranquil atmosphere of worship – but still, here was life going on: real, everyday life, for many, perhaps for most. In a doorway there was a beggar, asleep. People stepped over him, walked round him. Nobody troubled to see if he was just asleep or ill, or unconscious. Another young man, similarly dressed, came over and shook him awake, and together they shambled away.

In this story Jesus and Peter, James and John are confronted even more directly with the need of the father and his son, whom the other disciples had failed to cure. The glory of what they had seen on the mountain must suddenly have seemed far away as once more they are pitched headlong into the world and its demands. But Jesus does not hesitate to heal the boy.

We want to spend time in worship; of course we do. But we may not linger too long. The world is suffering. If we don't help, who will?

Heavenly Father, where there is need, let us be the ones who step forward to help.

Readings in Matthew   Susan Hibbins

Readings in Matthew 13–19

Teaching of the kingdom

Notes based on the *Good News Bible* by

Glory Befeke Anye

Glory Befeke Anye is an ordained minister with the Presbyterian Church in Cameroon. She is currently serving as parish pastor of New Town Airport parish and chaplain to the Douala Colleges. She also teaches pastoral studies at the Ecumenical Bible Institute, Douala. She is married with two children.

Preparing for the week

Community life in most parts of Cameroon is expressed when the father, mother and children, as the basic unit of the family, gather around a three-stone fireside in the evening, sharing their news and stories. This fellowship space provides an opportunity for members to demonstrate their zeal to know each other better, even as they struggle to understand the meaning of real life in, and through, each other. In this space, members engage in dialogue as a means to nurture love, unity and care for one another. Love, care and unity are some of the core models for the survival and growth of any community or kingdom. With the absence of these fundamental human values, life in a community will turn out to be inactive or inhuman.

This week's study focuses on kingdom values and virtues. It will expose us to the life Jesus Christ advocated for his followers – a life to be lived in the kingdom here and now, yet a mirror also of the life hereafter. This week's study is also a movement that will engage us with one another in sharing, like the community that gathers at the fireside – something that is only possible when one sees oneself in the other. This is the self-sacrificial life Jesus Christ calls his followers into. In this way, we will model life in the kingdom of God in our own global world, replete with respect and care for each other.

For any community, family or group to discover itself and its mission, it must build solid foundations on trust and truth in and for one another. These values are essential when differences or any type of crisis set in. In the gathering around the fireside, different members relate through dialogue in such a way that each one gets to know who the other is. In trying to know the other, you discover the truth about who you really are. As Jesus embarked on the journey to know the other, he was concerned to explore what others thought of him, in that space of family get-together with his disciples. Thanks to their varied opinions of him, Jesus confirmed who he really is – the Messiah. This was only possible when Jesus considered the opinions of the others in respect, thus coming to understand how he was perceived by them.

To know who we are is a call to kingdom living where each person inter-relates with respect for each other. Respecting the varied nature, identity and opinion of the other, gives a chance for truth to emerge and prevail. And where truth prevails in the kingdom of God, varied opinions and differences can become tools that enhance the celebration of community life. In this way each person benefits as new knowledge and revelation are gained.

Does what you know about the other enhance your vision of community life? Think of some concrete examples.

God help us that, in the process of knowing the other, we may discover and understand who we really are.

Knowing yourself in the other

Matthew 16: 13–20

Knowing your direction guides your movement

Matthew 16: 21–26

An African proverb holds that anyone who knows his/her direction cannot be misguided. To know your objective in life serves as a springboard to community-building. Even when confronted by adverse conditions, such as suffering, you can never be deterred from your dream. Rather, setbacks become stepping-stones to the achievement and fulfilment of that dream.

Jesus Christ, knowing his identity and his mission, knew where he was going. Hence not even suffering nor death could stop him from reaching his destination. Even when his followers sympathised with his suffering, he did not get distracted or derailed from his mission. His mission was one of self-emptying – accepting the necessity of saving the other through great suffering, being willing to offer the sacrifice even unto death. Life in the kingdom calls for such selfless saving of the other, yet we discover that, by so doing, we are saved ourselves.

In what ways are you called to accept suffering as an option to save the other?

Lead us, O God, towards the right direction, so that our mission in life might be fulfilled.

Glory Befeke Anye

Readings in Matthew

Most religious traditions in the world today, at least in some of their manifestations, continue to treat children and women as though they were not human – as though they were commodities to be traded for profit, objects of the 'master's' interest. In such traditions the opinions of children (or other 'insignificant' members of the community) and their welfare, are not respected. They are sacrificed for the profit of others. In contrast, when we gather around the three-stone fireside, children's opinions don't go unconsidered. They often enliven and spice up the conversation with their humble innocence, sense of humour and humility.

There is a general saying that any educated person is known by his or her humility. Humility, properly understood, is a great kingdom virtue that should be cherished. It is not abasement so much as a natural freedom of the self, a capacity to focus away from the self towards what is of most importance. Children are often endowed with this capacity – something Jesus beckoned his followers to adopt. Jesus demonstrated that, for our general welfare, all must be saved or included, irrespective of age, gender, nationality and race, and none should be excluded. 'Masters' or parents need the virtue of humility if God's kingdom is to prevail here and now. In God's kingdom all, including children and those different from us, are members. None are traded or excluded for self-interest or self-gain.

Who might be considered the insignificant members of your family, society, community or country? What would it mean to exercise humility in relation to them?

O God in heaven, teach us not to take advantage of the other in pursuit of self-gain.

Do not sacrifice the other for self-gain

Matthew 18:1–14

Debtors to each other

Matthew 18: 21–35

Global economic statistics often portray Africa as the only continent that owes huge amounts of debts to foreign banks. The burden of repaying such debt has caused this continent to deny her members many basic human needs, such as the supply of clean water sources, electricity, and so on. Yet looking more dispassionately at the global economy, we see that all countries are entangled in such a way that we each find ourselves debtors to the other. There is increasing recognition of the huge economic as well as moral debt owed to Africa for the way in which Africans were used as slaves for the self-gain of European countries.

Paul says that *all* have sinned and fallen short of God's glory (Romans 3:23). In this light we understand that all are debtors to each other, and especially to God. God, however, rather than holding us in thrall to this debt, sent his only-begotten son to overcome our debt. Through this generous gesture of self-sacrifice and forgiveness, we are committed to God to do the same for others. We are to live a life of forgiveness knowing that we all share a common destiny and purpose – which is to care for others, for all to belong and for all to live. This is the kingdom life that Christ calls all his followers into.

The supposed debts Africa owes the World Bank – can they not be forgiven rather than impoverishing them further through foreign aid that goes with onerous burdens?

What can you do to work for a relief of the debt for poorer countries?

God in heaven, teach us to know that we are indebted to the other, so that each one can be forgiven and set free.

To live is to share

Matthew 19: 16–22

It is common knowledge that some people are poor because wealth is concentrated in the hands of a few. In birth, there is no such division between poverty and wealth. Each individual is born naked, possessing nothing, only acquiring clothing and food as a gift from parents or other carers. Without sharing at its most basic level, there can be no life.

Due to greed, and the worship of Mammon, the world is currently faced with climate change and global economic crisis. If such facilities as we have are shared with all, this situation can be minimised. In the light of this danger we read the story of Jesus' encounter with the rich young man – a character who represents the minority of the rich in our world today. He was instructed to go and sell all he had and give the money to the poor in order that he might have spiritual life. This is a kingdom value which cannot be avoided if justice and well-being for all are to be established in the here and now. To accumulate riches for oneself while depriving others of the basic necessitites of life is actually to accumulate death, even for unborn generations. It is to build up global warming and increase the chances of global death and destruction.

People's welfare needs to be given the utmost priority over property and possessions. This is the call to the life with which Jesus challenges the rich. Jesus calls us to enter the kingdom of sharing so that all can live.

What action can you take to work towards equitable distribution of wealth in the world?

Our God, who shared your life with us, teach us to live by the values and virtues of your kingdom so that we share our lives with each other.

Readings in Matthew   Glory Befeke Anye

Planting God's kingdom in the global world

Matthew 19: 23–30

In view of the contemporary world of globalisation, it may sound naive, idealistic and impracticable to speak of 'planting God's kingdom'. Yet moving by faith with kingdom principles, impossibilities become possible. The kingdom life of God brings breakthrough. Where there is humility, sharing, self-emptying for the other, there is breakthrough. In this kingdom the reward is not only in heaven but also in life here and now. Where there is neither rich nor poor, young nor old, child nor parent, white nor black, but all commune together in love and freedom, each person in that love and freedom reflects the self-image of the other – which collectively constitutes the image of God. In such a kingdom there is no discrimination nor segregation; difficulties are seen as blessings and, by faith, the realisation of this kingdom is grasped as possible in the here and now.

What may seem impossible in human terms is very possible with God – if we believe the words of Jesus.

Dear God, let your kingdom reign here on earth as it does in heaven.

Marriage

1 Marriages good and bad

Preparing for the week

Renate and I were married at Queen's College (as it was then) in 1970, and have a daughter and two sons, one of whom is adopted. For ten years we were part of a Christian community consisting of two families and two single people, sharing a couple of houses in Aston, Birmingham. Two of our children are married and there are three grandchildren. Between us all, parents and children include British and German nationalities, white and black ethnicities, and Anglican, Lutheran and Baptist Christian traditions. Three of our respective parents have died, but Renate's mother celebrated her 100th birthday in December 2009. So between us and our extended family, we represent quite a range of the varied human experiences of family life and different patterns of marriage, community and household arrangements. It is out of that experience, as well as what we have learnt from others and from the scriptures, that we offer our reflections on marriage in the coming two weeks.

Notes based on the New Revised Standard Version by

John Wilkinson

John Wilkinson is an Anglican priest who has recently retired from being a vicar in Birmingham, England. He has worked in a variety of parishes and as a tutor at the Queen's Ecumenical Foundation, Birmingham. John has written about the black presence in mainstream churches in England, making what he calls 'a white response and testimony'.

A gift of God in creation

Genesis 2:18–25

Catholic theology lists marriage among the seven sacraments. This helps us understand it as a 'means of grace', but it's also the odd one out – the only one which is not Christian 'property'.

Marriage not only pre-dates Christianity by thousands of years, but the committed pairing of male and female is written deep into the genetic codes of the animal kingdom. Who has not thrilled to hear David Attenborough describe the courtship ritual of a magnificent bird, or the ferocity of mammals guarding their young? All this is our inheritance as humans; we feel *our* desire in the eagerness of buck and doe for each other, *our* protectiveness in the lioness guarding her cub.

What, then, is the 'image of God' (Genesis 1:28) in us? It is this: we alone on earth can objectify our existence, reflect upon it rationally, understand it as gift. Marriage brings together the primeval and the rational, the urges necessary for reproduction-survival and the divine image.

And it has been so in every culture and every race. Picture the betrothal of a young couple arranged by Indian parents in consultation with astrologers, the Christian joining of hands and exchanging of rings or a Hindu couple walking seven times around fire: it is always the couple who 'confer the sacrament' upon each other.

Eternal God, grant that the bonds of our common humanity, by which all your children are united to one another, may so be transformed by your grace that your will may be done on earth as it is in heaven.

John Wilkinson   Marriage

Marriage liturgies use these words of Jesus at the solemn joining of hands. But the officiating minister knows that dotted through the congregation are those who have divorced. One or both of the couple may be among them; so might the minister.

Although the Pharisees ask Jesus a question about divorce, his answer is about marriage, an answer which takes us back to Genesis and the 'gift of God in creation'. Their motive is to trip Jesus up by involving him in a sectarian dispute about how to interpret Deuteronomy 24:1. Jesus responds by affirming God's gift, marriage as the lifelong joining of persons in a profound union.

But there is always 'hardness of heart', an expression which bears the weight of the stereotypical man out drinking, the 'nagging wife', the inability of either to apologise and the psychological hinterland of such behaviour. It also includes dysfunctional personalities, the pressure of work, the sharpness of radical suffering, the corrosion of materialism, the brutality of abuse, the tragedy of illness and unemployment, and the social reality which underlies these and prises couples apart.

Verses 13–15 which follow speak of the kingdom of God belonging to otherwise rejected children. No one has bargaining chips with God, neither does failure disqualify us. The lives of both the happily married and the painfully separated alike are sustained by the blessing of God.

Those whom God has joined together, let no one put asunder

Matthew 19:3–12

God, may the life of those who marry be a sign of your love in this broken and disordered world; may unity overcome estrangement, forgiveness heal injury and joy overcome despair.

Marriage   John Wilkinson

'Am I not more to you than ten sons?'

1 Samuel 1:1–18

These verses and those in tomorrow's reading tell the story of the birth of Samuel, the great prophet and judge of Israel who would one day crown both Saul and David as kings over his people. The story is told to signify that from birth Samuel was a special child, conceived by Hannah, who was childless, in answer to prayer. She called him Samuel because 'I have asked him of the Lord' and dedicated him to lifelong service of God.

Hidden within this story of historical, political and religious significance for Israel we are given glimpses of moving and tender moments in the relationship between Hannah and her husband Elkanah. Within a society in which to be childless – especially not to have given birth to a son – is shameful, Elkanah says to his wife, 'Am I not more to you than ten sons?'

Is not this the heart of marriage, as of every covenanted relationship, that it is the love one has for the other which sustains the commitment, 'to have and to hold, for better for worse, for richer for poorer, in sickness and in health . . . within the love of God' (from the Marriage Service of the Church of England)? It is a costly love that knows of struggle, of pain and sacrifice. It is also a love that is life-giving.

Loving God, uphold us in the agony and in the joy of all our loving.

In thankfulness for the birth of her son, Hannah dedicated Samuel to lifelong service of God. This reading may help us consider what our hopes are for our children's faith.

In Western society there are many voices that question the right of parents to bring up their children within a faith tradition, regarding it at best as a purely private matter, at worst as a violation of the freedom of the child. Religious education in school is criticised for influencing a child's choice before the child is old enough to decide for him- or herself.

But a child is not an isolated individual and does not grow up in a vacuum. From birth, the family into which the child is born, and the world in which he or she grows up, shape the adult that the child will become. As we feed a child's body and a child's mind, so his or her spirit needs to be nurtured in order to develop into maturity. As Christian parents we will want our children to experience the life of our faith community, its worship, its common life and its engagement with the world.

It is painful if our children grow into adults to whom the life of faith is irrelevant or if their understanding of the gospel is very different from our own. But we have to let them find their own way in the knowledge that wherever they go, they are held in God's love.

Eternal God, Mother and Father of us all, we commend our children to your care and protection.

Nurturing faith

1 Samuel 1:19–28

Marriage

John Wilkinson

David danced before the Lord with all his might

2 Samuel 6:12–23

In some marriages, one partner exercises power and responsibility and enjoys fame and popularity. What was it like to be the wife of Ghandi, John F Kennedy or Nelson Mandela, or husband of Marilyn Monroe, Margaret Thatcher or Queen Victoria? This is a tension that 'ordinary' marriages are not necessarily spared. In many different scenarios, one partner is compelled to ask, 'is he/she so important that I must give myself up to supporting him/her for the greater good?'

A recent television play gave a searing presentation of Winnie Mandela's courage and suffering during the 27 years of her husband's imprisonment and the tragedy that her attempts to build a power-base for herself led to: the ignominy of being complicit in the murder of 14-year-old Stompie Moeketsi.

Michal loved David and chose him and his welfare over the wishes of her father Saul. David's bringing of the Ark into Jerusalem was a crowning achievement of his reign, but Michal could not bring herself to rejoice with him. Her apparent disgust at his dancing before God was a thin cover for her envy.

It's not clear whether her childlessness is inflicted by David or by God but, either way, her inability to bask in her husband's glory is seen by the writer as a serious and potentially calamitous weakness.

God, may we show kindness, born of a gracious heart, to each other in generosity of spirit.

The opening of this passage repels because the man is active and does the finding, whilst woman is passive, the object who is 'found'. But that is not fair to the passage as a whole, where the woman is revealed as shrewd and pragmatic, and as one who 'fears the Lord' and is preoccupied with doing God's will. She is possessed by Holy Wisdom, the key category for understanding Proverbs.

We need to immerse ourselves in the wonder of divine Wisdom to learn from this woman. Divine Wisdom is the first thing God made; beside him 'like a master worker; . . . daily his delight, rejoicing before him always, . . . delighting in the human race', she sounds like a wife for God (Proverbs 8:30–31).

Proverbs 8:31 is not eternal law, but is given to help us fashion our understanding of a 'good' spouse. If we let scripture, tradition and reflection on our context guide us as we look at this wife, then she can be both yardstick and inspiration. Caring industriously for her family, busy in the purchase and cultivation of land, she was a fulfilled woman, strong and dignified, who became all she could be in her day. By contrast, many women who also 'fear the Lord' (verse 30) in our day are denied the dignity and standing this 'good wife' enjoyed.

'Good' wives and husbands

Proverbs 31: 10–29

Grant, O God, that those who marry may have such awareness of the bonds of their common humanity that their work, their family and the open hospitality of their home may be sources of dignity, respect and delight.

Marriage   John Wilkinson

Marriage

2 Marriage as metaphor

Notes based on
the New Revised
Standard Version
by
**Renate
Wilkinson**

Renate Wilkinson is a
minister of the
German Protestant
Church whose
ministry has been
based largely in
England, where she
has worked on an
inner-city housing
estate in Birmingham,
as a hospital and
hospice chaplain, and
finally as Chaplain at
the Queen's
Foundation.

Preparing for the week

Last week John looked at the basis of marriage; marriage understood as rooted in the providence of God and the 'givens' of human nature – it's not a fortuitous by-product of transitory social structures. And we looked at some of the challenges and delights involved.

Now I shall look first at the practical details of daily life, beginning the week with three readings containing what Martin Luther called *Haustafeln* ('house rules') for daily life.

Then, by contrast, we look at the ultimate basis of marriage which exists not only by God's providence but also arises out of God's very nature and being. So, Jesus is himself a bridegroom and we, the church, are his bride; God and God's people bind themselves together in a covenant, which the marital covenant reflects; the compassionate love of Christ poured out for the world informs the love of a married couple for each other; the hopes and the potential of a couple and their family are a foretaste of not simply a heavenly family but a celestial metropolis of light and glory.

These passages are not prescriptive eternal law, but neither are they merely inspiring, helpful tales. God asks us to bring to scripture an eagerness to understand what shaped and formed those who wrote it and attention to what shapes and forms us. The dialectic of this interplay is one definition of life in the Spirit.

Christian faith flowed from new life in Christ, but the early Church found that living it from day to day required the creation of a new ethic – a *Christian* ethic – the details of which simply did not yet exist. However: there were principles, there were resources from the past, and there were issues which needed addressing. The unexpected delay to Christ's return lent urgency to the task.

The guiding *principle* was love (see chapter 13). The main *resource* was the Hebrew scriptures, including its image of Israel as God's bride, but pagan philosophers were also a resource – in their writings *Haustafeln* were common. *Issues* included family life, church organisation and offering food to pagan idols.

If in doubt, a church could always write to its apostle for guidance: note how Paul distinguishes between principles ('not I but the Lord') and his opinion ('I say, not the Lord'). The house rules of the New Testament are not eternal law but prompt us to fashion our own code. We today must also be guided by scripture and tradition and listen to what *our* philosophers, scientists and artists show us.

Concerning the matters about which you wrote

1 Corinthians 7: 1–16

For reflection and prayer:

Christians marry like everyone else, and beget children but do not cast them off; they share their tables but not their marriage beds . . . they are 'in the flesh' but do not live 'according to the flesh'.

Epistle to Diognetus, *c.* 25 AD

Marriage

Renate Wilkinson

If you have then been raised with Christ

Colossians 3: 12–19

The whole of Colossians 3 depends on these words because Christian existence depends on the triumph of Christ's resurrection. Without his victory, the fledgling Christian community at Colossae would not even exist. However, the battle that Christ won continues to be fought in us. A long list – from sexual immorality, coveting and destructive anger to defaming others and regarding our socio-ethnic identity as superior – shows how 'lower nature' we still are.

When the divine nature operates within us, says the writer, we join in Christ's victory as he renews our wills. We are then overtaken by thankfulness, which issues in patience and reconciliation and blossoms in our worship.

Only then can he begin his 'Haustafeln' (house rules), of which our reading gives us but two verses, both about marriage. We today are to follow the method by which he devised it (reflection on scripture, tradition and the contemporary context) in writing our own. To us, language of 'subjection' is not acceptable and the injunction not to be 'harsh' is inadequate, to say the least. But mutuality of obligation, each partner to the other, continues to flow from new life in Christ, now as then.

This passage exults in the quality of Christian life which can enable us to live in joyful harmony with God, with each other, with creation – and even with our spouse!

Eternal God, may we drink deeply from your boundless love and know in our hearts the delights of your Holy Spirit.

Renate Wilkinson   Marriage

This list of 'house rules' is profoundly Christ-centred. As God had sought Israel as a bride, so now Christ seeks the church – through his sacrificial death! Let the explosive power of this image – the bride whose suitor died for her – sink in, before turning to the somewhat problematic details.

The problems include: issues of grammar and the logic of the analogy, which commentaries address; the offence of exhorting wives to be 'subject', and the power of the image of Christ's passion, misused down the ages to compel women to accept the unacceptable. Despite references to mutuality, the patriarchal context of the times remains evident.

Nonetheless traditional patriarchal 'rule over' has shifted remarkably to (patriarchal) *'love for'*. The husband is still the head of his wife, but only in the way that *Christ is head of the church* (verse 25). In the 1993 film *Shadowlands*, C S Lewis summarises his feelings for his terminally-ill wife:

Why am I so afraid? I never knew love could hurt so much. Yet I love you, and all I want is to love you.

There is love that cannot hold back or protect itself from risk, from paying the price. This is what it means for a man to love his wife as he 'cherishes his own flesh', as 'Christ loved (his body) the church and gave himself up for her' (verses 25, 28).

As Christ is united with his bride, the church . . .

Ephesians 5: 21–33

Christ, may your passion for us be the ground of our covenanted relationships. May the passion of our covenanted relationships be the ground of our love for others.

Marriage

Renate Wilkinson

The compassionate God

Isaiah 54:1–8

I am writing this on Holocaust Memorial Day. It therefore seems appropriate to begin by acknowledging the debt we as Christians owe to the Jewish faith. Into that faith Jesus was born and nurtured, and out of it he fashioned his life and his teaching. Throughout history, Christians have been tempted to disregard that continuity. Instead we read the Old Testament as 'law' and the New Testament as 'gospel', see the God of the old covenant as the God of wrath and the God whom Jesus calls Father as a God of grace. Today's passage shows us the error of such understanding.

As in the passage from Hosea that we will read tomorrow, the relationship between Yahweh and Jerusalem and the people of Israel is described as that between husband and wife. But that relationship is broken, and in extraordinary images the prophet describes the plight of the city – 'barren one, 'desolate woman', 'ashamed', 'disgraced', 'a wife forsaken and grieved in spirit', 'a wife cast off' – expressions of the depth of despair in the experience of the exile. But into that abandonment the prophet speaks words of hope. He reminds Israel that their God of judgement is also a God of mercy, of everlasting love and compassion, their redeemer.

It is this God, judge and redeemer, whom we encounter in Jesus Christ, now no longer the God of Israel alone but the redeemer of the world.

Merciful God, look with compassion on your broken world and strengthen in us the hope of redemption.

Renate Wilkinson   Marriage

Hosea is the prophet who imaginatively and beautifully uses the image of love and marriage when he speaks about the relationship between Yahweh as the faithful husband and Israel as the unfaithful wife. This imagery cannot be found in the time before Hosea. It may have its source in the prophet's own experience of marriage and betrayal, of brokenness and graciousness (see chapter 1).

Covenanted living

Hosea 2:14–20

Our text has to be read together with the beginning of chapter 2 (verses 2–13). There Hosea speaks of Israel, the unfaithful wife who has broken the covenant between Yahweh and his people. But in his graciousness Yahweh woos her back into relationship with him and renews the covenant he made of old. In moving and tender words the prophet describes this gracious act of Yahweh. 'You are my people,' says the Lord, as he said to the people of Israel in the desert. And as then, the people are called to choose between life and death (Deuteronomy 30:15ff) and place themselves again into a renewed relationship with God.

The Methodist Church has preserved the covenant tradition in its covenant service which emphasises the relationship between God and the believer. The custom of the renewal of marriage vows is an echo of the tradition within the covenant relationship of two people. In Christ, God has made a new covenant that reaches beyond Israel to all people.

Where are we called to choose between life and death, between faithfulness and betrayal?

Faithful God, woo us back into the embrace of your love.

Marriage   Renate Wilkinson

The glory of God in the city

Revelation 21: 2, 9–11

As the Book of Revelation is full of Old Testament imagery, it should not surprise us that here too the images of bridegroom and bride, of husband and wife, express fundamental truths about the relationship between God and his people, and about the history in which this relationship unfolds.

In the struggle between the Lamb and the Beast (chapters 13 & 14), between God and all that is evil and oppressive in this world, the final victory – begun in the Lamb that was slain – is God's. He will again live with his people in whom he delights. And the glory of God will fill the new Jerusalem, in whose streets heaven and earth will be one.

John wrote down his vision in order to comfort and encourage the early Christians living under oppression and even persecution, but also as a challenge to those who were tempted or even willing to align themselves to the powers that be.

Do you see life-denying powers at work in your life, in the church, in society? Does your hope in God's final victory over all that is evil empower you to resist and to endure?

Immanuel, may your will be done on earth as it is in heaven.

Renate Wilkinson   Marriage

Order now for 2012!

It may seem early, but the copies of *Words for Today 2012* and *Light for our Path 2012* are now available to order.

Order now:

• with your local IBRA Rep*
• in all good bookshops
• direct from IBRA

online: http://shop.christianeducation.org.uk/
email: sales@christianeducation.org.uk
phone: 0121 472 4242
post: using the order form at the back of this book

If ordering direct, postage is free of charge.

*If you purchase 6 copies or more, and you live in the UK, you can sign up as an IBRA Rep and claim the 10% IBRA Rep discount on all IBRA products. You will also receive a free poster and samples to help you share IBRA more easily with family, friends and others in your church. Contact staff at IBRA to sign up now!

A whole year's Bible reading notes for only *17p* a week!

Consider a legacy

Help us to continue our work of providing Bible study notes for use by Christians in the UK and throughout the world. The need is as great as it was when IBRA was founded in 1882 by Charles Waters as part of the work of the Sunday School Union.

Please leave a legacy to the International Bible Reading Association.

An easy-to-use leaflet has been prepared to help you provide a legacy. Please write or telephone (details below) and we will send you this leaflet – and answer any questions you might have about a legacy or other donations. Please help us to strengthen this and the next generation of Christians.

Thank you very much.

International Bible Reading Association
1020 Bristol Road
Selly Oak
Birmingham
B29 6LB
UK

Tel. 0121 472 4242
Fax 0121 472 7575

Readings in 1 Kings

1 Solomon and the temple

Preparing for the week

This part of the book of Kings tells of the events leading up to the establishment of a strong Israelite kingdom by King Solomon, and culminates in the establishment of the new Temple as the religious centre of Israel. David favours his younger son over his brothers and crowns him king even before his own death, in order to prevent his older brother, Adonijah, from ruling. Solomon proves his wisdom and goes on to build the temple in Jerusalem.

The selection of readings leaves some open questions and points for reflection. Solomon was a king full of wisdom, as the text repeatedly tells us, and yet also very tyrannical in his ways. He also took upon himself some aspects of religious leadership, which most others left to the priests.

It is important to study the texts with an open mind, confronting difficulties when they arise, not always accepting all that is written. Questioning will lead us to a better understanding.

Praised are you, our Eternal God, Sovereign of the universe whose mitzvot (commandments) add holiness to our life and who gave us the mitzvah (commandment) to study the words of the Torah.

Notes based on *Tanakh: The Holy Scriptures* (Jewish Publication Society, 1985) by **Irit Shillor**

Rabbi Irit Shillor serves the Harlow Jewish community as well as the Jewish Community in Hameln, Germany. Born in Jerusalem, she moved to the UK in 1982, where she taught Mathematics for many years. She was ordained in 2002.

Strife

1 Kings 1:5–13

David was a warrior-king who created the great kingdom that was going to be handed to Solomon. And yet, David was not allowed to build the Temple, although he did bring the Ark of the Covenant to Judea, to David's city. This was because David's hands were stained with blood.

Strife formed a large part of David's life and that of his many sons. These fought over the kingship, hoping to achieve their desire by the sword. Each of the sons in turn attempted a coup d'etat, with little success and at enormous cost. In the end it was Solomon, whose name refers to peace, who reigned after David.

Adonijah, one of the sons, was a favourite of the generals, while Solomon was favoured by the priests. David was by then old and not particularly interested in matters of state, but he had to be the arbitrator in this case. It was left to Bathsheba to convince him that quick and decisive action needed to be taken. Bathsheba, the woman behind the scenes, David's love – it was to her that the priests turned, knowing that she would be able to guide him in the right direction.

May it be your will, God of all generations, to cancel all wars and the spilling of blood in the world. May you bring a great and wonderful peace to the world, when no nation shall take up sword against nation; they shall never again know war. (Isaiah 2:4)

Solomon was crowned as king. The ceremony could have been modest, with family and close advisers in attendance. But that would have defeated the object. After all, Adonijah was seen as a promising lad, definitely a possible future king. So the crowning of Solomon had to be in the public eye, a ceremony of pomp and circumstance to warm the most doubting of hearts and to show the people that this, David's chosen, was indeed also the choice of the people.

Solomon was a wise politician, choosing not to engage in strife against his brother Adonijah, leaving that to the priests and to his mother, and later choosing not to harm Adonijah, who was, after all, the favourite of the people. This wisdom will continue to manifest itself later in Solomon's reign. Yet his wisdom was not always used for the good of Israel, rather to get Israel to fall in with his various projects, as we read later in the book.

Perhaps David recognises this political canniness of his son and worries that in the interest of power he might forget that all comes from God, and therefore enjoins him to walk in the ways of Adonai.

Pomp and circumstance

1 Kings 1:32–2:4, 10–12

Let all who work for the congregation do it for the sake of heaven. Then the merit of their ancestors will come to their aid and their righteousness will last forever.

Sayings of the Fathers

The wisdom of Solomon

1 Kings 3

'And Solomon . . . loved the Lord and followed the practices of his father David' (3:3). In the Torah the love of God is its own reward, yet Solomon himself is King David's reward for having obeyed God. And Solomon, what is his reward? It seems to me that Solomon was twice blessed. He was able to talk to God, albeit only in a dream, and when granted a request, was given wisdom and the ability to be a just judge, using this wisdom to resolve what seemed to be insurmountable problems. Surely the request for wisdom was in itself a display of wisdom. Was Solomon being very crafty here, doing everything right, so that all would recognise 'that he possessed divine wisdom to execute judgement' (3:28)?

Our sages explain that Solomon asked for an understanding heart because he said:

'A pagan prince may judge in any way he wishes, to hang, to strangle, to have a man beaten or to set him free. He is responsible to no one, for his word is law. But a Jewish prince may judge only by your law and your teachings and if he fails to judge aright, he is then responsible to you.'

From the Midrash

God, give us grace to accept with serenity the things that cannot be changed, courage to change the things which should be changed, and the wisdom to distinguish the one from the other.

Reinhold Niebuhr

Judah and Israel were as numerous as the sands of the sea.

1 Kings 4:20

God endowed Solomon with wisdom and discernment in great measure, with understanding as vast as the sands on the seashore.

1 Kings 5:9

Riches and wisdom?

1 Kings 4:29 – 5:12

Grains of sand stand as a symbol for a very large quantity. Can people be as numerous as grains of sand? Clearly not, but the Midrash tells us that it is forbidden to count people as one counts objects: people are to be counted according to their worth and their good deeds. Under Solomon, so says the Midrash, the people lived according to God's commandments and therefore had infinite worth and were regarded as numerous as grains of sand. Similarly the greatness of Solomon's wisdom is regarded as vast, and therefore likened to grains of sand.

'And they ate and drank and were content' (1 Kings 4:20) – clearly observance of God's commands is rewarded by riches. Is Solomon's wealth similarly the product of his wisdom? And if so, what kind of wisdom? I would like to suggest that Solomon was wise in many different ways. One of these was his wisdom in judgement. Was the flip side cunningness, which enabled him to amass all his riches?

[Hillel] used to say: . . . The more property, the more worry; the more slaves, the more robbery; the more Torah, the more life; the more dedicated study, the more wisdom; the more advice, the more understanding; the more justice, the more peace . . .

Sayings of the Fathers

Readings in 1 Kings   Irit Shillor

The temple

1 Kings 6:
1, 11–28

In Exodus 35 Moses was instructed to build the Tabernacle, which was to house the Ark of the Covenant. The people were commanded to bring gifts, each according to their abilities and the goodness of their hearts. The Tabernacle was made of the finest wood and of silver. The Ark itself was adorned with gold. The temple that Solomon built was constructed of wood, which was brought from afar and decorated with gold.

Of course that edifice was vastly richer than its predecessor, the Tabernacle. This is due to the change in circumstances of the people and the kingdom. But there is another major difference between the two structures. The temple has two Cherubs. These were sculptures of creatures with the body of a lion, the wings of an eagle and a human head. These may have been borrowed from the mythology of the surrounding peoples. One can similarly find sculptures of eagles, modelled after the Roman eagle, in synagogues from the time of the Mishnah and the Talmud. The Rabbis have no issue with these and we must conclude that the faith of the Israelites and later the Jews was so strong as to cause no concern. It is not clear what the function of these Cherubs was – are they there purely for decorative purposes, or do they serve as protectors in some way?

Today, when there is no temple, we pray for the safety and rebuilding of Jerusalem and hope that it may become a symbol of eternal peace.

Irit Shillor   Readings in 1 Kings

Solomon is not only the political ruler of Israel but here he is also the religious ruler. There was no separation between religion and state and by definition the state became a religious entity. This lack of separation is, to some extent, still evident in Israel today – one of the few states in the world to be governed partially by religious principles.

Solomon not only blesses the people (verse 14), he then offers a prayer to God in his own name and in the name of the people (verse 30). A large part of his prayer is devoted to history, namely the history of his father, David, who was God's faithful servant and walked in God's ways.

How many people, I wonder, were standing in that crowd and thinking of the sins of David, which led to God's prohibition against his building of the Temple? Or perhaps there was none such in that crowd, since the memory of the people is very short. After all, after the years of warfare under David's rule, Israel was now able to enjoy a time of peace, a time of celebration of their newly erected Temple.

Is there a God in this place?

1 Kings 8:1–6, 10–30

May the maker of peace in the highest bring this peace upon us and upon all Israel and upon the whole world.

From the Siddur

Readings in 1 Kings   Irit Shillor

Readings in 1 Kings

2 The demise of the kings

Notes based on
*Tanakh: The Holy
Scriptures* (Jewish
Publication
Society, 1985) by
Pete Tobias

Pete Tobias is Rabbi
of the Liberal
Synagogue, Elstree, in
Hertfordshire, UK. He
also has two
published works:
*Liberal Judaism:
A Judaism for the
Twenty-First
Century* (2007) and
*Never Mind the
Bullocks!* (2009),
and many articles. A
devoted fan of
Watford Football
Club, Pete can be
heard regularly
offering a 'Pause for
Thought' and other
reflections on BBC
Radio 2. He lives in
Hertfordshire with his
wife, Robbie, and
family.

Preparing for the week

This week's title makes it clear that the kings are doomed – yet the monarchies of Judah and Israel continue for several centuries after the demise of the readings' key characters – Solomon and Jeroboam. The books of Samuel and Kings, which tell the stories of the biblical monarchy, make it clear that being a king in Israel or Judah was not only challenging, it was also frequently challenged by the prophets. A ditty I once wrote about the biblical kings included these lines:

*With all of these prophets telling them how they
    had lapsed
It's hardly surprising their kingdoms collapsed.*

And it is no surprise. The prophet Samuel predicts that a king will bring misery to the Israelite people. And history proves him right. It's a sad account of the failures of leadership, with plenty of relevance to our modern world . . .

'The day will come when you will cry out because of the king whom you yourselves have chosen; and the Eternal One will not answer you on that day'.

I Samuel 8:18

Welcome to the coronation of King Solomon! A grand affair of state, as the son of David takes his rightful place on the throne, and is anointed as the ruler of a kingdom that stretches – according to the book of Kings – from the Euphrates to the borders of Egypt.

Long live the King!

1 Kings 8:63 – 9:9

What a marvellous occasion it was, this royal inauguration! Thousands and thousands of animals sacrificed before hundreds of admiring guests and onlookers. How this resembles a modern state occasion, with all its pomp and ceremony, cheering crowds watching an indulgent display by their leaders.

But when the party is over, the ruler is left to reflect on the responsibilities that go with leadership, the expectations of the people and the requirement to honour and respect the will of God. The prospect of failure haunts the thought of every leader of people. And those fears come knocking not at the moment of acclamation, but in silent, lonely moments of self-doubt. The scene is set; Solomon has been told what is expected of him. In his moment of uncertainty he is humbled and turns to his God. Is he up to the task?

Eternal God, whose dominion embraces the universe, we ask your blessing . . . for those who govern our country and influence the quality of its national life. Make them conscious of their responsibility and teach them to exercise it in accordance with Your will.

Siddur Lev Chadash, p. 484

Readings in 1 Kings   Pete Tobias

Lifestyles of the rich and famous

1 Kings 10:1–25

One of the attractions of power and leadership is the opportunity it offers for mixing with the rich and famous. There's no doubt that our biblical ancestors would have been bewildered by our modern culture of celebrity – but if there is a biblical equivalent of some of our modern icons, then it is surely the Queen of Sheba.

Solomon, the king of a relatively modest kingdom (the borders described in an earlier section of Kings are somewhat fanciful) suddenly finds himself thrust into the limelight. Having heard of his wisdom, the Queen comes to question him. Again, his reputation is on the line. Can this unheard-of monarch from an insignificant land cut it with the 'A-listers' of his day?

Solomon emerges from this challenge with his reputation enhanced, and proves that Israel has talent. This talent earns Solomon fame and wealth, and raises his standing in the ancient world. But whereas he was reflective and humble after his coronation in Jerusalem, there is now no room for any humility or self-doubt: Solomon has entered the world of the rich and famous, and his head is about to be turned from his divinely charged task.

Sovereign of all worlds, we lay our supplications before you, relying not on our own merit but on your abundant mercy. For what are we? . . . Are not the mightiest of us as nothing before you, the famous as though they had never lived?

Siddur Lev Chadash, p.123

Solomon's legendary wisdom, on which his fame and fortune were based, seems to have deserted him. Seduced by the attractions of mixing with the rich and famous of the ancient world, Solomon is also attracted by hundreds of foreign women. It would seem that Solomon's love of grand occasions was matched by his love of women from different tribes. If the biblical figures are true (always questionable), Solomon would have celebrated a royal wedding roughly every three weeks during his 45-year reign!

Several hundred weddings and a funeral

1 Kings 11:1–12

More troubling than this – and Solomon's greed – was his turning away from worship of Israel's one God. This goes against the biblical author's insistence that a good monarch is one who walks in the ways of King David (and at least he only had six wives!). Solomon has committed the ultimate sin for a king in Israel: he has turned away from his God – just as he was warned not to do immediately after his coronation.

Solomon's reputation was buried under the dangerous trappings of fame and wealth. This holds up a light by which we should consider our own shallow times. For the future of Solomon's kingdom, the consequences were fatal.

There are days when we seek material things, and measure failure by what we do not own. Let us seek not to acquire, but to share, to open our hearts to the needs and rights of others.

Siddur Lev Chadash, pp. 88–9 (adapted)

Readings in 1 Kings   Pete Tobias

'We have no share in David!'

1 Kings 12:1–24

Solomon's death may well have been a cause for celebration in the northern kingdom – more so than his many weddings! The arrival of his son Rehoboam, offering to make life even worse than it had been under his father, is unlikely to have been welcomed. Revolution is in the air. The rebellion of Jeroboam against Solomon's son had already been anticipated by the prophet Ahijah (and also in God's words to Solomon at the end of his life). It is further explained when God announces to Shemaiah that all is unfolding as planned.

Rehoboam's stubbornness and Solomon's weaknesses are, therefore, not their fault – they can claim that they are simply playing their part in the unfolding of Israelite history. For the author of Kings, this may be an explanation for the behaviour of David's son and grandson, but it does not stand up to scrutiny. The consequences of Rehoboam's intransigence are death, rebellion and political upheaval. These events may well have been inevitable, given the historical reality, but they might have been avoided if Rehoboam had behaved differently and taken responsibility for his actions. So we too must take responsibility for the state of our world, not simply blame it on fate.

We would do better to acknowledge that if the society around us is ugly with selfishness, falsehood and violence, the fault must lie not in our stars but in us.

Machzor Ru'ach Chadashah, p.72

This is the moment when, according to the author of the books of Kings, the fate of Israel was sealed. And this is also, perhaps, where the fact that history is written by the winners (or at least those who survive a little longer) becomes clear. The House of David is held up as the paragon (despite the behaviour of David's two successors) while that of Jeroboam is derided. Why? Because the kingdom of Israel was destroyed 150 years before Judah – and the Judahite authors needed someone to blame.

Jeroboam's actions, although heavily criticised, were little different from those of Solomon, and were politically astute. In fact, he established a successful kingdom that thrived for two centuries before the Assyrians destroyed it. But to a writer in neighbouring Judah, Jeroboam's rejection of Jerusalem's rule was a political and theological affront. When the history of Judah gets written, Jeroboam is going to be held responsible for everything that went wrong.

When we see political systems that differ from our own ideology or theology, we tend to be suspicious of them. Let the story of Jeroboam teach us to be more objective when judging the political actions and institutions of others.

'To your tents, O Israel!'

1 Kings 12:25 – 13:10

Do not let us imagine that we are 'Children of Light' while others are 'Children of Darkness'. Keep us from making judgements that serve only ourselves, and from the urge to rise by our neighbour's fall.

Siddur Lev Chadash, p. 297

Readings in 1 Kings

Pete Tobias

Jeroboam's fate is sealed

1 Kings 13:11–34

The author of the books of Kings, sitting in Jerusalem after the destruction of the kingdom of Israel, has to explain why his northern neighbours have been wiped out by the Assyrians. And he chooses Jeroboam, he who took the ten tribes of Israel away from the House of David.

But David's dynasty wasn't so terrific either. The key to the monarchy lies in the silent conversation between Solomon and God with which this week's readings began. Solomon failed to live up to his responsibilities. This is why his son lost the ten tribes to Jeroboam – who was blamed for everything that went wrong thereafter. The author of Kings needs a hero. And that hero is King Josiah.

Josiah is the archetypal good king, destroying altars and banishing foreign gods – including that established by Jeroboam. In time, Josiah's descendants would also need explanations as to why Judah was destroyed by the Babylonians. But that's another story.

The story of Israel's kings is, for the most part, one of failure. It is a tale of opportunities missed, abuse of power and poor leadership, despite the noble aspirations expressed at the start of Solomon's reign. In the end, the test of good leadership lies not the leader's promises but in the achievements and the legacy they leave behind. And that's as true today as it was 3000 years ago.

All depends on leadership. When the leader is good and upright, the flock follows.

Siddur Lev Chadash, p. 326

Readings in 1 Kings

3 The prophetic ministry of Elijah

Preparing for the week

'Elijah, come soon with the Messiah!' These are the words Jews sing every Saturday evening while ceremonially marking the division between Sabbath rest and working week. Other prophets – Moses, Samuel and Nathan, for example – preceded Elijah, but Elijah is very important. In Malachi 3:23 – 24 God says Elijah will appear and reconcile parents and children, thus averting destruction. In post-biblical Jewish tradition, because he ascended to heaven but did not die, he brings God's messages to earth. He protects the vulnerable; his presence is invoked at circumcision ceremonies when eight-day-old Jewish baby boys are welcomed into God's covenant. He will provide the solution to complicated debates the rabbis could not resolve, and proclaims the imminent arrival of the Messiah; in both these roles he is welcomed at every Passover *seder*, when a cup is filled for him. In one story in the Talmud, the fifth-century Jewish compendium of law and lore, Rabbi Meir was pursued by Roman soldiers intent on killing him. He ran into the nearest building then realised it was a brothel; Elijah answered Meir's prayers by appearing appropriately disguised and embracing him so his presence was not questioned. In another episode Elijah declares two jesters will go to heaven because they make people laugh and use that laughter to effect reconciliations.

Notes based on the Hebrew Bible by

Rachel Montagu

Rachel Montagu teaches Judaism and Biblical Hebrew. She believes teaching people to understand the Bible in Hebrew without translators' interpretations empowers them as readers. She has been involved in inter-faith dialogue for many years. She lives in London.

'I know God's word in your mouth is truth'

1 Kings 17

It is tempting to read this chapter as comedy. The widow, her son and her household have all been sustained by God's miraculous effect on her flour supply and oil jar for a substantial period of time in the midst of a famine so severe that even the brooks have dried; the Hebrew *yamim*, 'days', can mean a year. Once the brook that has been his water-source dries up, God tells Elijah that the widow has been commanded to provide for him. She clearly is, and remains, unaware of this. She obeys Elijah's command to bring him some of the last morsels that she thought were all that stood between her and her son and death by starvation. Presumably she has reservations about his claim that God has promised that her rations will not fail, since only when Elijah revives her lifeless son does she acknowledge that there is something rather special about the lodger, who must indeed be a man of God – and what is more, his promise that her food will not fail is truth. Nothing is said about whether she provides for others from her unfailing supplies; is her sin (verse 18) lack of hospitality?

Think of all those who sustain and support you, and those dear to you, in different ways; and think if there is anything you can do to make life easier for them.

Blessed are you, Eternal God, who provides for my every need.

This section could also be read as mocking comedy: Obadiah is brave enough to hide a hundred prophets from Ahab and feed them through the famine. Yet when Elijah asks him to tell Ahab that he wants to speak to him, Obadiah (who bravely enacts the meaning of his name, 'servant of God', and resists Ahab and Jezebel) does not trust that Elijah is conveying God's message. Instead he panics, thinking that Elijah will get him killed rather than being confident that Elijah is obeying God. Once Ahab sees Elijah he calls him 'troubler of Israel'; this is a classic example of someone projecting their own difficulties onto others. In a similar way, Jepthah uses the identical word 'troubler' to his daughter after his rash vow to sacrifice whatever meets him on his return home after the battle, if God gives him victory. His vow caused the trouble, not his daughter's loving welcome (Judges 11–12).

Ahab is confusing Elijah and Elijah's troubling message from God, conveyed in chapter 17, that there would be prolonged drought. It is actually Ahab, as Elijah points out, who has caused the trouble – in 1 Kings 16:33 we learned that Ahab made an *asherah* (idol) and did more to enrage God than any previous king. And the extent of the panic of Obadiah, Ahab's trusted minister, shows that Ahab is a cruel tyrant, whose loyal servants expect unjust punishment.

You who trouble Israel

1 Kings 18:1–20

Blessed are you, Eternal our God, who graciously gives us self-knowledge.

Readings in 1 Kings

Rachel Montagu

**Answer me
and the people
will know you
are God**

1 Kings 18:21–46

Elijah describes himself as God's only remaining prophet – presumably this is an exaggeration, since we know Obadiah has a hundred prophets safely stashed in two caves! Perhaps Elijah feels isolated because he is the only prophet in his generation with the stage-presence to carry off this public trial. So he must confront Ba'al's prophets alone, while fearing Ahab and Jezebel's retribution.

Ba'al does not answer his prophets when they call while limping round his altar. The same word *p'sach* is used in verse 27 when Elijah tells the people that they can no longer halt between God and Ba'al. Elijah mocks the idiocy of Ba'al worshippers' beliefs and practices. In contrast to the God of Israel in Psalm 121, who never sleeps but continuously protects Israel, their Ba'al may need waking or even to relieve himself. The Bible forbids the self-mutilation practised by the prophets of Ba'al (Leviticus 19:28). After the long day of fruitless pleas to Ba'al, Elijah adds to the drama by pouring water over his offering, which is consumed by fire as soon as he prays. The people acknowledge God with the words that end the Yom Kippur prayers for forgiveness: 'The Eternal is God.' Now the long drought can end; Elijah emphasises to Ahab that the rain comes from God in response to the people's return to faith.

Listen to Mendelssohn's oratorio *Elijah*, which conveys the drama and poetry of Elijah's life.

Blessed are you, Eternal, who listens to prayer.

Rachel Montagu

Readings in 1 Kings

Elijah's despairing hope for death is assuaged by the comforting cake the angel brings. The angel's command to eat, because the way is too much for him without support, can be read as assurance that God brings us the comfort we need.

Mount Horeb is synonymous with Sinai. Elijah's cave is presumed, by traditional Jewish commentators, to be the cleft where Moses, after receiving God's commandments, heard God's self-definition as merciful and forgiving (Exodus 34:6–7). When God asks Elijah how he is, Elijah voices his distress that, even after his valiant efforts for God, he is alone, his life at risk. God passes Elijah, as he passed before Moses. But Elijah, unlike Moses, does not seem to perceive God's presence: not in the wind, or the storm or the fire where it cannot be found, but also not in 'the still, small voice' or, perhaps a better translation, 'the reverberation of utter silence'. When God again asks Elijah how he is, he repeats his earlier statement unchanged: the 'still, small voice', which we often quote as a supreme manifestation of God, seems not to move Elijah at all. This explains why God then tells him that Elisha will succeed him as prophet, reassuring him that he is not alone, and relieving him of the role he could no longer bear.

The fine sound of silence

1 Kings 19

Surely goodness and loving-kindness will pursue me all the days of my life and I will dwell in the house of the Eternal forever.

Psalm 23:6

Rachel Montagu

The power of repentance

1 Kings 21

This episode is a byword for the abuse of political power. When Nabaoth says that his ancestral inheritance cannot be replaced either by money or a better vineyard, that should have ended the matter. However, Samuel had cautioned the people that having kings would lead to exploitation of their subjects – including taking their vineyards (1 Samuel 8:14). When Ahab's 'spirit turned away' (verse 4) at Nabaoth's refusal, Jezebel assured Ahab that his rule over Israel entitled him to it.

Elijah goes to deliver God's message that, whatever Ahab and Jezebel might hope, kings may not murder and dispossess, and that they would share the fate they had engineered for Nabaoth. Even then Elijah has to remind Ahab that it is his own actions that caused the encounter and reproach, not any hostility from Elijah.

Like Jonah, this episode teaches the power of repentance and God's delight in forgiveness. Even after everything Ahab had done, when he fasted and wore sackcloth, God accepted his repentance and postponed the decreed punishment. His son could also have repented and averted punishment, but chose idol worship instead. And as Elijah prophesied, Jezebel did share the fate that she had engineered for Nabaoth (2 Kings 9:30–37).

Write a letter that enhances someone's life, using the written word for good not evil (as Jezebel did).

Blessed are you, Eternal, who desires repentance.

These verses describe the end of the reigns of Ahab and Jehoshophat and the transition to their sons. A similar transition to a successor can be seen in the account of Elijah's end in 2 Kings 2. Just as Ahaziah continues his parents' Ba'al worship, and Jehorum continues his godlier family traditions, so Elisha continues Elijah's prophetic work. To do this, he asks for a double portion of Elijah's spirit. As a symbol of his inheritance from Elijah, Elisha picks up Elijah's cloak which falls as the whirlwind carries him up to heaven. Elijah's mantle divides the water for Elisha as it had for Elijah (verses 8 and 14), a quick reassurance that he had inherited Elijah's strength.

Accepting inherited tradition

1 Kings 22:1–2, 29–45

God willing, today is my son's bar mitzvah. He will read from the Torah during the Sabbath morning service. Today's reading includes the verse telling us to teach our children Jewish beliefs (Deuteronomy 6:7). I hope for my son that the mantle of tradition will feel comfortable on his shoulders, and will help him hear God's presence, do good to others, delight in living as a Jew and, in turn, teach that to his children.

Hear O Israel, the Eternal is our God, the Eternal is one. And you will love the Eternal your God with all your heart and with all your soul and with all your strength. And you will repeat these words to your children and will talk about them while sitting at home, walking on your way, at bedtime and on rising.

Readings in 1 Kings   Rachel Montagu

Openings and closings in the New Testament

Greetings and blessings 1

Notes based on the New Revised Standard Version by

Winston Halapua

Winston Halapua is Bishop of the Diocese of Polynesia in New Zealand. Born in Tonga, he served the Church in Fiji for many years. He is based at St John's College, Auckland, and teaches at the School of Theology, Auckland University. He is married and has two grown-up sons.

Preparing for the week

I begin with ancient words of my mother tongue 'Si'oto ofa'. Older people in Tonga may sometimes use this ancient form of greeting meaning literally 'all my love'. This may be understood as 'You are embraced and safe.' The greetings speak of a concern for well-being and blessing which continues in the life of the one greeted.

The opening greetings and the closing blessings in the readings chosen for this week are very much entwined. These opening and closing words are not shallow, superficial greetings or a mere rounding off of the letter. The greeting, 'Grace and peace to you' (you may like to trace how many times these words are used), is part of a deep desire and underlying prayer that Christians may experience and live out the life of God. The words are a prayer that believers may be embraced by the power and love of God. As we launch into this week, I offer a blessing from the Pacific, which you may like to pray each day:

The waves of a mighty ocean of God's love embrace and carry us forward.
With Christ, our mast and master, may we voyage courageously.
The Spirit of peace and power flow in us to strengthen and guide
through calm and storm. Emeni.

We all appreciate being greeted warmly by people who care for our well-being. We often feel diminished when people only acknowledge us superficially. One of the common forms of greetings in the Fiji Islands and one of the first words strangers learn is the word 'bula'. 'Bula' means life. 'Life!' What a wonderful greeting, and even more wonderful when this greeting expresses the desire that a person may have fullness of life.

Paul combines the Greek and Roman heritage in his opening greetings to the church in Rome. 'Grace to you and peace.' These are love-laden words. Paul, writing with great sincerity and boldness, is saying, 'Life to you!' What gives him this great sincerity and boldness is the life he himself has been given – a life transformed by the immense love of God, which came through his encounter with the risen Christ on the road to Damascus. There, Paul experienced for himself the power of God which turns enmity to friendship. This power enabled him to reach out to a church he did not found – to both Jews and Gentiles. Paul writes with great kindness and humanity – he is one who prays and encourages others in the life-giving faith of Jesus Christ.

Consider how you might go through the day with the prayer in your heart that everyone you greet may experience fullness of life.

Life to you!

Romans 1:1–17

Risen Jesus, as I know the embrace of your unconditional love, so may I reach out to others and relate to them with sincerity and warmth.

Counting blessings

Romans 16:1–27

Names sometimes tell a story. I was named Winston, which is not a Tongan name. I was born in 1945 when peace was declared after World War II. I was named after the Prime Minister of Great Britain, Winston Churchill. Because of threat of invasion, American troops were stationed in Nuku'alofa, the little capital city of Tonga. Tongans on the island were asked to move out of their homes and take refuge further inland. When peace was declared families returned joyfully to their homes. My name, Winston, was a celebration of the peace that embraced even faraway Pacific islands.

The names listed by Paul at the end of the letter to the Romans tell a story. They tell the story of the way the church was experiencing the immense love of God. 'Grace and peace to you from God our Father and the Lord Jesus Christ,' Paul prays at the beginning of the letter. In Romans 16, it seems, Paul recognises that deep prayer is being answered in the grace and peace evident in the lives of the people he names. The names of people to whom Paul sends personal greetings are listed lovingly with appreciation of their particular contributions. Paul is counting blessings. Many names are Gentile names, and the list includes women and men. The church in Rome embraced a diversity of people with many gifts. Paul concludes by encouraging wisdom in the service of a God whose peace embraces us.

Count your blessings – take time to name people whom you know, acknowledging their particular gifts and qualities.

God of peace, you embrace each one. Help us to celebrate and live out your peace.

At the beginning of his letter to the Corinthians, Paul speaks in various ways of what it is to be called by God. He has been called to be 'an apostle of Jesus Christ' (verse 1). The church in the cosmopolitan port of Corinth was struggling with many problems. The people are nevertheless 'called to be saints' (verse 2). 'God is faithful,' Paul writes, 'by him you were called into the fellowship of Jesus Christ, our Lord' (verse 9). The way Paul greets a people struggling with divisions is to focus on the significance of being called by God.

When I think of being called in the Pacific Islands, I think of the conch, a large shell used as a trumpet. Although a wooden drum is often used to call people to worship, on particularly significant occasions a conch may be used. The sound of the blown conch has a resonance that seems to speak from the very depth of the ocean.

Paul is sounding a conch. He reminds the Corinthians of the significance of their calling which arises from the infinite depth of God's love. The love of God is deeper than any ocean and embraces all. When communities of faith understand the profound significance of the call of God – the flowing life of God's grace and peace – then rivalries and divisions are shown up as stagnant pools preventing the flow of the Spirit's life.

A profound calling

1 Corinthians 1: 1–17

Faithful God, thank you that from the depths of your love in Jesus Christ you call us into life-giving relationship with you and with one another.

Openings and closings in the New Testament   Winston Halapua

Sharing with the saints

1 Corinthians 16: 1–24

In 2009 a tsunami hit islands in Samoa and also a tiny island in the Tonga group. Lives were lost and villages devastated. As the news unfolded in New Zealand, stories of how Pacific Islanders were responding to the needs of their own people were marvelled at. The Government of New Zealand promised aid for relief-work, and other organisations began to respond to the needs. The churches' mission boards appealed for help. I was alongside Samoan families who had lost loved ones. My ancestral home, Nuiatoputapu, has a very small population, but some precious lives were lost and the hospital and other buildings flattened. Supplies of food were short. In Auckland, the extended families of people in Nuiatoputapu collected sufficient bags of flour and tinned food to fill a container which was shipped to offer immediate relief.

'My love be with you all in Christ Jesus' (verse 24), writes Paul at the end of his letter. The beginning of chapter 16 makes it clear that Paul expects the spiritually gifted Corinthians to respond to the needs of others in practical and carefully worked out ways. Love is sharing and caring in relationships. Because of the generous love of God which embraces all people, the Corinthian church is kin with the different people of the mother church in Jerusalem, and it is important that the needs of family are met.

Reflect and pray on Paul's greeting, 'My love be with you all in Christ Jesus.' How will you put this into action today?

Winston Halapua   Openings and closings in the New Testament

A younger Fijian woman came to live with us for a while. She was seeking medical help for cancer. She was away from her husband and children and missed them. She had never been out of Fiji and the big city was strange to her. Her future was uncertain. She was ill. She prayed frequently. Although she had little formal education, like other devout Pacific Islanders she read her Bible, which was a great source of comfort to her. She even slept with it under her pillow. She returned to Fiji and died shortly after. We shall never forget her gentle presence and faith. It seemed that, through her troubles, she was ministering to us.

Paul, the pastor, identifies with people. He knows suffering and even the experience of being 'utterly, unbearably crushed' (verse 8). Here is empathy. In extreme, tough times Paul learnt about the faithfulness of a God who is there even in the most desperate situation. In his experience of weakness and being crushed Paul has been open to God's tender mercy. With deep understanding of that tender mercy Paul reaches out to others.

In Fiji the creeper commonly called 'mile a minute', when crushed, brings relief to the pain of hornet stings. Crushed lavender heads release perfume. When we feel 'crushed' there may be new possibilities opening for us.

Compassionate God, in tough times help me to know your great comfort through Christ.

Tough times and tender mercy

2 Corinthians 1: 1–14

Openings and closings in the New Testament   Winston Halapua

235

Life in the strength of God's power

Ephesians 6: 10–24

In Fiji, there is a stone called a bashing stone, an instrument of death. In the days when cannibalism was practised people's brains were bashed out on the stone. Now this stone stands in a Methodist church in Bau, a village associated with the Paramount Chief Cakobau, who enabled the Christian faith to take root in Fiji. It has been formed into the baptismal font, an instrument of life.

Chained to a Roman soldier, the prisoner is able to observe the military apparatus of his guard. This prisoner uses his immediate experience to reflect on the power of God, which is stronger than any armoury or weapons of destruction. With the conviction that the power of God is far greater than the forces of evil, the writer of the letter to the Ephesians addresses the wider church and exhorts them: 'be strong in the Lord and in the strength of his power' (verse 10).

Sadly, the Pacific Islands, known sometimes for the friendliness of the people, have not been immune from militarism, political turmoil, violence and wrong use of power. But the scriptures encourage us towards a life transformed and protected by the loving power of the God of peace.

The writer of the Ephesians writes, 'Pray in the Spirit at all times' (verse 18). So, dear reader, I ask you to pray for the peoples of the Pacific Islands, and I offer a prayer for you:

As you read the scriptures and meditate on God's word, may you know the transforming power of the love of God in Christ Jesus. Life to you!

Winston Halapua   Openings and closings in the New Testament

Openings and closings in the New Testament

Greetings and blessings 2

Notes based on the New Revised Standard Version by

John Fairbrother

Preparing for the week

Openings and closings, greetings and farewells, are the thresholds of relationships. Some we cross frequently; some less so; some once only. On each occasion the speaker has mere seconds to communicate their identity and provide their hearer(s) with reason and/or feeling to listen. Such thresholds are precious for the intensity of the moment. Each presents an acute challenge for speakers who are concerned to connect meaningfully with individuals or communities.

It is little wonder, then, that early Christians gave so much attention to the form of their greetings and blessings. The forms and content that have come down to us reveal a concern for clarity about the identity, commitment and purpose of the speaker and their relationship with the hearer(s). Clearly, there was need to communicate much within a few words, if hearers were to find sufficient confidence to risk declaring their faith in what were often less than sympathetic social environments.

For Christians, greetings and blessings are much more than salutation. They are prayers of invitation to be with another in a spirit that transcends distance, offering the embrace of Christ and thereby revealing the heart of God.

Be with me, Holy Spirit, in my approaching and leaving of those I meet. Fill my thoughts with life, words with love and heart with grace that I might recognise Christ always before me.

John Fairbrother is an Anglican priest from Aotearoa, New Zealand. He has served in a variety of ministries, including former Archdeacon of Wellington and Dean of Waikato, and is currently Director of Vaughan Park Anglican Retreat and Conference Centre at beautiful Long Bay (www.vaughanpark. org.nz). He is married to Margaret, a natural-health therapist. Their three adult children provide plenty of opportunity for family greetings and farewells with addresses in Birmingham, Rome and Auckland.

In the heart of friends

Philippians 1:1–14

Physical distance from those one loves may be a painful experience. For many New Zealanders with family and friends in the northern hemisphere it is an ever present reality. The heart can long for reunion in a manner that may render otherwise pleasant memories as pain. Such separation may all too easily become loneliness.

Imprisoned, Paul might have good reason for feeling alone, separated from those he loves. Yet this greeting of his is rather upbeat for one with cause to feel down.

He overcomes his present difficulty by inviting the recipients of his letter to share with him in the grace and peace of God as they continue to experience their faith in Jesus Christ. Paul's greeting to the church in Philippi is a wonderful example of how Christian faith may transcend the otherwise impossible difficulties presented by distance.

Paul's greeting is a prayer. He is assuring the community of believers that in prayer the faithful are always in communion with one another. Physical distance may separate loved ones; however, the heart of God holds all believers within the one embrace.

God, in whom we all live and move and have our being, lift my love for those I know beyond the limits of space and time to hold us all in your compassion and universal presence.

In these closing words we who, as it were, eavesdrop on Paul's letter are privileged to hear a succinct and profound personal summary of what it means to share life in the spirit of Christ. Paul is leaving his friends with an outline of the values and outcomes that identify and shape the life of those who declare Christ as Lord.

Characteristically of Paul, his closing is entirely positive. He calls to mind the depth of compassion and understanding he shares with his dear friends. In this, he and they are as 'a fragrant offering, a sacrifice pleasing to God' (verse 18).

At the very edge of the threshold he leaves them, and, thankfully, we who read his words now have the perspective that all any of us do is done within the realm of God's patient, inexhaustible love.

Grace and peace indeed: Paul knew how to say goodbye.

Forever loved

Philippians 4:8–23

May the grace and peace that reveal God continue with all who share in the way of Christ: in Jesus' name may such grace and peace be found in me.

Openings and closings in the New Testament   John Fairbrother

Beloved in Christ

Philemon 1–16

'I am sending him, that is, my own heart, back to you'.

(verse 12)

This short letter, which in form is little more than a greeting and farewell, may be read as something of a distillation of Paul's priority for love being witness to a life lived in faith towards Jesus Christ.

He recalls the love of his friends to one another and for all the members of the church, and how such love is an expression of faith. Feeling safe in that love of friends and their faith toward Jesus, he puts his authority aside, trusts that love and returns Onesimus to his master. More than a mere return, Paul urges the master to receive Onesimus as 'a beloved brother' (verse 16).

Paul's witness for us who read now might lie not in the generosity of returning Onesimus, or his keeping of the law in this regard, but more in the fact that Paul is giving up one who has become so close to him, as to be part of his heart. He could have kept Onesimus with him.

Paul offers to those he loves something he dearly needs. His love for Onesimus, the master, local church and thereby for Christ is demonstrated in his willingness to do what is best for them all. Paul's meaning and hope rests in trusting that the response of his friends will be of the same quality. That expression of faith invites mutual commitment to Christ, one another and the church.

Eternal God, in Jesus I see the gift and cost of your love: for your love's sake, grant me strength and resolve to offer the best I have in trust to those who share your name.

Christians have good cause for empathy with oppressed minorities. The greetings and farewells of this letter address church communities in Asia Minor, where the faithful were a relative few within a dominant pagan culture. Their Christianity was an alien practice to accepted conventions.

Both greeting and farewell reflect the intensity of the situation. The brevity of greeting emphasises the significance of the hearers' solidarity with the church in Rome. It assures the communities their current situation is God's purpose and therefore blessed.

The farewell reiterates God's purpose and ultimate protection. Through steadfast discipleship oppression will be subverted and God's glory revealed to their everlasting reward.

The situation described in the letter is no less true for contemporary culture. Wherever the values and morals of Christians' conflict with surrounding culture, this letter, particularly with its greeting and farewell, may remind the faithful of the ultimate worth of seeking to live in the Way of Jesus, and remaining at one with the wider church.

Of ultimate worth

1 Peter 1:1–2, 5:6–14

Grant me courage, dear God, to seek your purposes and live well: ready to respond where truths that would otherwise disturb and challenge might tempt me to turn away for quiet and safety's sake.

Openings and closings in the New Testament   John Fairbrother

Take heart to make plain

1 John 1:1–10

Now for something quite different from the more traditional forms of greetings we have been reading. Here the writer has such a sense of urgency to communicate that he appears to burst over the threshold with the declaration of purpose. The intensity communicates a sense of: 'Let there be no mistake of what is to be said: we are attesting to the truth that we have seen.'

It is not uncommon to hear laments about the current state of the contemporary church. It is not difficult to find evidence of denominations engaged with internal debates about issues of scriptural interpretation, doctrine, sexuality, morality and financial affairs. Some churches question the validity of other churches. Agreement about truths, understanding and tolerance are no more apparent now than they perhaps were at the time of this letter of 1 John.

We may take heart from such difficulty. The writer of 1 John is concerned that the church he speaks to does not stray from the love of God as lived by Jesus. His proclamation was up against competing beliefs, competing voices calling people away from the gospel the writer knows as the 'word of life' (verse 1). He is calling the churches to be honest about their condition, 'to walk in the light', to confess sins in order that we [may] have fellowship with [God]' (verse 7).

The writer of 1 John deserves some thanks for the emphatic beginning to this letter. It offers a ready example of how important it is to make plain what one believes and values if understanding another's point is to be possible.

Gracious God, grant me the grace to listen, to accept what is offered and respond in manner and meaning that builds relationships contributing to the presence of your realm.

Perhaps Jude was something of a politician. The opening and closing of this small letter are gentle words highlighting supremely human values, hope for the recipients' well-being and glorification of God through Jesus Christ. These are fine words and refined sentiments. Between them lies a text that confronts, challenges, exhorts, warns and offers a little encouragement. Jude seems concerned to greet and conclude on good terms.

Each day will challenge most people with a journey through a variety of emotions and moods. The journey is begun with sun lighting our world with the energy of life, and the journey draws to a close as night invites rest. The rising and rest, rest and rising, provide a context for greeting and blessing life. The greeting is when we may place all our hopes on God's grace, the closing a time when we may, as it were, entrust ourselves to the protection of angels watching over us.

The Christian way is about living with zest to engage the difficulties and sometimes arbitrary events of a day. Faith is the means by which doubts in our own strengths to achieve challenges, or even cope, may be placed within the context of God's gentle gift, waking us to life and trusting protection when falling into rest.

Jude's letter, while retaining a literal message for Christians now, also provides in form and type of content a metaphor that may aid a disciple's prayerful approach and conclusion to a day or week.

Angels watching over us

Jude 1–2, 24–25

Within the energy of life and wonder of each day, keep me awake, Lord God, to present opportunities for personal growth and community involvement. May difficulties become challenges, and joys thanksgivings, all for the good of each day.

Openings and closings in the New Testament   John Fairbrother

Readings in Matthew 20–25

Going up to Jerusalem

Notes based on the New Revised Standard Version by

Helen Stanton

An Anglican laywoman, Helen has worked for Christian Aid; in university chaplaincy; and in promoting social justice. In recent years her work has focused on training people for ordained and lay ministries. She is closely associated with the Anglican Poor Clares, who live in Freeland in Oxfordshire.

Preparing for the week

The pace of a fast-moving Gospel quickens, and parables and narratives are crowded together breathlessly, offering us a teacher and a saviour who is bewildering. The writer of this Gospel expects us, like the first disciples, to work hard, to use our imaginations. The parables and narratives are not spelled out, Jesus does not explain what he is trying to say, and we face some of the most challenging, and frankly rather odd, passages of scripture. We cannot sit back and think 'how very interesting'. It is as if the text is somehow incomplete, and only we can complete it. We become part of the text itself as we try out answers to the questions Jesus raises. And like the disciples, even the twelve, we will sometimes misunderstand, be confused or just plain wrong. What is important here is our openness to learn. We are called to engage, not necessarily to understand everything that happens or is said. We are called, as Jesus called the disciples earlier in this Gospel, to follow the way of Jesus. And that calling is to take up our cross daily and to accompany Jesus as he goes up to Jerusalem to die.

'God made the animals for innocence and plants for their simplicity, but Man [*sic*] he made to serve him wittily in the tangle of his mind' (words ascribed to Thomas More in *A Man for All Seasons* by Robert Bolt). What might these words mean for our understanding of scripture?

This chapter begins with one of those parables that challenges a Western, liberal sense of fairness. Like the end of the preceding chapter, it is part of the undermining of our ordinary understanding of things, a reversal of what might be called the thinking of the world, in contrast with the thinking of the kingdom. This reversal can be seen as culminating in the death of Jesus, a death towards which Jesus turns in this chapter. Just as a humiliating and appallingly cruel death is not what would be expected for the Son of God, so '. . . the last will be first, and the first last' (verse 16). The death of the cross is to be seen as an expression of God's extravagant and overwhelming love, and so is this parable.

One can understand the carping of those who had worked hard all day: surely they deserved more than those who had only put in an hour? But none of us earns God's love; all of us are dependent upon God's abundant, even excessive, grace. God's love is not depleted when God is generous to everyone, nor is our worth devalued.

Where have you seen God's extravagant love at work today?

God of tenderness and compassion, grant us the generosity to rejoice in your love for others, and long for their well-being.

All shall have prizes

Matthew 20:1–16

Servant leadership

Matthew 20: 17–28

The concept of servant leadership is something much bandied about in the churches today, but I wonder how often it is practised. It is as if the power that inevitably comes with leadership, and in some societies and at some times also the status and kudos, make being a servant leader extremely difficult, and sometimes unpopular with those whom leaders seek to serve. It is hardly surprising that *we* find it so challenging when those who were closest to Jesus didn't understand what he was all about.

Jesus has just spoken of his being 'handed over', given into the control of the powers that be, who will disempower him, and finally subject him to torture and an horrific death. And James and John and their mother, instead of being dismayed by this prospect, seek power for themselves. Jesus makes the connection that they have failed to make – discipleship means identifying with the Jesus who will accept the cup of disempowerment and suffering. Again he reverses the thinking of this world, true greatness in the kingdom of God means handing oneself over, becoming a slave.

How may we be servant disciples while maintaining our identity as those made in the image and likeness of God, and, therefore, worthy of respect?

I am no longer my own but yours.
I freely and wholeheartedly yield all things
to your pleasure and disposal.

Extract from the Methodist Covenant Service

What do you want?

Matthew 20:
29–34

When asked what she wanted, the mother of James and John had said power for her sons. A few verses later, and in answer to almost the same question, two blind men ask for their eyes to be opened. Here is a theme that resonates throughout the Judeo–Christian tradition. Those who should know God well so often fail to understand, and it is those who come to God with their raw need who so often get it right. The two men might be said to have more insight than James and John. They certainly have more insight than the crowd. The two men understand (see) clearly that Jesus is supremely compassionate. They recognise, or at any rate hope, that they will take priority, and this story is an embodiment of the last being first, for Jesus turns aside and the men receive their sight.

The two blind men also recognise whom it is that they are addressing. In calling Jesus 'Son of David' (verses 30 & 31), they use a royal title that prepares us for the narrative of the entry into Jerusalem. The crowd seeks to silence them, but still they cry out.

How can we seek to listen to the voices of those who are silenced in our church or society or world?

God of the silenced, give us grace to bring our neediness to you, that our lives may be transformed, and we may shout your praises.

Humility and power

Matthew 21:1–17

Again Jesus subverts and reverses the thinking of the world. This time the crowd takes up the cry of the blind men, and acclaims Jesus as son of David. The people, again like the blind men, call Hosanna – come and save us! And again Jesus defines his royalty as that of humility, for his 'triumphal entry' is mounted on the foal of a donkey. Humility does not mean accepting the *status quo*, however. Rather it means asserting the reign of God. Servant leadership does not mean keeping quiet in the face of error or evil, it means telling the truth. Proclaiming the kingdom of God does not mean treating all equally, it means prioritising those who suffer, even at the cost of the anger of those who are thought to be good.

In these verses Jesus directly confronts the religious authorities: he is neither polite nor conciliatory. He might be described as a little like a bull in a china shop, as he reclaims the temple for God. And, as I read these verses and the protests of the authorities, I wonder what it is about *our* religious practice that Jesus would wish to overthrow in order to reassert the reign of God.

Who are those in our church, society or world who call for change most passionately? What truth can we find in what they are saying?

Abba, our loving God, give us wisdom and courage to speak and act clearly and with strength whenever your truth is compromised.

Helen Stanton   Readings in Matthew

The story with which these verses begin is an uncomfortable one, for surely Jesus should have compassion on this tree? The evangelist seems to have found the story uncomfortable too, for uncharacteristically we are given its meaning, and it is linked with the power of prayer.

I have another understanding of the story, however, and one that links it with the encounter between Jesus and the religious authorities that follows. If a tree that does not fulfil its purpose withers, will not the same thing happen to the authority of religious leaders who do not fulfil their function, of leading people in the way of God?

These religious leaders question Jesus' authority, and in a piece of exquisite dialogue, Jesus exposes their inability to tell the truth, thus calling their authority into question once again. Are they fit religious leaders? They give that appearance, but like the second son in the parable they say the right thing but don't do it. As he has overturned the tables in the temple, Jesus overturns religious authority: those who were at first obdurate, or scandalously sinful, but who did what was right, are those who are fit for purpose in God's kingdom. It is doing God's will that counts.

Try to attend to the wisdom of those who carry least authority in your church.

God of all, give us grace not only to accept your word, but also to do it, that those demeaned and rejected in this world may be lifted up as your kingdom comes.

Fit for purpose?

Matthew 21: 18–32

Readings in Matthew   Helen Stanton

No pasaran

Matthew 21: 33–46

For the last few days we have read of an uncompromising Jesus, one who is prepared to provoke the anger and violence of the authorities. This parable would have been seen as offensive in the extreme. Yet the parable draws upon the very tradition that religious rulers depended on for their authority. It is they, Jesus implies, who not only failed to believe the Baptist, but who maltreated and abused and ignored the prophets. They have been called to account repeatedly, and repeatedly found wanting. Finally, in rejecting the son they will draw God's wrath upon themselves. Here again, Jesus pulls no punches: a miserable death awaits them, and they will be crushed. It is difficult to hear the voice of the one who came to serve in this parable. The language is angry in the extreme: it offers a dire warning.

The Christian faith is committed to truth-telling, to exposing and, where possible, overthrowing evil. In this we are called to be as uncompromising as Jesus in these verses. We cannot be reconciled with evil. Apartheid South Africa is a classic example of this where the acknowledgement of truth was a prerequisite for reconciliation. There can be no love without truth.

What evils in your society need exposure? How can you encourage your church to issue a dire warning where it is needed?

God of all truth, enable us to examine our own lives with your uncompromising gaze of love. Set us free to oppose all that diminishes that love in your world.

Readings in Matthew 20–25

Conflict

Notes based on the New Revised Standard Version by
Helen Stanton

For Helen's biography see p. 244.

Preparing for the week

If any of us has a residual sense of 'gentle Jesus meek and mild', that image will be destroyed by this week's readings! In them Matthew's Jesus offends everyone who is anyone in the world of first-century Judaism. He begins by calling into question the whole concept of election, proceeds to argue passionately and systematically with the Pharisees, the Herodians and the Sadducees – and then argues with the Pharisees all over again.

In chapter 23 passionate argument turns to condemnation and threat. This Jesus is straight out of the tradition of the prophets such as the eighth-century Amos, who told the people that on the day of the Lord, 'I will not revoke punishment' (Amos 2:6). Jesus' anger, like that of Amos, was on behalf of the vulnerable and poor, but it was still a consuming anger. We ignore that anger at our peril, especially those of us who are leaders in our churches, or in our societies. But at the end of chapter 23, it is as if Jesus collapses from anger and frustration into grief and compassion, and our motherly saviour laments over us, his obdurate children.

Use this week to think about how you deal with your own anger and that of others. Pray that God may use your anger so that God's reign of justice and peace may be promoted.

The clothing of the reign of God

Matthew 22:1–14

Some Christians see this as a parable that indicates the end of the special relationship between God and the Jewish people. They identify the church with those who come to feast at the great banquet of God's reign after those originally invited refuse. But the text deserves a deeper engagement than that reading suggests, for it undermines any possibility of Christian self-satisfaction.

Those who were invited – perhaps 'the great and the good' – made light of an invitation from a king. So, having done away with the expected guests, the king invites everyone who can be found, good and bad. Ordinary understandings of worth and status are superseded. I believe that, at least in part, these verses remind us to expect the unexpected to feast with us too – in the reign of God the vulnerable and low of status become the most important.

The final verses make it clear that there is no room for us to be smug or complacent because we have accepted God's invitation: if we fail to clothe ourselves with the clothing of God's reign – perhaps to welcome those unexpected guests – then it is clear what will happen to us also. We become no better than those who have refused God's invitation in the first place, those who are replaced by the humble and lowly.

God of the feast, clothe us with the values of your reign, that we may feast with the unworthy, and rejoice.

Today's episode reminds me of one of those radio programmes where the audience is invited to question public figures. In the text, the questions are asked by public figures who, the evangelist says, seek to 'entrap him'. And the questions asked are ones that have been significant for the Church throughout the ages. First, what is the relationship between those who follow the way of God with a state government that may be alien to God's reign? Christians have argued throughout history about what Jesus meant by 'Give therefore to the emperor the things that are the emperor's, and to God the things that are God's' (verse 21).

For the most part the church has believed that Christians should be obedient to the state except when it is contrary to the reign of God, and many believe that disobedience to the state should only happen in extreme circumstances. Dietrich Bonhoeffer and the Confessing Church in Germany did just that during the 1940s. But I wonder whether this does not also apply to less extreme situations? The coin that Jesus handles in this story bears the image of the emperor, but surely all human beings bear the image of God, and therefore we should all be treated with respect and compassion.

All things are God's

Matthew 22: 15–33

Lord our God, your reign gathers together the whole life of the world. Help us to offer you not a part of our lives but our whole selves in the service of the life that has no end.

Readings in Matthew

Helen Stanton

253

God, others, self?

Matthew 22: 34–46

In my youth, this was the order of priority for love, as though human beings only had a certain amount of love available, and it had better be wisely used. Although in the community to which I belong now this is certainly not what is taught, many of us, and perhaps especially women, have internalised this story to mean that our wishes and desires, and even our physical and psychological well-being, must be considered only after others are cared for. I think this entails a fundamental misunderstanding of what Jesus was saying.

In Matthew's Gospel, the evangelist makes it explicitly clear that there is no competition for love between God, neighbour and self. For what happens when we love God? Our own lives are transformed and enriched, because meeting God means meeting with the most extravagant and absurdly excessive love we can imagine. As beings whose hearts and souls and minds (and, I would want to suggest, bodies) are united, we come to God with the whole of our lives, lived in society with others. We can never be isolated individuals. And as we love God and neighbour and self, that love simply grows and increases.

All love is God's love and, like the loaves and fishes of an earlier story, there is enough for all, and overflowing.

God, who loves us tenderly, give us grace to love ourselves and others that we may reflect, and rejoice in the face of Jesus Christ.

Helen Stanton

Readings in Matthew

Jesus returns to his earlier theme of servant leadership, again contrasting this with the practice of the religious authorities. 'They tie up heavy burdens, hard to bear' (verse 4), he says, and goes on to point out that these leaders do not do their share of the carrying. I suspect it is not just that religious leaders tie up heavy burdens for others to bear, but that we, religious leaders and others, tie them up for ourselves too. These verses always remind me of the saying of Jesus earlier in this Gospel, 'my yoke is easy, and my burden light' (Matthew 11:30).

In the context of these later chapters that move Jesus towards the cross, it would be inept to suggest that the way of Jesus is not a difficult path. But it is often our unwillingness to be set free that makes it unnecessarily hard for us.

Jesus calls us to take up our cross, but that cross is good news and brings us to life eternal. The choice of what gives life, rather than the kind of behaviour that is life-denying, is surely a neglected virtue in the Christian tradition. Let us burden ourselves neither with guilt, nor with supererogation, but seek and rejoice in the life God gives freely to us.

God, you set us free from the burden of sin and death.
Help us to accept your freedom and rejoice in the life
you give.

Pharisees and theologians

Matthew 23: 13–28

Jesus continues in prophetic mode: woe to those who are obsessed with the minutiae of religious observance but neglect what is really important! The words are addressed to Scribes and Pharisees, and the word 'pharisaical' has come to mean one obsessed with unnecessary details. But Jesus had many things in common with the Pharisees, and some scholars believe that he may, in fact, have been a Pharisee – robust disputation being a characteristic of Pharisaic search for the truth.

Like Jesus, the Pharisees seem to have called into question elitist and hierarchical approaches to religion. They tried to popularise Judaism, seeing religious observance as the task of every Jew, not just a priestly caste. Pharisaic schools promoted love of neighbour, and attitudes to divorce and to women that are similar to those of Jesus. Both Talmud and Mishnah provide oral commentary on and discussion of the scriptures that is comparable with the processes of Christian tradition.

So why are the Pharisees so often viewed as downright wicked by the church? I suspect that this is an example of the anti-Semitism that originally arose through an attempt by the early church to distinguish itself from Judaism. At various times and places this has escalated to cause a level of anti-Jewish violence and hatred that has marred the history of the church.

God of Abraham and Sarah, Abba of Jesus Christ, forgive our hatred of one another; grant us *shalom* as we seek your truth.

How often do we do precisely what Jesus describes here? How could our ancestors have accepted slavery, engaged in the brutal killing of Muslims in the name of Christ, or have regarded women as second-rate children of God? Yes, we must tell the truth: our ancestors allowed and sometimes caused evil to flourish; but to point the finger at them is so often an evasion of our own responsibility. Slavery continues to flourish, in the factories and brothels of the world. The war against terror is easily interpreted as a war against Islam. And women continue to be devalued even in the so-called enlightened West. Our words of condemnation rebound on us.

Christ our mother

Matthew 23: 29–39

But the end of this chapter gives us cause for hope: for at last Jesus laments over Jerusalem, expressing God's motherly love for God's children. The words of God's demand for justice that have torn through these last two chapters, leaving us exposed and desolate, are replaced by the shelter of wings, warm and downy: the wings of the outstretched arms of the cross, the 'wings' of the protecting cloak of the *theotokos*.

And as Jesus goes to the cross, we remember that it is God who takes responsibility for the suffering of the world, and breaks the cycle of violence and revenge. God demands of us not less than everything, but only in response to the divine love that gives itself to the uttermost.

Motherly Saviour, 'hide me under the shadow of your wings'.

Readings in Matthew 20–25

Signs at the end

Notes based on the New Revised Standard Version by

Helen Stanton

For Helen's biography, see p.244.

Preparing for the week

The chapters set for this week provide the run-up to the Last Supper, arrest, trial and crucifixion of Jesus. They contain some of the most strange writing of the New Testament – the genre called apocalyptic. It is as if the penny has dropped, at last, for the disciples, and they realise that some absolute change is about to happen. The talk is of the end of the age, of living in the in-between time after the death of Jesus has brought in the reign of God, but before that reign is realised in its fullness. According to scholars, the early church thought that the full realisation of the reign of God would come soon after the death and resurrection of Jesus, but we are still living in this in-between time. At many times in the history of the church it looked as if the end time had come, but the message to us is that only God knows the time, while we must persevere and not be led astray. These strange chapters encourage us above all to maintain our hope. We must resist despair, for things really have changed absolutely – evil really is defeated: the reign of God is about to come of age.

This week think about the things that give you hope. Are there actions you can take to cultivate that hope? Write them down and return to them when you are tempted to despair in this complicated, violent and suffering world.

At times of persecution Christians must have longed for the end of the age – the end of suffering, the vindication of their beliefs. Some of us in the 21st century share that longing: the state of our world seems too much to cope with, and modern communication leaves us flinching with horror at natural disasters and the cruelties imposed by human beings on one another. It feels as if there is no let up. We recognise the randomness of much suffering, but we also see how good and wise people are frequently attacked, and how churches tear themselves apart – unintentionally undermining the message of God's love. The new age has indeed come, but the powers and principalities of this world still infiltrate even the most virtuous of structures.

In the light of this it is tempting to retreat to the fortress of our homes. But towards the end of these verses, Jesus states that 'this good news of the kingdom will be proclaimed throughout the world, as a testimony to the nations' (verse 15). The reign of God is not only about our 'private lives'; it is also about the ways in which our communities, societies and world are structured. If the world is to be claimed for God, then our faith must be taken into the public realm also.

Powers and principalities

Matthew 24:1–14

Holy God, you are the King of the Universe. Grant us courage to speak and to embody the values of your reign in the world.

Death throes

Matthew 24:
15–31

I remember the first democratic elections in South Africa in April 1994. In some parts of South Africa there was a good deal of violence, and a British journalist asked one of those standing in the queue to vote for the first time what she thought of this violence. She said that the violence was the death throes of apartheid – like a poisonous snake striking out as it died. Those who hold power, perhaps especially those who hold great power, do not give it up easily and will usually fight to maintain their power. This applies even to those who merely protect their vested interests – which is most of us in the West.

Change can be a bloody business, but these are but the death throes. God's reign is coming. Sometimes it seems as if we must make things worse before God's reign can come in fullness. We must protest loudly about injustices, about the distribution of wealth across the world, about the degradation of the planet, our sister earth. Change always brings in its wake great challenges, and frequently great hardship, but we have the promise that the new age has come, evil has been defeated absolutely, and we have to reach forward to grasp that hope in our world.

Spare us, God of justice, from all that would harm us, but give us grace to promote change, even when it requires of us great suffering.

The apocalyptic language can seem strange to our ears, to be somehow foreign or plain 'weird', but it is language that makes sense to those who are in great crisis – in the wars that accompanied the Reformation for example, or in the violence that people face in Darfur or on the West Bank. Perhaps it is only 'weird' language that can do justice to such extreme situations.

Jesus says we must keep awake in these times of extreme crisis. We must read the signs of the times and recognise that, in crisis most especially, we must maintain our faith in God's reign. *Kairos* is the Greek word for crisis, but it also means opportunity; in crises, whether personal or societal or global, we are called not to bury ours heads in the sand, nor give up our Christian witness in despair, but to continue to practise the faith that has given us hope in the past.

Change, as I have indicated, is not easy. Hannah Ward and Jennifer Wild in their book *Guard the Chaos* (DLT, 1995) point out that 'For the new situation to "live", the old must "die"' (p.16). So often we try to avoid that death by hanging on to the familiarities of the past, even when they cause stagnation. We need to accept a necessary death in order that new life may flourish.

God of change, help us to rely upon your eternal changelessness, as we take risks for the coming of your reign.

Crisis and change

Matthew 24: 32–51

Readings in Matthew

Helen Stanton

Maintaining our vision

Matthew 25:1–13

Today's verses always leave me uneasy. Surely if the wise bridesmaids had shared, everyone could have gone to the wedding? But the uncompromising Jesus of these verses says it will not do for us to be unprepared – we must make provision for a long wait.

The long wait for justice is something that affects all of us in the world, whether we experience injustice in a way that makes us suffer acutely or as merely a frustration in relatively comfortable lives. How can we make provision? Well, keeping a store of oil suggests to me what Jesus said in previous verses: 'Keep awake.' Keep awake to injustice, and offer all our frustrations and suffering to God as we seek God's compassion. But also keep our antennae tuned to God's reign so that we can rejoice and celebrate with the bridegroom when we see small steps made towards justice – be it changes in legislation, personal acts of generosity or understanding suddenly coming to someone with the power to change things.

In the past, Christians sometimes said, 'Count your blessings.' I used to think this was to provide an anaesthetic from difficulties, but I now believe that we must use the signs of God's goodness, however small, to stretch forward and maintain our vision of a world in which that goodness will shine from our lamps.

God our strength, light our lamps in times of trouble with signs of your gracious love.

The church has struggled to interpret this parable throughout its history. Is it a defence of capitalism? Is it about our individual gifts and talents, which may atrophy if we do not use them? In the last couple of years I have been aware of another reading that links this parable more clearly with the previous verses. This kind of inter-pretation says that we need to keep lots of oil ready if we are Christian because the world will treat us unjustly. It suggests that the implications of following Jesus are that we will be so out of kilter with the world that our 'lords and masters' – the powerful in this world – will set things up so that we suffer. We will be counted worthless, in a world where making money is the criterion for valuing anything.

I don't know if this is a correct reading of the parable, but it does make some sense, for nowhere in the text is the master likened to God. How could he be, if God is the gracious one whom Jesus called Abba? And this parable does seem to be linked with the previous story.

What do you think? Is it true that just as crucifixion was the inevitable result of all that Jesus did and said, so the Christian life is likely to lead us to be devalued and even punished in a world that denies God's reign?

Deliver us from evil, and grant us the grace of your reign.

An unjust God?

Matthew 25:
14–30

Helen Stanton

Easy virtue?

Matthew 25: 31–46

This final parable of chapter 25 is one of my favourites. Although on first reading it sounds grim, I believe it is a hopeful and enormously positive parable. It also contains a joke. Those of you reading this in Africa, and in some other parts of the world, will understand this well, but others may need the joke explained.

The Son of Man divides the sheep from the goats, but that will have been difficult, because sheep and goats looked much alike. Even now, when I go to a local farm with my young friend Miriam, we have difficulty telling the more ancient breeds of sheep from the goats in the pen next to them. Everyone looks alike in this parable; you can't tell the virtuous from the wicked.

But it is not, I believe, really a parable about the virtuous and the wicked. Jesus has already warned the disciples about following false prophets and messiahs. Here he tells us exactly how we will know we are relating to the real Christ. We will encounter him among people who are poor, who are strangers, who are prisoners. Those of us who engage in that encounter will find ourselves looking into the face of God, and that will be the cause of joy and of eternal life. For as we embody God's love for others, we will find ourselves transformed into the full stature of Christ.

Christ, our brother, help us to recognise your presence wherever it is found.

Helen Stanton   Readings in Matthew

Angels

1 Angels in the Old Testament

Preparing for the week

Rapid communication is a wonder of the modern world. Through mobile phones, text messages and emails we can speak to almost anyone, anywhere and at any time. In the scriptures, the masters of the art are the angels, literally 'messengers', sent by God to communicate God's guiding will or guarding presence. In the Old Testament one angelic figure stands out above all others: the Angel of the Lord. This angel can be a dread warrior, slaughtering the Assyrian army at the gates of Jerusalem (2 Kings 19:35); or a comforter providing food or drink to Hagar (Genesis 16:7; 21:17–19) and Elijah (1 Kings 19:7) in the wilderness. Angels surround God's throne, like the Cherubim upon whose wings the Lord rides the air, or like the Seraphim of Isaiah 6 singing God's praise. Guardian angels are like personal bodyguards, sent out to protect the righteous from all harm (Psalm 91). Some angels have names, like Michael (Daniel 10:13) or Raphael (Tobit 12:15); others conceal their names, like the angel who wrestles with Jacob until dawn (Genesis 32:29). Angels are everywhere in the scriptures, appearing and disappearing when least expected but most needed. Are our ears and eyes open enough to receive such messengers in our information-soaked societies? Are we aware that God is powerfully present with us at all times?

Notes based on the New Revised Standard Version by

Nicholas Alan Worssam SSF

Brother Nicholas Alan is a member of the Anglican religious community, the Society of St Francis. He has been a friar since 1995, and has lived at Glasshampton Monastery in Worcestershire, England, since 2002.

Seraphim

Psalm 103:19–22

It has been well said that we can never begin to pray; we can only join in the unceasing prayer and praise of the angels since the beginning of creation. 'Where were you,' says God to Job, 'when I laid the foundation of the earth . . . and all the heavenly beings shouted for joy?' (Job 38:4–7). Every night and day the heavens proclaim and rejoice in God's handiwork (Psalm 19:1). Here in Psalm 103, the angels, God's ministers gathered around his throne, are like the seraphim seen in a vision by Isaiah. Each had six wings, calling to one another: 'Holy, holy, holy is the Lord of hosts; the whole earth is full of his glory' (Isaiah 6:3).

Dionysius, a Syrian monk of the sixth century CE, wrote in *The Celestial Hierarchy* of nine orders of angels. The highest are the seraphim, closely followed by cherubim and thrones. These heavenly beings dwell in the Holy of Holies, the intimate presence of God, and proclaim God's praises throughout creation.

The word 'seraph' comes from the Hebrew word meaning 'to burn'. As John the Baptist says of God's messenger Jesus: 'he will baptise you with the Holy Spirit and fire . . . the chaff he will burn with unquenchable fire' (Luke 3:16–17). Dare we face the unquenchable fire of God, to throw ourselves into God's presence and be consumed in love and praise? Truly our God is a consuming fire (Hebrews 12:29).

Bless the Lord, O you his angels;
Bless the Lord, O my soul.

Psalm 103:20, 22

Nicholas Alan Worssam   Angels

Angels are never far away in the book of Genesis. Here Hagar meets the angel of the Lord; later the same angel stops Abraham from sacrificing his son Isaac (Genesis 22:11, 15). Moses too sees an angel at Horeb, the mountain of God, 'in a flame of fire out of a bush' (Exodus 3:2–6); and it was 'the angel of God who was going before the Israelite army' as they fled from Egypt (Exodus 14:19) and as they entered the Promised Land (Exodus 23:20).

In many passages it is difficult to know where the boundary lies between God's angel and God's self. The retelling of Hagar's story in Genesis 21 uses the word 'God' where today's passage speaks more of God's angel. Are they really the same? In the story of Elijah in the wilderness in 1 Kings 19, first the angel of the Lord appears to him as he had to Hagar in today's story, then 'the word of the Lord came to him' (verse 9). Both expressions show a respectful distance from God in the use of language, taken one step further by the later Jewish use of the phrase, 'the daughter of the voice (of God)'. The angel, and the word, are the communicative and sustaining power of God, who speaks all things into being (Psalm 33:6). God's message is simply his love, his willing us into existence and enabling us to respond in thankfulness and praise.

Our soul waits for the Lord;
he is our help and shield.

Psalm 33:20

The angel of the Lord

Genesis 16

Angels   Nicholas Alan Worssam

Stairway to heaven

Genesis 28:10–17

Jacob in his dream has stumbled across an entrance to heaven. Here angels come down for their earthly patrols before reporting back to the Most High God (see Job 1:6–7). The prophet Zechariah has a vision of these angels saying: 'We have patrolled the earth, and lo, the earth remains at peace' (Zechariah 1:11). This is a comforting thought: that God has angelic UN peacekeepers patrolling the nations, holding back the weapons of war. But in fact these angels are only waiting for the command to enter battle themselves, to restore the fortunes of ruined Jerusalem. The heavenly host, God's army of angels, is a terrifying force. Nothing can withstand them when God sends them out to execute justice and restore the poor of the land.

We like to think of angels as comforting beings, wisp-like and downy-feathered. The angel that appears to Balaam has a drawn sword in his hand, and terrifies the donkey that the prophet rides upon. But this saves him, as the angel admits: 'If the donkey had not turned away from me, surely just now I would have killed you and let it live' (Numbers 22:33). Those who strive for justice and peace in our own day need the strength and courage of angels – God's warriors sent to right wrongs, 'not by (human) might, nor by power, but by my spirit, says the Lord of hosts' (Zechariah 4:6).

Where are the angels fighting today?

How awesome is this place!
This is none other than the house of God,
and this is the gate of heaven.

Genesis 28:17

Nicholas Alan Worssam   Angels

Chariots of fire

2 Kings 6:8–17

This reading echoes the earlier story of Elijah's ascension into heaven in a chariot of fire and horses of fire (2 Kings 2:11). Here Elisha's servant learns of the presence of the Lord of hosts, the Lord of armies, stronger than the most well-equipped human force.

God is often depicted in the Old Testament as a king surrounded by his council of war (e.g. 1 Kings 22:19). Moses sings of the Lord coming from Sinai to help his people: 'with him were myriads of holy ones; at his right, a host of his own' (Deuteronomy 33:2). God is like King Arthur, surrounded by his knights of the round table. He gives territory to each of his knights, like a feudal monarch parcelling out land: God 'fixed the boundaries of the peoples according to the number of the gods' (or 'the angels of God' in the Greek version of the Old Testament) (Deuteronomy 32:8). Each nation has their angel or holy one, but the Lord is 'a God feared among the council of the holy ones, great and awesome above all that are around him' (Psalm 89:7). None dare challenge the overriding authority of the Lord.

Yet these images of God as a warrior need balancing in our war-ravaged world. So we look to Isaiah's suffering servant, and to Jesus, armies of angels at his command (Matthew 26:53), who disarms the powers of evil by the power of his death.

O Lord, please open my eyes that I may see.

Angels   Nicholas Alan Worssam

A face like lightning

Daniel 10:4–21

Daniel's vision of an angel has many echoes in the New Testament. John the Divine sees Jesus, 'one like the Son of Man', in very similar terms, with 'eyes like a flame of fire' (Revelation 1:13–14). The greeting here, 'Greatly beloved . . . do not fear', reminds a Christian reader of Mary being greeted by the Archangel Gabriel. Perhaps it is indeed Gabriel who speaks to Daniel, as he goes on to mention Michael, the other of the two great archangels in Jewish and Christian teaching.

Michael, the 'great prince', fights for the people of Israel against the prince of Persia, and Gabriel (if it is he) must go to help him. In the Jewish tradition Michael is the ruler of the archangels. He defeats the chief of the fallen angels and prevents them from learning the sacred name of God. He is like the 'commander of the army of the Lord' who mysteriously appears to Joshua by Jericho (Joshua 5:13–15).

This idea of heavenly battles as counterparts to the battles on earth may seem strange to us now. One such picture from the Apocrypha in 2 Maccabees 5:1–4 seems almost like science fiction. But it is hard to deny that in the dark arts of statecraft, powers stronger than human resourcefulness seem to be at work. If we are to overcome the manifest evil that surfaces in war, we must truly put our trust in God's higher, unconquerable power.

Let my lord speak, for you have strengthened me.

Daniel 10:19

Nicholas Alan Worssam

Angels

This psalm is traditionally chanted at the end of every day in the monastic Office of Compline. It is a statement of trust in God who 'will command his angels concerning you to guard you in all your ways' (verse 11). Even Satan knows this psalm, and quotes it in his temptation of Jesus in the wilderness (Matthew 4:6); but Jesus defeats Satan, and the angels minister to him (Matthew 4:11). Jesus finds refuge under the wings of the Most High. He himself wanted to gather the people of Jerusalem under his wings (Luke13:34), yet they were not willing, unable to respond to his maternal care.

In an age before electricity, the dark of night would have been a time that angelic protection was especially welcome. But angels not only guard, they also guide. The psalmist prays: 'O send out your light and your truth; let them lead me; let them bring me to your holy hill and to your dwelling' (Psalm 43:3). So too the angel of God brings the Israelites into the Promised Land: 'an angel . . . to guard you on the way and to bring you to the place that I have prepared' (Exodus 23:20). Angels lead us into the presence of God, here and now, just as Jesus leads us into his Father's house of many rooms to dwell in the place prepared for us since the foundation of the world (see John 14:2–3). Angels guide us into eternal life.

Cover me with your pinions;
let me find refuge under your wings.

The shadow of your wings

Psalm 91

Angels

Nicholas Alan Worssam

Angels

2 Angels in the New Testament

Notes based on the New Revised Standard Version by

Nicholas Alan Worssam SSF

For Nicholas' biography see p. 265.

Preparing for the week

St Francis, the patron saint of my community, had a great devotion both to the angels and to the mother of Jesus. Fourteen times a day he would say: 'Holy Virgin Mary . . . , pray for us, with St Michael the Archangel and all the powers of heaven and all the saints, to your most holy and beloved Son, our Lord and Master.' He was particularly delighted that the church just outside Assisi, around which the mother house of the order was built, was dedicated to St Mary of the Angels. There he felt the presence of the angels very strongly, and he entrusted himself to their protection.

In our own chapel here at Glasshampton Monastery, people have sometimes felt the presence of angels. In fact, anywhere that praise has been consistently offered to God, something of the angelic worship in heaven can be felt here on earth. I found this particularly true in a prison where I once worked as a chaplain. At the centre of the grim Victorian wings of cells, the chapel seemed an oasis of peace, a place from which grace flowed out like the rivers from the temple of Ezekiel's vision (Ezekiel 47).

Angels surrounded Jesus' earthly life: from his conception in the womb of Mary to his agony in the garden of Gethsemane. Many times his disciples are rescued by angels in the Acts of the Apostles; and John's Revelation is full of angelic scenes. Maybe we too would know angels at our side, if only we had eyes and faith to see.

Nicholas Alan Worssam   Angels

This has to be the most famous angelic visitation recorded in the New Testament. Every Christmas we sing of this encounter between Mary and the Archangel Gabriel. His name means 'God is my hero', and the angels bring out something of the heroic in us all. Mary certainly is granted absence of fear and the favour of God; and generations of Christians have celebrated her faith in the 'Hail Mary' prayer as they repeat the Archangel's words.

The Lord is with you

Luke 1:26–38

Already in Luke's Gospel, this angel has made himself known. Appearing to Zechariah he says: 'I am Gabriel. I stand in the presence of God, and I have been sent to speak to you and to bring you this good news' (Luke 1:19). In John's Gospel, Jesus echoes this by saying: 'I have come down from heaven, not to do my own will, but the will of him who sent me . . . I declare what I have seen in the Father's presence' (John 6:38; 8:38). Jesus even declares that all those who will enter God's kingdom 'are like angels and are children of God, being children of the resurrection' (Luke 20:36).

An angel is a messenger of God. How far do we act as messengers of what we have seen and heard of the Lord? Is there someone we can speak to today, to reassure them of their blessing by God, to help them know that God is indeed with them?

Here am I, the servant of the Lord;
let it be with me according to your word.

Luke 1:38

Angels   Nicholas Alan Worssam

The time of trial

Luke 22:39–43

At the beginning of his ministry Jesus is driven out into the desert to be tempted by Satan, but eventually the devil leaves him until an opportune time, and angels minister to his needs (Matthew 4:11). Here at the end of his earthly life Jesus is tempted again to abandon the way of the cross he sees stretching out before him. Once more he passes through the trial and angels give him strength. Some early manuscripts of the Bible lack these verses, but early Christian writers knew them, and the description of sweat dripping like blood from the brow of Jesus vividly brings out the agony of Jesus' prayer. A parallel scene in John's Gospel shows the angelic encouragement from heaven as being not just for Jesus, but also as a revelation to all of the glory of God's name (John 12:27–33).

Angels may strengthen us in our trials, but they do not necessarily make things easy for us. Jesus truly goes through agony in Gethsemane, even with the angels by his side. The angels reappear on the first day of the week at his garden tomb (Luke 24:4), but where were they when he needed them most as he suffered on the cross? Maybe it was the penitent thief who maintained God's angelic presence, encouraging Jesus by his words, and accompanying Jesus into Paradise (Luke 23:42–43). Angels can sometimes be very fallen flesh and blood, yet still messengers of God's power to save.

How can we strengthen others in their trials?

Not my will but yours be done.

Luke 22:41

This encounter echoes the story of Jacob's ladder from last week's readings, where squads of angels patrol the earth and report back to God. Now Nathanael too will see these angels, and their descent will be upon the Son of Man, the name by which Jesus refers to himself. Lifted up on the cross, Jesus will himself become the ladder between heaven and earth (John 12:32).

The figure of the Son of Man, or Human One, is often associated with angels. In Daniel 7:13 he ascends to the throne of the Ancient One, surrounded by thousands of holy ones or angels. So too, Jesus the Son of Man will ascend to heaven where he was before (John 6:62), and will send out his angels to judge the earth and gather his elect (Matthew 13:41; Mark 13:26–27; John 5:27–29). But here Jesus says that the separation of good from evil will be witnessed even by Nathanael, sitting in peace under his own fig tree (see Zechariah 3:10), who cries out: 'Rabbi, you are the Son of God!' Only God's anointed one could accomplish these things.

But was it as simple as Nathanael hoped? Jesus didn't drive out the hated Romans or give Israel temporal peace, but he did bring judgement to the earth (John 12:31) by disarming evil on the cross. And he pulls us back up the ladder of his broken body to feast at the banquet of heaven.

You will see heaven opened

John 1:47–51

You are the Son of God!
You are the King of Israel!

John 1:49

Angels

Nicholas Alan Worssam

The dungeon flamed with light

Acts 12:1–11

One of my favourite hymns is 'And can it be' by Charles Wesley. Even though angels cannot tell the depths of love divine – ''Tis mystery all!' – yet they participate in our salvation. Truly Peter's release is an allegory for all Christians.

The belief in guardian angels is deeply rooted in Jewish and Christian tradition. Jacob, at the end of his life, blesses his son Joseph and his grandsons in the name of 'the angel who has redeemed me from all harm' (Genesis 48:16); Tobit says of his son Tobias, 'A good angel will accompany him; his journey will be successful' (Tobit 5:22); and Jesus says of the young and more vulnerable around him, 'in heaven their angels continually see the face of my Father in heaven' (Matthew 18:10). In the Catholic Church the Holy Guardian Angels even have their own feast day on 2 October.

Being confronted, even shaken awake, by an angel may be accompanied by a blaze of light, but the angel still may not be recognised. At first Peter has no idea what is going on around him here. But when the angel suddenly departs, realisation dawns. Are these beings real? The other disciples are more ready to believe Peter's angel has knocked on their door rather than the imprisoned Peter himself (Acts 12:15). Is it not possible that we are surrounded by a great 'cloud of witnesses' (Hebrews 12:1), both human and angelic, showing us how to be free?

My chains fell off, my heart was free;
I rose, went forth, and followed thee.

Charles Wesley

Nicholas Alan Worssam   Angels

This vision draws deeply from the prophets Ezekiel and Zechariah. The 'mighty angel' of verse 2 is like the angel of the Lord from Zechariah 3; the scroll is the record of God's judgement (Ezekiel 2:9–10); and the living creatures are the cherubim of Ezekiel 1:5–14, guarding the throne of God. And then in the midst of them all appears a Lamb – Jesus, once sacrificed on the cross, now risen in glory. Jesus is surrounded by angels, receiving their worship, together with the One already seated on the throne. Now Jesus shares that throne, 'having become as much superior to angels as the name he has inherited is more excellent than theirs' (Hebrews 1:4).

Yet we are not excluded. Jesus bears the name of God's Son, a relationship into which he gathers us also, 'for the one who sanctifies and those who are sanctified all have one Father. For this reason Jesus is not ashamed to call them brothers and sisters' (Hebrews 2:11). We share in his glory, by first sharing in his suffering and death (Romans 8:17). We are his body, his life abides in us, who receive his flesh and blood (John 6:53–57). When we celebrate the eucharist we not only remember the last meal of Jesus; we join with the angels in their worship of the Lamb, and are transfigured, leaving Jesus standing alone.

Worthy is the Lamb

Revelation 5

To the one seated on the throne and to the Lamb
be blessing and honour and glory and might forever and
ever!

Revelation 5:13

Angels   Nicholas Alan Worssamlain Roy

Clothed with the sun

Revelation 12

Mary, the Mother of the Messiah, and Michael the Archangel were intimate companions to St Francis. In their honour he fasted each year from the feast of Mary's Assumption into heaven (15 August) until the feast of St Michael and All Angels (29 September). It was during this retreat in 1224, two years before he died, that Francis had a vision of an angel, a seraph on a cross, blazing in light. Then looking down at his hands he saw the marks of nails, and felt the pain also in his side and feet of the wounds of his Saviour. He had become one body with Christ, literally conformed to the image of God's Son. Many of the friars in his Order believed that Francis was the Angel of the Sixth Seal from the Book of Revelation, bringing in a new age of the Holy Spirit before the end of time.

Whatever may happen in the future, God is present both as comforting refuge and fearless guide. Mary embodies for us the all-embracing compassion of God, whom she carried in her womb; and Michael and all the angels proclaim the holiness and power of God that lead us through the wilderness to the Promised Land. Satan has already been defeated: Jesus saw him fall like lightning (Luke 10:18). Our work now is to rejoice with the angels in heaven, and to look and labour for the coming of God's kingdom of righteousness and peace here and now.

Rejoice then, you heavens
and those who dwell in them!

Revelation 12:12

The prophecy of Jeremiah

1 Prophetic words in action

Notes based on the *Tanakh: The Holy Scriptures* (Jewish Publication Society, 1985) by **Pete Tobias**

Preparing for the week

What does one need to be a prophet? Prophecy is more than just being able to foretell the future, though that is a key part of the role. But we are not looking for divination or inspired guesswork; the best way to predict the future is to have a keen awareness of the present and of the circumstances, political, social, theological, that may combine to shape the future. The ability to recognise in natural phenomena the hand of the Divine and to be able to interpret and present these phenomena to one's audience is also a useful addition to the prophetic toolbox. To that must be added the confidence and courage to speak out about what one sees and believes in, despite the likelihood of opposition, hostility and even ridicule.

Jeremiah had all of these characteristics and he turned his insight, his inspiration and his visionary zeal on the troubled and turbulent world of Judah. He was not believed, but he was right.

Where are the prophets, the visionaries, the Jeremiahs of our day? What must they tell us, how would they seek to make us aware of what is ahead – and who are they?

For Pete's biography see p. 216.

Eternal God of all humanity, you have called us to your service, and summoned us to bear witness to you among the peoples of the earth. Give us grace to fulfil our task with zeal tempered by wisdom and guided by regard for the faith of others.

Siddur Lev Chadash, p. 225.

Where are the visionaries?

Jeremiah 1:4–17

The call, when it comes, is overwhelmingly powerful and at the same time profoundly simple. And once we have received the call, once we have been granted the insight, we can no longer deny our knowledge of it or pretend that we have not heard it.

Our modern, secular world seems to have little time for religion, or for those who would speak in its name. And yet it could be argued that never has our world been more in need of a religious message, of a prophetic vision to guide it through troubled and tempestuous times.

It would be simple to block our ears to the voice that speaks within our hearts and cries out within our souls. But in our time we see, just as Jeremiah saw in his, signs and portents that speak to us of societies that have lost their way, of dangers that lie ahead, seen perhaps, but not recognised or understood. We must get ourselves ready, we must stand up and say to them what we are commanded by God to say. And we must not let ourselves be terrified, for the consequences of not speaking out are more terrible still.

There is a mystery here that reason cannot solve, nor cynicism dismiss. We can deny it, or we can humbly recognise it, and each resolve to be a part of it, saying to God: 'Hinneini: Here am I, send me.'

Machzor Ru'ach Chadashah, p. 311

Pete Tobias   The prophecy of Jeremiah

Disaster is coming. It comes not from the ancient kingdom of Babylon with armies borne on chariot and horseback, but from a world that has grown self-indulgent and lazy, that has casually exploited the earth's resources and turned our world into a barren landscape, parched and fruitless with no thought for future generations.

We are the prophets!

Jeremiah 4:1–18

We see this world, what we have done to God's creation. We see parched land and parched souls, thirsting for human compassion and God's love. We watch as warning after warning is visited upon our world, our only world, torn apart by poverty and hunger, mistrust and hatred.

Can we, having seen and recognised all this, dare to keep silent? Can we fail to speak out against the untruths and deceptions of our time? Can we, people of faith and understanding, who recognise our duty to God and to future generations, turn our backs on our responsibilities and block our ears to the warning signs all around us?

We must be the prophets of our day, anticipating disaster and calling on those around us to mend their ways and our world. The need for prophecy has never been more urgent. We must be the Jeremiahs of our day, speaking out against injustice and corruption.

The Eternal One, my God, does nothing without having revealed the divine purpose to God's servants, the prophets. A lion has roared, who can but fear? The Eternal one my God has spoken, who can but prophesy?

Amos 3:7–8

The prophecy of Jeremiah   Pete Tobias

We are the visionaries!

Jeremiah 8:1–13, 20–22

And what of the protests that are faced by those of us brave enough to speak out against the injustice and cruelty in our world? What of those who seek to contradict and silence us? Though we are confident of our own perceptions of the world and its future, we cannot assume that all will think as we do.

But the role of a modern-day prophet is not to correct; it is to advise. It is not to chastise; it is to remind. Convinced as we are of the legitimacy of our concerns and the genuineness of our perceptions, we can speak with the confidence and authority with which Jeremiah and other biblical prophets were imbued.

Can there be any doubt that human beings have been created to have respect and compassion for one another? Is it not obvious that we must cherish and respect the planet on which we live, for the sake of ourselves and future generations? Is not the cause of the problems in our world, our own actions and attitudes? Why then can we not correct these and so save ourselves and our world?

'What need have I of all your sacrifices', says the Eternal One. 'I have had enough of the burnt offerings of lambs, the fat of oxen and the blood of bullocks . . . Devote yourselves to justice; help those who are oppressed. Uphold the rights of the orphan; defend the cause of the widow.'

Isaiah 1:11, 16–17

Pete Tobias   The prophecy of Jeremiah

Spoken by prophets, spoken by those who refute the prophets: whose words are to be believed?

For every assertion that our world is in danger of self-destruction, there is a counter-claim that this is all exaggeration. For every voice that cries out for peace and understanding, there is another seeking to promote discord and hostility. In a world of global communications and instant information, how can we know any more whose opinion is to be believed and whose to be dismissed?

Must we wait for the jackals to prowl through the ruins that our world must surely become if we do not pay heed to our failings? And when our food turns bitter and the waters are poisoned, whom then shall we blame?

We need to differentiate between those who speak falsely and those who would seek to guide us in ways of truth. We must once again search for the truths that reside within God's teachings: those that demand of us that we respect our fellow human beings and care for our world. If the words we hear spoken do not measure up to these simple yet powerful standards, then they are not to be trusted and we must reject them – or we shall be rejected.

Words, words, words

Jeremiah 19:1–15

Who among you loves life and longs to enjoy good for many days? Then guard your tongue from evil and your lips from deceitful speech; turn away from evil and do good; seek peace and pursue it.

Psalm 34:13ff

Questions and answers

Jeremiah 18:1–23

Now the big questions are being asked of us as we step ever closer to accepting our task as prophets in this troubled century. We know that our prophecy is needed. We have seen the deception and falsehood that would seek to distract us. We are aware of the multitude of opinions that would voice their opposition to what we might have to say, what we must say, to bring the world back to God. And the questions are those that Jeremiah, all the prophets, had to answer when their moment came: will we have the courage to speak aloud?

And, assuming that we do, how shall we address our reluctant listeners? What symbols might we use to depict or portray our concerns about the world? What metaphors might we employ to impress upon the unheeding descendants of those who lived in the doomed days of Jeremiah the frightening future towards which we are stumbling blindly?

Whatever we choose, we know that the reaction will not be favourable. Like Jeremiah, we may find ourselves cast into a pit, our words twisted and condemned, our visions derided and rejected. But like Jeremiah, we must hold fast to our vision, even when the taunts of our detractors might dissuade us. The truth must guide us.

When others curse me, may my soul be silent and humble as the dust to all. Dissuade those who seek to harm me and let not their plans prevail.

Siddur Lev Chadash, p. 102

And when the fate of nations has been decided, the shouts of victory have subsided and the dust has settled on the ruined cities of the defeated, what then should be our role as modern-day prophets?

We should not turn away, despondent and downhearted, nor allow our voices to grow silent or our vision to be dimmed. For more powerful than all the forces that might have conspired to convince us that there is no hope, must be our unfaltering belief in justice and compassion, and our unwavering commitment to the nobility of the human spirit. If we believe in our prophetic vision, in the goodness of humanity, and in God's love for us, then, like Jeremiah, our hope shall never diminish and we shall carry its torch for ourselves and for future generations.

Will it always be like this? Shall we never toil to some avail? It need not always be so. For what is divine in us is our refusal to surrender. 'To suffer woes which hope thinks infinite; to forgive wrongs darker than death or night; to defy power which seems omnipotent; to love and bear; to hope till hope creates from its own wreck the thing it contemplates . . .'

Gates of Repentence, including quotation from Percy Bysshe Shelley, *Prometheus Unbound*, IV, 570

This is the task of the prophet. May we seek to make it ours also.

Hope for the future

Jeremiah 24:1–10

The prophecy of Jeremiah   Pete Tobias

The prophecy of Jeremiah

2 A prophetic life: memoirs

Notes based on the New Revised Standard Version by

Jane Wallman-Girdlestone

Jane Wallman-Girdlestone is a Research Fellow at the Divinity School of the University of Aberdeen, UK. She is a writer and artist and runs a small retreat space in the Highlands of Scotland.

Preparing for the week

Jeremiah was an independent thinker. He speaks out publicly during a period of economic and political upheaval. While the military forces and politicians are concerned with borders, potential conflict and economic prosperity, Jeremiah asks where God is and what is God doing in his own locality.

The writings of Jeremiah draw together material that expresses a dynamic, poetic and, at times, painfully frustrating relationship between Jeremiah and God. There is a sense that God punishes those nations that are not obedient to God's will, although this is not actually borne out by salvation history. Jeremiah is preoccupied with *sheqer* – falsehood or, rather, illusion. In today's parlance we would talk about people who are 'in denial'. Jeremiah speaks what he believes to be a prophetic truth concerning God's displeasure. He finds himself caught between a rock and a hard place as he tries to remain faithful to God whilst being largely ignored by the community. Perhaps it was just too difficult for them to hear the truth that they needed to change their ways dramatically to find faith with God?

God, who called Jeremiah to proclaim your will, inspire us with your sacred word to be your prophets to this generation.

Jehoiakim has no interest in pleasing God. Jeremiah has spoken at the Temple and in the streets. It is clear from the authorities' response that following God's law is a long way from being top priority. A political agitator, Jeremiah is determined, despite the overpowering threat in verse 8: 'You shall die!' He places the future of Jerusalem in the hands of the people. Judah must claim the Torah or face destruction like Shiloh. Yet the prevailing teaching stated that the Torah was no longer central and the old covenant tradition was unimportant for Judah.

Jeremiah is charged with prophesying. His defence is that he utters only God's words and he is offering God's people an opportunity to be rescued. He is acquitted on a technicality.

In today's church we are experiencing challenges as society turns from religious truth. We stand with the people hearing Jeremiah and hear the challenge to 'amend your ways and your doings, and obey the voice of the Lord your God' (verse 13).

The Jeremiah code

Jeremiah 26:1–16

God of compassion and mercy, I confess that I have often failed to follow your word and the prompting of your Spirit in the outworking of my life. Give me strength to become a faithful witness to your love.

The prophecy of Jeremiah   Jane Wallman-Girdlestone

Home is where the heart is

Jeremiah 29:1–14

There is an underlying tension after 598 BCE between those who have been deported and those who continue to live in Jerusalem. In this pastoral letter to those in exile, Jeremiah is pragmatic, reflecting political realism and encouraging the exiles to be obedient to those in power. The exiles are warned not to listen to false prophets, and to recognise that God is keeping God's promise of homecoming (verse 10). God has seemed distant and absent to the exiles. The letter encourages acts of devotion and obedience; the dispossessed must claim life and put down roots, even in exile. Through repentance they will find that God has remained faithful even when they have turned from God's ways (see verse 14).

Verse 7 reminds us of the intricate relationship between prayer and being a servant of God. How do you pray? How do you listen for the whispering of the Spirit? What is God laying on your heart at this time? How are you a servant of God in your circumstances?

Verses 11–13 remind us of the covenant God has made with each one of us and that when we are faithful disciples of God's vision, we can anticipate an intimate, caring relationship with God. How do you celebrate this relationship? How do you tell of God's love in the world?

God of love, I know you are waiting to hear from me, yet so often I choose to be distracted. Help me to place you first in my life and in doing so to delight in the love we share for each other.

Jane Wallman-Girdlestone   The prophecy of Jeremiah

Jeremiah makes a very public show of confidence in the future – he buys a piece of land. In purchasing in economically uncertain times, he wants to show God's people that God's promise to be faithful is real and tangible and can be trusted. He is telling them that they should be building houses, tending fields and building communities.

This is an act of theological as well as political significance. The exiles have a legal claim in owning a piece of land. In their action of ring-fencing their claim, obeying God's edict to be prosperous and faithful, they are making a claim on God; but they are also stating their purpose politically and socially. Jeremiah is encouraging people through his action to show the world that they are a people of identity and purpose.

It can be difficult for us as members of the community of faith to stand up for God's vision in a public arena. Yet when we manage what we possess ethically and with care for the needs of the world, we too are claiming a place in this ancient tradition of celebrating what God does for us. When we offer an open heart, generous mind and willing body in order to achieve justice and bring hope to those who do not know the love of God, we are staking our claim on God's word. Then we become those who possess God's promises in abundance.

God of land, make me mindful of all you have given me, and make me powerful in the service of others.

Political prisoner unfairly held

Jeremiah 36:1–4;
37:1–21

This section of Jeremiah holds an important place in the outworking of the story. Hans Kremers suggests that this is Jeremiah's 'passion narrative', tracing how a righteous prophet and innocent man moves towards his unjust end. Another way of viewing this passage is to see it from God's point of view. God's will for humanity is repeatedly ignored and dismissed by those in authority. God's word is constantly revealed but falls on deaf ears.

Chapter 36 begins with an account of how the scroll is written. In chapter 37 we join the story of Jeremiah's trial, in an unstable political climate. The king is weak and depends on Jeremiah's prophecy – the oracle from God. The oracle explains that Pharaoh will withdraw but the Babylonians will invade. The result will be complete desolation. Jeremiah's public utterances result in his life becoming endangered. The king hears Jeremiah's petition from prison and is able to recognise that he is a prophet who speaks God's will and seeks nothing for himself.

In chapter 37 we see what happens when truth speaks to power. Telling the truth in the light of God's action in our lives and in the life of creation is hard; it's open to misunderstanding and we risk being branded as strange or misguided. Jeremiah reminds us that although ministering in God's name is not without cost, God supports and upholds in a time of crisis.

God of truth, give me strength and resilience when the path is demanding, that in all I undertake your will may be done.

Jane Wallman-Girdlestone   The prophecy of Jeremiah

The contrast continues between a weak monarch who is trying to survive and the prophet determined to proclaim God's will. Jeremiah is a traitor who is undermining the war effort and surely he must die.

We pick up the story in chapter 40 with Jerusalem destroyed. Some have fled, but many remain and the need for some kind of ordered government grows. However, the theological truth is still presented that the destruction of the city is the will of God. This narrative is highly favourable (as much of Jeremiah is) to the Babylonians who are portrayed as a just retribution for disobedience.

Jeremiah is released but the irony is intensely real. He has proclaimed downfall at the hands of the Babylonians and is now freed by them. He is seen by some as a collaborator. He can't have been in a comfortable position. He agrees to support the temporary government of Gedaliah and remains true to his earlier prophecy that Babylon would gain power and he would not flee. Jeremiah becomes a walking symbol of God's promise to his people. Even as a new chapter begins in the lives of God's chosen, Jeremiah stands firm, proclaiming God's will to God's people.

Reprieve and freedom?

Jeremiah 38:6–10; 40:1–6

God of vision, you do not promise us an easy path; yet you remain with us and with your beloved creation. Strengthen us for your service that we might speak freely of your love and bring life to others.

The prophecy of Jeremiah   Jane Wallman-Girdlestone

'God is dead!' Read all about it!

Jeremiah 44: 20–30

Imagine how it felt to the Egyptian Jews who believed in the severity of Jeremiah's prophecy. The sacrificial offerings made at the altars of other gods were not only unacceptable to God but brought divine judgement on God's people. God is removed from the sight of the community. God has no further concern for them, God is dead to the community.

God is set apart but continues to watch. In a spiritual sense this is even harder than the death of God. God has personally removed from the action but is still working out the destruction and judgement of the people. Like Cain, the community knows the desolation of separation from the protection and love of God.

There are times in our spiritual journey when we experience powerfully the absence of God, perhaps during bereavement or a major life transition. It is tempting to feel betrayed by God or of little interest to God. This reading reminds us that God is present – whatever.

In the light of Jesus' ministry, death and resurrection, we believe that God has made a new covenant with us; always to hold creation and humanity close to God's active purposes in the universe. Even when God feels far off, we need not fear; God is enveloping us with love and generosity. Hope teaches us to trust and believe.

God, I am here. Only just. Hold on to me.

Jane Wallman-Girdlestone — The prophecy of Jeremiah

The prophecy of Jeremiah

3 Chanting down oppressive nations

Notes based on the New Revised Standard Version by

Renato Lings

Preparing for the week

Jeremiah turns his critical attention to the oppressive policies of nations such as Ammon, Assyria, Babylonia, Egypt, Elam, Moab and the Philistines. Their idolatrous practices and destructive military campaigns will inevitably make them stumble and fall. At the same time, while punishment in the form of defeat, humiliation and tragedy is approaching, it is possible to imagine a day of future restoration.

His focus on foreign arrogance does not make Jeremiah overlook the political and theological mistakes of his own people. In his view, the kingdom of Judah is far too focused on the reshuffling of military alliances in the region. Weapons provide false security. God's faithfulness to Judah rests on the people's willingness to walk by the commands of the covenant. Hence, for years, the prophet preaches about, and laments over, impending doom. Yet when defeat is at hand his message is one of hope.

Over the next few pages the words of Jeremiah are placed in contemporary settings. Today nations continue to embark on misguided military adventures; they turn a blind eye to the mounting challenges of climate change; they fail to learn from the mistakes that led to the current financial crisis; and powerful church shepherds still mislead their flocks, as they force lesbian and gay Christians into exile.

Do rulers in your part of the world act peacefully?

In which ways does the Bible inspire you to face oppressive policies?

Kjeld Renato Lings is a Danish translator/ interpreter. He holds a PhD in theology from the University of Exeter, UK. Renato's doctoral thesis 'Restoring Sodom: Towards a Non-Sexual Approach' (2006) proposes a fresh, language-based interpretation of the biblical drama. Renato currently lives and works in his native Denmark. His main occupations are teaching, translating, interpreting, lecturing, writing and singing.

They have stumbled and fallen

Jeremiah 46:1–24

With the benefit of hindsight, Jeremiah's utterances of doom against one of the most powerful nations of his day seem perfectly understandable. The legendary empire of Egypt was coming to an end. Yet to some of Jeremiah's contemporaries such considerations may not have seemed obvious.

History shows that the Spirit of God at all times stirs human beings to speak out in the face of injustice, oppression and militarism. Obedience to this impulse may come at great cost. In today's Russia prophetic voices denouncing their government's atrocities in Chechnia expose themselves to persecution and assassination.

In recent years my own country, Denmark, broke a century-old tradition of non-aggression as our government joined imperial war efforts in Iraq and Afghanistan. Given the absence of political persecution within our borders, prophetic opposition to such misguided adventures has been remarkably muted. Very costly military interventions overseas seem to have become acceptable. A self-assured parliamentary majority in Denmark has set itself up as an arbiter of life and death abroad.

Apparently my part of the world has succumbed to the idolatrous notion that Western democracy is infallible. According to the prophets of the Bible, including Jeremiah, nations and empires built on arrogance, greed and idolatry will stumble and fall.

Where are the prophetic voices in your community?

Eternal God, have mercy on the victims of my own government's war efforts. Grant me compassion, wisdom and courage.

Certain parts of Denmark along the North Sea coast are susceptible to flooding under extreme weather conditions. Particularly during the autumn months, fierce westerly winds may cause salt-water invasion of low-lying areas. For this reason, a system of flood-proof dikes was put in place in the early 1970s. Thankfully, this country has not experienced disasters on a major scale in decades.

Waters are rising out of the north

Jeremiah 47:1–7

As I write, Jeremiah's vision of waters rising out of the north strikes a chord. In recent years, and because of global warming, large chunks of icebergs have been melting in the Arctic region at an alarming rate. According to scientific observers, this is contributing to a gradual rise in the water level of all oceans. The implications for the coastline of Denmark, and other sea-level nations and areas, are going to be dire.

The verdict of the experts, including prominent Danish scientists, has been clear for years: a major contributing factor to global warming is our civilisation's obsessive reliance on fossil fuels. Instead of harnessing renewable sources of energy, which are already available, powerful decision-makers around the world are turning a blind eye to the mounting environmental challenges facing our planet. The allure of short-term profit overrules long-term foresight. The habitat of future generations is in jeopardy.

Is your community preparing for the future?

Creator God, open our eyes to the pulse of this living planet. Stir me to act responsibly and creatively.

The prophecy of Jeremiah   Renato Lings

He magnified himself against the Lord

Jeremiah 48:1–9, 42–47

Geographically, the biblical nation of Moab is situated on the eastern side of the Dead Sea. The Moabite language is closely related to Hebrew. Throughout the Hebrew Bible, the relationship between Judah and Moab oscillates between the peaceful co-existence described in the book of Ruth and the open hostility unfolding in Numbers chs 21–25. In Genesis 19:32–37 the mythological origin of Moab is described in very unflattering terms.

The whole chapter of Jeremiah 48 reflects this permanent tension of conflicting emotions between Judeans and Moabites. On the one hand this Judean prophet laments the impending destruction of Moab while, on the other hand, he declares that they have brought it upon themselves by acting arrogantly. Despite their false steps, they are promised a new beginning.

A few centuries ago my own part of the world was rife with skirmishes between neighbouring nations. In certain ways the history of Denmark may be likened to the story of Moab. Some moments of arrogance have come at huge cost, making this country lose four provinces. Since the late-nineteenth century Denmark has lived in peace with its neighbours. In the twentieth century, Danish forces have participated in international peacekeeping operations overseas. However, the trap of arrogance remains. At present my country is at war in countries that are not our neighbours.

Almighty God, lead us away from the temptation of arrogance.

Renato Lings   The prophecy of Jeremiah

As I write, the latest international financial crisis is in its second year. Its sudden eruption took the vast majority of Western governments and economic gurus by surprise. Astonishingly few decision-makers have paused to reflect on the deeper causes of this global malaise.

Crises bring opportunities for change. Yet, in today's corridors of power, alternative thinking is virtually unheard of. Instead of turning defeat into victory through innovative schemes and procedures for the benefit of the global environment, most heads of government have hurried to bail out an unhealthy, highly speculative financial system. At huge cost to national budgets, they have salvaged sinking ships unfit for navigation. Apparently the most important thing in modern politics is to ensure that business continues as usual. Put differently, Mammon-worship matters most.

Jeremiah offers no consolation to those who trusted in their now devalued treasures. On the contrary, he warns them of impending destruction. At the same time, and intriguingly so, the prophet continually looks ahead to a time of restoration for all the nations he is chanting down. Clearly the omnipotent God Jeremiah serves is not simply determined to chastise those who have made mistakes. If we come to our senses, a better way ahead is possible. The challenge is to seek it.

Is your community facing the current crisis in creative ways?

Heavenly teacher, let me act justly in all financial affairs.

You trusted in your treasures

Jeremiah 49:1–6, 24–27, 34–39

The prophecy of Jeremiah   Renato Lings

Their shepherds have led them astray

Jeremiah 50:1–20

Many church leaders around the world habitually exclude certain Christians from church life. Despite their commitment to Jesus Christ, lesbian, gay and bisexual believers are deemed unfit for participation solely on the basis of their sexual orientation. Transgendered people are met with similar hostility. In these churches, faith in God and neighbourly love are insufficient criteria for admission. Only heterosexuals need apply. In other words, the good news of the gospel is replaced with the bad news of exclusion, condemnation and bigotry. All too often, hatred and persecution are added. As a result, tens of thousands have been forced to leave the church folds in which they grew up.

Jeremiah 50:6–7 speaks powerfully of these lost sheep of God whose shepherds have led them astray. In 23:1 he declares: 'Woe to the shepherds who destroy and scatter the sheep of my pasture! says the Lord.'

Ezekiel 34 castigates the shepherds of Israel who look after themselves but fail to strengthen the weak, heal the sick, bind up the injured, bring back the strayed or seek the lost. Instead, they rule their flocks with force and harshness. In the Gospel of Matthew, Jesus rebukes the shepherds who lock fellow believers out of the kingdom of heaven (23:13) or who put stumbling blocks before young people (18:6).

Does your own church preach good news or bad news?

Heavenly parent, remember your children driven into exile by harsh shepherds.

Renato Lings   The prophecy of Jeremiah

The harsh way in which lesbian, gay, bisexual and transgendered (LGBT) people have been treated makes their situation comparable to the sufferings endured by the people of Judah. In fact, Jeremiah's description of this last group reveals a story of original blessing followed by hurt, pain and alienation. Where the two stories differ is in relation to sin and guilt. The Judeans have been faithless by worshipping other gods while LGBT believers have striven to remain faithful to their Creator.

Despite the numerous efforts to exclude me and my LGBT brothers and sisters from the churches, I have not given up hope. Time and again I take comfort from the Bible, including Jeremiah. In 30:22 God extends this powerful promise: 'You shall be my people, and I will be your God.' This echoes the prophecy of Hosea 2:23 in which God accepts those who have been regarded as outsiders.

Divine love is far greater than the human tendency to marginalise. Thus, Isaiah predicts that God will offer a special welcome to outsiders (56:5). In John 10:16 Jesus mentions the 'other sheep', declaring that he himself will bring them into his fold. Inspired by this biblical inclusiveness, an international ecumenical network exists to support and nurture Christians excluded from the churches. Its name is Other Sheep – Multicultural Ministries with Sexual Minorities.

Dear heavenly shepherd, thank you for inviting me in.

Trade between the nations

Notes based on the New Revised Standard Version by

David Ford

David Ford is an Anglican priest working in parish ministry and school chaplaincy in the city of Leeds, England. He is also a member of the Religious Society of Friends. Prior to entering ministry he was Managing Director of a marketing and public relations company. His primary theological interest is in discipleship: the equipping of Jesus' followers for a life of commitment to God's creation.

Preparing for the week

This week's readings – which focus on King Solomon – explore the implications of international trade for both biblical and modern times, and the impact this has on our lives of Christian discipleship.

The land that became Israel was the great trading centre of the known world, a cosmopolitan mix of migrants, merchants and travellers, exchanging ideas, images, stories, commodities, luxuries, tools, livestock and people. It was also a world of competing empires as kingdoms grew – and declined – in economic, political and military might.

Today the known world may have gone global, but a similar pattern of relationships can still be discerned between economic activity and political power. We too live in a world of empire. In some respects little has changed.

As you travel through the week, explore your relationship with the issues that emerge from each day's reading and reflect on how God is calling you to respond.

Is Joseph's story a simple case of sibling rivalry that has gone a step too far? Large families can create unhealthy dynamics, and the weak position of the youngest brother, Reuben, is striking. He cannot stand up to his other brothers, so instead tries to create a situation from which he might rescue Joseph. Are there echoes here of Miriam looking out for her brother Moses?

The significance of this story lies in its location. Dothan is to be found along an important trade route between Syria and Egypt. The possibility of selling Joseph only existed because of where the brothers had chosen to pasture their flock. Ironically, this almost certainly saved Joseph's life. But there was another motivation too: the brothers' belief that blood cannot be concealed, that if they killed Joseph, in time their sin will be uncovered. 'Trafficking' Joseph solves a 'problem' with no unwanted side effects.

The primary motivations for human trafficking – poverty and greed – have changed little since Joseph's day. It remains true that wherever there is international trade, there exists the possibility of human trafficking.

As it eventually unfolds, Joseph's story shows us that God can – with our help – turn this situation around. But how many more Josephs will it take before we become fully engaged with the issues?

Are you aware whether human trafficking is taking place within your own community?

Trading in humanity

Genesis 37:12–28

Help us, Lord, to strengthen our voices against human trafficking, so more Josephs are rescued from the clutches of slavery.

Trade between the nations   David Ford

Solomon the arms dealer

2 Chronicles 1: 14–17

Before getting ordained I ran my own marketing company. It was a small business, nothing grandiose or pretentious about it. But it was successful, and as the years passed I discovered that a rapidly increasing income became deeply unsatisfying. Wealth simply creates the desire for even more wealth, and eventually the practical challenge of how to protect it.

Solomon faced the same problem but on a grand scale. Part of his solution was to become an arms dealer. His trade in horses and chariots was as much to do with defending and protecting his economic and military interests as it was to do with generating even more wealth.

The same pattern can be seen clearly today in the economic and military behaviour of the most powerful nations on earth. The arms trade is a logical consequence of uncontrolled economic freedom and a necessary consequence of disproportionate economic and military power. Wherever there are the prospects of new wealth, military interests and activity will not be far behind. But elsewhere the world's poor suffer, and horrendous regimes go unchallenged.

Jesus was unequivocal in his condemnation of the hypocrisy inherent in political, military and religious alliances. You cannot serve God and Mammon, nor God and Caesar. Discipleship is solely about following God in Christ.

How is your discipleship constrained by the forces of global economic and political power?

Generous God, help us to trade responsibly, earn justly and spend our wealth wisely.

A few years ago I had the pleasure of visiting Cape Town. It was a paid-for business trip and so I stayed in one of the plushest international hotels in town: a far more extravagant environment than I would ever have been able to afford myself. A single night in the hotel cost more than a successful taxi driver would earn in a month. Where, I wondered, did all the money go? Was the profit from my visit staying in the country or returning to the United States, home of the hotel chain?

A similar question arises with Solomon's temple. This fantastic symbol of Solomon's reign was achieved at a cost, as the wealth, skill and culture of neighbouring countries and peoples was plundered in the process. Nor was the trade with King Huram of Tyre as innocent as it seems. A past ally of King David, his complicity in Solomon's plans was built on short-term self-interest (the commercial success of Tyre) rather than the long-term interests of his own people. It was a very special relationship.

We can draw parallels too easily sometimes. But the economics of the Old Testament world and the economics of the 21st-century world look remarkably consistent. When will we learn?

Is the wealth of your culture threatened by international economic interests? Do you think this is a legitimate area of Christian concern?

Forgive us, Lord, for those times when our trading has weakened or eroded another nation's culture and wealth.

Whose wealth built Solomon's temple?

2 Chronicles 2: 3–16

Trade between the nations

David Ford

The politics of celebrity

2 Chronicles 9:1–9

Throughout history, success in any sphere of life has attracted those who might feel threatened or envious or simply inquisitive. Solomon bears all the hallmarks of an A-list Old Testament celebrity, with his wealth, power and reputation for wisdom. His success rapidly came to the attention of the leaders of the known world, concerned no doubt about his rise in power and influence. Yet where there is wealth there is opportunity and even the most powerful need allies.

So it was no surprise that the Queen of Sheba should find her way to Solomon's palace. Her motives might not be clear but Solomon's impact upon her is beyond dispute. Following extensive cross-examination, the Queen surrenders to Solomon's wealth and hospitality: 'There was no more spirit left in her,' we are told (verse 4).

This part of the story may be more about the wisdom of the Queen of Sheba than the wisdom of Solomon. One can sense her strategic thinking taking shape. How should I play this guy? Perhaps this is reminiscent of international trade agreements today that are dominated by the politics of commercial diplomacy. Yet who is speaking for God's people in all this? Where is their voice?

If governments are so controlled by vested interests, should Christians waste energy trying to voice the needs of the poor and powerless in the corridors of power?

Lord God, help us to keep our feet grounded in the gritty reality of life and our voices committed to the needs of the poor and powerless.

David Ford   Trade between the nations

More than any of our other readings this week, today's passage overwhelms us with descriptions of Solomon's material wealth. Yet by verse 31 he is dead.

Death of wisdom

'You can't take it with you' is a frequently heard phrase in England. It refers to the brutal reality that death separates us from our wealth as well as from our loved ones. So – the saying implies – you may as well spend what you have now.

2 Chronicles 9: 10–27

Solomon's reputation for wisdom has barely been noticeable in our readings this week. Yet surely it was such wisdom that prevented him from embarking on a self-indulgent spending frenzy. True, he built an extravagant temple for God and an extraordinary palace for himself. Yet the first reflected loyalty to his nation's faith whilst the second was an appropriate response to his stature and success. We should not judge Solomon by the standards of today's Christian economic ethics.

We can wonder, though, whether he felt the gift of the temple cancelled out his personal extravagance on the divine weighing scales. Yet we now know that such bargaining with God is unnecessary. The cross shows we cannot do anything to make God love us any more – or any less – than he already does. What we do with our wealth may reflect our priorities as Christians, but it cannot make us any more worthy in the eyes of God.

How can you use your wealth more effectively to benefit the kingdom?

Creator God, nurture in us the wisdom to recognise your priorities in our lives.

Trade between the nations   David Ford

Gospel economics

Acts 19:23–41

The silversmiths of Artemis were right to be worried. The early church cared greatly for the integrity of their economic life together. It mattered how money was spent.

Some argue that it is impossible in a complex modern world of international trade to ensure integrity in trade. They suggest that changing individual behaviour will never change corporate policy. Sacrificing personal integrity, however, seems a high price to pay. Better to run the risk of failure than to guarantee it.

But history tells a different story anyway. Economic boycotts have changed history. The boycott of South Africa was a foundation stone in the abolition of apartheid. More recently the fair trade movement shows that it is possible for consumers to vote with their wallets and influence change.

Nevertheless, all this is far removed from the high ethical principles of the early church. Certainly in the West most Christians appear reluctant to let their faith get too close to their livelihood. Perhaps it comes down to a lack of trust. Jesus came to offer us life in all its abundance. Yet many of us seem happier finding life in consumerism. Here is a clash of values as momentous as any in the history of thought. 'Follow me,' called out Jesus to his disciples. He still does, and he still means it.

When do you find it most difficult to trust God?

Patient Lord, as we struggle to come to terms with the implications of your good news, help us to trust in your promise of abundant life.

Gratitude

1 How to give thanks

Preparing for the week

Thanksgiving is a key part of being a Christian. It is important because it makes us look outwards from ourselves and our self-centredness and brings us into a closer relationship with God and our fellow human beings. Thanksgiving is an act of responding with love and thanks to God who is with us and present in this world. Blessings may lead us to thanksgiving. But the core of thanksgiving comes from our heart, with joy in God and God's good will. The theme for this week reminds us of the importance of gratitude – of not taking things for granted – in the Christian life, and gives practical illustrations from scripture.

Let us aim to be passionate and sensitive to the Holy Spirit who inspires us to give thanks for God's works, and for abundance wherever we find it in our lives. Pray with an attitude that focuses on God's grace for you, and sing a song with thanksgiving.

Notes based on the New International Version by
Eun Sim Joung

Dr Eun Sim Joung is a visiting lecturer at Baekseok Culture University, Korea, and the author of *Religious Attachment* (Cambridge Scholars, 2008). She is especially interested in the affective and relational dimensions of faith development, and how this can be applied to pastoral care and education, particularly for women.

Give thanks to whom?

Psalm 147

This is a great song. It instructs us about the One whom we are to thank. The greatness and goodness of the Lord are praised. The psalmist praises the Lord with thanksgiving. God is good and great. God is almighty and wise. God heals and comforts. God provides and protects. God strengthens and blesses. God grants peace and satisfies with the right things at the right times.

God is worthy of our praise. We should thank God for what God is and for what God does. Thanksgiving opens our eyes to see the Lord who is good and great. Thanksgiving opens our heart to feel the Lord who provides and protects. Thanksgiving enables us not only to see what we have but also to see that what we have comes from God. One who gives thanks truly worships. Our soul rejoices and sings to the Lord.

When we give thanks, we are satisfied with what we have. Thanksgiving generates more things to give thanks for as our appreciative spirits become more aware of all that we have been given. Above all, we give thanks for the fact that God has saved us to live in God's grace. This is a blessing beyond compare.

Lord, thank you for your Holy Spirit who inspires us to give thanks. You who are good and great are the source of all that is good and the abundance in our lives.

This song bursts with a sense of fullness of joy. Hannah's prayer is both powerful and delightful, but perhaps somewhat puzzling too. It may be hard to credit her joy when she is about to hand over her child, dedicated to the temple, the following day. We should notice that her song was sung, not after she gave birth to her son, but after she dedicated him to the service of the Lord. What other mother would sing such a powerful and delightful song just before separating from her little child? Returning home to her husband, we might imagine that he would perhaps accuse her of cruelty. And certainly, it is likely that Peninnah would ridicule her.

From where did Hannah's soul get such strength to praise God in the midst of such loss? Rather than looking at her circumstances, her faith was focused only upon God. Her joy and strength came from the Lord who is good and faithful. This enabled her to overcome Peninnah's mocking, to dedicate her son to the temple and to give thanks with a full heart to the Lord. This song communicates to us something of her joy, the satisfaction of her soul, her salvation and her freedom. Her faithful prayer issued in a joyful song.

Pray, focusing on God's grace for you, and sing a song of thanksgiving.

Thanksgiving with fullness of joy

1 Samuel 2:1–10

Gratitude

Eun Sim Joung

Thanksgiving with our whole being

Colossians 3: 12–17

Music is, perhaps, the most basic and pure form of thanksgiving that we can offer, a means of thanking God with our whole being. People who enjoy music are blessed with a certain purity of spirit. I know a pianist who served in churches for years. I was impressed by her, not only because of her music but also because of her beautiful attitude towards music. She said, 'The more I appreciate music, the more I come close to God. The more I worship God, the more I give thanks for the music.' Music for her was a blessing and a gift of God.

Music is a language in which we may speak our affection for God's love. It is a form of expressing our thanksgiving for God's grace. It can also be a way through which we can grow closer to God. Words and rhythms, melody and harmony, vocal and instrumental sounds can stimulate different aspects of our being, allowing thanksgiving to come from every part of our being: heart, mind, body and spirit.

I once saw a group of lepers praising God. Though their bodies were decaying, their spirits were passionate. It was a most moving sight that has been ever since imprinted on my heart.

We only need a grateful heart to sing praises. Then, our heart overflows and even our body becomes suffused with God's goodness.

Praise the Lord, O my soul; all my inmost being, praise his holy name.

Psalm 103:1

David gave many materials to his son Solomon for building God's temple (1 Chronicles 28:10–19). Then, in the prayer we read today, he expressed his thanks to God in these words: 'Everything comes from you' (verse 11).

We know that everything comes from God, but we may not be so generous in thanksgiving. It is easy to give thanks for big things, but it is not so easy in small things or in our weakness and struggle. 'Give thanks for the day, for the sun and the moon. Give thanks for roses, for their odour and thorns.' These words are part of a gospel song that I like very much, because they encourage me to give thanks here and now for what I have been given.

We do not need to look far away to find a cause for giving thanks to God. We do not need to envy others. What we need to do is to appreciate what we have, even if what we have is little. When we give thanks, the little we have becomes a blessing – to ourselves and to others. When a small boy shared his two fish and five loaves, five thousand people could eat. When a widow served Elijah with her last supplies of flour and oil, she experienced God's miracle of sustenance for three and a half years.

Thank you, God, for everything you give us today. Increase our generosity in thanksgiving.

All things come from God

1 Chronicles 29: 10–19

Gratitude

Eun Sim Joung

How can we not be thankful?

Luke 18:9–14

This parable is addressed to those who trusted that they were righteous. The Pharisee gave thanks for who he was and for what he did. According to his standard, he thought he was already righteous and for that he thanked God. He compared himself with the outcast, a tax collector. He justified himself by claiming that he was better than the tax collector.

If we compare ourselves with others, we may become arrogant. Pride is the sin that leads to other sins. Pride does not allow the Holy Spirit to work in us. The parable teaches us that the tax collector – the one who thought himself unrighteous and pleaded for God's mercy – went home justified before God. He did not compare himself with others. He was humble. He asked for God's mercy. He did not justify himself but was able to receive God's gift of justification.

This parable tells us that we cannot be righteous by ourselves. Nobody can be justified by their own deeds or status. Yet everyone can receive God's free gift of justification. How can we not be thankful that we are justified by God's grace alone!

Lord, forgive us when we compare ourselves with others, and believe we are righteous. Thank you for your grace and the righteousness by which alone we are righteous.

Thanksgiving for others' attributes and good deeds can come naturally at times. But it is not so easy when you feel that you are weaker and have less than others. There is a Korean saying, 'Someone else's cake looks bigger than mine.' When we compare our life with that of others, we are never satisfied.

Paul's letter to Philemon is full of gratitude for his 'faith in the Lord Jesus' and his 'love for all the saints (verse 5). Paul expresses his joy and excitement for Philemon. Paul is a model of a thankful and generous spirit, grateful in every situation. Some of his letters to the early churches were written when he was in prison, others were written when he was unwell, others again when he was in dispute with his recipients. Yet whatever the situation, he always begins his letters with words of grace and thanksgiving. Thanksgiving was a habit with Paul.

We too need to nurture that quality, practising thanksgiving until it becomes habitual. Thanksgiving is a secret source of happiness, a means of forming good relationships and a sign of spiritual maturity. Thanksgiving for other people can make our relationships richer and fuller. It is also contagious and spreads its own spirit of generosity naturally and gracefully.

How might you train yourself to be grateful in every situation, and learn the habit of thanksgiving?

Nurturing thanksgiving habits

Philemon 4–7

Give thanks for those who generate joy and thanksgiving by their own positive spirit. Pray to be genuine and faithful in thanksgiving.

Gratitude   Eun Sim Joung

Gratitude

2 What to give thanks for

Notes based on the New Revised Standard Version by

Maureen Edwards

Maureen Edwards, a former editor of *Words for Today* and of the *Methodist Prayer Handbook*, is a lay preacher of the Methodist Church.

Preparing for the week

'Thank you'? Do you always mean it? How often are you just being polite? Gratitude goes much deeper. It is a way of life, and it is never wholly destroyed by crises and sadness.

All our worship begins with praise and thanksgiving and at the heart of it is the celebration of the Eucharist (Greek: *eucharisto* – 'I thank'). Read Luke 22:14–23. When Jesus broke the bread and gave thanks this was no formal saying of Grace, but a thanksgiving offered at the very moment when his life was threatened. How does that aspect of thanksgiving challenge you? Look at Psalm 69, verses 1–3, 20, 21, and then see verse 30. Think of its echoes in Jesus' experience.

Breaking bread and giving thanks were habitual for Jesus (John 6:11) and a recognisable act (Luke 24:28–31). He was also profoundly thankful for the insignificant – the lessons to be drawn from the world of nature, for those who are often bypassed in society – women, children, those with leprosy and mental illness, the poor.

Thank you for the gift of life,
for the wonders of creation that delight our senses,
for the diversity of people through whom you reveal to us
the many facets of your love and above all
for all that you have given us
through your Son, Jesus Christ our Lord.

This letter is addressed to one of Paul's faithful travelling companions, a thoroughly reliable fellow worker, advising him as he helps new members and seeks to encourage the right kind of church leadership. By this time, false ideas about Christ and Christian behaviour were rampant – an early form of Gnosticism – and the more gullible members fell for it. They thought of body and spirit as separate entities opposing each other, claiming that Christians must be 'spiritual' people, denying their so-called 'sinful' physical appetites by fasting regularly and practising celibacy even within marriage.

For our daily food

1 Timothy 4:1–10

The writer of this letter emphasises that all created things come from God and are by their very nature good. Read Genesis 1:31 and Psalm 24:1. We are to enjoy to the full all that God has provided and be thankful. That does not of course extend to over-eating or sexual exploitation and so the writer balances thankful living with the self-control and discipline of the athlete (verse 8).

How often do you give thanks for your daily food and the many parts of the world from which it may have come? Think of communities gathering for a celebration meal – 'the banquet God has prepared for all people'. 'Enjoy!'

Loving God,
cleanse us from all greed and self interest
so that our thankfulness may flow spontaneously
in generosity to others.

Gratitude

Maureen Edwards

For other people

2 Corinthians 8: 16–24

Paul is profoundly thankful for the support and commitment of those who work with him and who can be relied upon to take his messages and letters to the churches he established. Titus is one of them, and there are two others he is sending to the church in Corinth. One is referred to as 'the brother' (verse 18), well known for his preaching and administration of the fund collected by Christian communities in the provinces for the many poor in the Jerusalem church. The other, known personally to the Corinthians, is referred to as 'our brother'. Paul's mission depends upon a vast network of men and women, such as these, whom he calls his 'fellow workers' (see Romans 16 for other examples).

Think of those who support you in whatever tasks you have to do, or who are just there for you when the going is rough: those with whom you work, your family and friends; those who challenge you and draw you beyond your 'comfort zone'. Think of those who have died, who have had a profound influence upon your life . . .

How easy or difficult do you find it to ask for, or accept, the help of others?

Sometimes, mysterious God,
you come to us in the guise of a stranger
and speak to us in ways that test and tease our thinking.
Make us ever thankful for the words of your messengers
even when they appear as unlikely as angels,
as poor as shepherds,
as unusual as wise men,
or as insignificant as a babe in a manger.

Maureen Edwards   Gratitude

This extravagant anointing of Jesus by an unknown woman happened at the very time when he was acutely aware of the plots being made on his life and the treachery of one of his closest friends. Some said her action was 'over the top': nard (spikenard) was an expensive oil and its price was equivalent to the average man's annual wages.

Her kindness and generosity were profoundly moving. He – the doer, teacher, healer and encourager of others – was surprised and affirmed by someone ministering to him when he most needed it. What thoughts ran through his head? Was it ironic that she was anointing his body before his death? Assassination would allow no time for burial rites: the body is hastily buried to conceal the evidence. Was he aware also of a hidden symbolism – that the Messiah his people had failed to recognise was here anointed by someone from the bottom of the social scale? His profound thankfulness to her lifted her up and gave her an unexpected honour. Happy are the poor . . .

How would you have responded? Would you have stopped her? We have been encouraged to believe that it is more blessed to give than to receive, but sometimes it is harder to receive. It calls for grace, humility and a readiness to see the dignity of the other person who desires to give or to be of service.

Jesus' gratitude was genuine

Mark 14:1–9

Living Christ, washer of feet and healer of wounds,
give us your grace that we may be truly thankful
for the gifts of others.

Gratitude   Maureen Edwards

317

Gratitude for the indestructible

1 Corinthians 15: 50–57

This strong statement from Paul about the freedom that comes about at death speaks of our need for a new 'body', a transformation of all that we are (physically and spiritually). 'The sting of death' – the sinful nature we find hard to let go but which alienates us from God – will be 'transfigured'. Wrongs will be forgiven, relationships healed and the tears of sorrow and pain wiped away. This is all made possible by the death and resurrection of Jesus Christ. Something infinitely new will emerge out of the destruction of the old: the new body can no longer be taken from us by death.

This does not mean that the scars of our guilt and human experiences will have gone: but they will be healed and will not hurt any more. We are accepted as we are, put right with God and 'glorified', but it is still the life we have lived and for the first time we are whole as God intended us to be.

This is 'good news'. It inspires and challenges the way we live here and now for we now know that divine forgiveness is real and that love and sheer goodness are indestructible. New beginnings are possible.

Help us, gracious God,
to show our thankfulness through a love that welcomes all
and so to work with you for the day when all barriers are
broken down and your kingdom comes.

Gratitude from the darkness

Luke 22:14–23

How did Jesus feel at this moment, acutely aware of mounting hatred, the threat of assassination, betrayal by one of his friends? Imagine how vulnerable he felt, yet he does something positive that arises spontaneously out of his life of faith and prayer. Like the woman (in Wednesday's reading) who, in her brokenness, did something for Jesus, so now out of his own sense of brokenness and vulnerability, he does something equally symbolic to strengthen the disciples in their weakness and confusion. Bread, which can be broken, is the object of his thanks. The wine, too, comes from a tree so fragile that it has to be supported by a wooden frame. The fourth Gospel puts into his mouth the words, 'I am the bread', 'I am the vine'.

Is Jesus then so embracing the suffering to come that he actually gives thanks for it?

Etty Hillesum, a Christian Jew who died in Auschwitz, speaks in her diaries of not running away from difficult feelings that seem to crush you. Facing them honestly, rather than being overcome by bitterness and the longing for revenge, denies the power of death from destroying both the individual and the world. Despair itself, if acknowledged honestly, can be absorbed by courageous living.

Loving God,
be with us in those moments when we are tested beyond our strength to endure;
and may our thankfulness for all that you have done for us in Christ sustain and help us to overcome.

Gratitude   Maureen Edwards

Gratitude and grace

2 Corinthians 4: 7–18

Turn to 2 Corinthians 11:24–29 for a list of Paul's sufferings and you will be able to reflect on his testimony of faith in today's reading. He also had a physical disability, 'a thorn in the flesh'.

Etty Hillesum (mentioned yesterday) was helped to face the insecurity of her early years and so discovered a new freedom which helped her to endure the more overwhelming suffering of life in a concentration camp. She held that it was essential 'to keep a small corner of one's soul unsullied'. If she could do that, no one would ever have complete power over her.

She developed a sense of solidarity with those who had suffered through the ages and with her fellow Jews in the camp. In her moral outrage against the Gestapo – whose unimaginable cruelty obliterated any resemblance to God's image within them – she always refused to hate the enemy. In her life in the camp, and when death became inevitable, she was aware of a sense of goodness and grace within her that was deeper, stronger and more endurable than the horrors and death that surrounded her. It gave her strength to comfort and encourage others. In spite of all that was happening, she could write, 'Life is glorious and magnificent.' Although she did not escape death in Auschwitz, she triumphed over it.

Loving God,
we give thanks that light is stronger than darkness,
that love dispels hatred,
that your grace is sufficient for each day,
and that in you the powerless find strength.

Readings in Matthew 26–28

Arrest

Preparing for the week

This week's readings come from the closing chapters of Matthew's Gospel. Normally we would expect to read these passages in Holy Week. However, as we come to the end of the year in which we have been reading Matthew's Gospel, it seems right to conclude with the final stages of Matthew's story. In the coming week we are looking at the familiar passages of Christ's passion, particularly through the senses.

Today is Remembrance Sunday. In many ways, Remembrance Sunday reflects a story leading to the suffering and death of Jesus. Both Remembrance Sunday and the Passion of Jesus express something of the sacrificial cost of loving.

Why not, today, read through the story covered in the week's passages, Matthew 26 – 27:10, in order to get an overall picture?

Notes based on the New Revised Standard Version by

Barbara Calvert

Barbara Calvert is a Methodist minister in the Orpington and Chislehurst Circuit, in England. Previously, she has been an RE teacher, worked for Christian Aid, and been a University Chaplain in Glasgow, Scotland.

Beauty in brokenness

Matthew 26:1–16

Darkness is closing in. In Britain, at this time of year, daylight is short and the hours of darkness long. Each day is darker, and in the leaden November skies hangs a sense of foreboding. So, as we near the end of Matthew's Gospel, the plot thickens. Conspiracy, denial, betrayal and death hang in the air. All seems lost, all is broken.

Yet in the midst of darkness and gloom, a woman appears with an alabaster jar of aromatic oil. She anoints Jesus' head, and the beautiful perfume entices our senses, blotting out the stench of death. It is a simple act of love, costly, without guile or forethought. She just does it, pouring out the oil as she pours out her love. In the midst of darkness, the light of love of this simple act of devotion glows and a beautiful fragrance fills the air.

Yesterday was Remembrance Sunday, marked by the symbolic red poppies growing through the cloying mud of Flanders fields, scenes of unimaginable human suffering and horror. We remember the dead as we remember this woman, unnamed – the lifeblood of love poured out. The red poppy, like the alabaster jar – a symbol of hope and new life, of love overcoming death.

In the darkness of conspiracy and denial, the beauty of selfless love shines and we are reassured by Jesus' three predictions that it is the God of love who is in control, not those who plan his death.

Where have you seen selfless, costly love this year?

Day by day, O God, may we see beauty in brokenness.

The days darken. Jesus has foretold his death and is surrounded by those plotting to kill him. Even his friends are prepared to deny him and betray him. A bleak and despairing picture of humankind is portrayed; yet in the midst of such darkness rays of light break in.

There are two meals in this chapter in Matthew. One is at the house of Simon the Leper, and now another meal, the Passover meal, is being shared and celebrated. We are invited to taste the bread and the wine. Jesus reaches out to us through our senses – touch, smell, taste and sight – and we hear Jesus speaking to us, 'Take eat; this is my body.'

The sacrament of the Last Supper, the simple act of breaking and tasting bread together and drinking from a shared cup, breaks through to our inner being. The act of sharing bread together is deep and profound. It has been practised everywhere, at all times and in places of darkness and despair: in concentration camps, in prisons, amongst refugees and in women's refuges.

At the end of life where words might fail, our senses continue to recognise the fragrant presence of Jesus in our midst, hope reaching our senses beyond words, nourishment for the soul. Taste and see.

Day by day, O God, may we taste the fruits of your Spirit.

Readings in Matthew   Barbara Calvert

The welcoming Trinity

Matthew 26: 36–46

The story of Gethsemane and Jesus' acceptance of his coming death reaches a climax in his prayer in the garden. Three times Jesus prays, three times Peter later denies Jesus, and three times in this story the disciples fall asleep. The three disciples who witness the praying are the same three who witnessed the mountain-top transfiguration of Jesus.

In Rublev's early fifteenth-century Russian icon, a print of which hangs in the hallway of our home, the three figures of the Trinity, God the Father, God the Son and God the Holy Spirit, sit around a single cup. Each of the three figures wears a garment of blue, the colour of transcendence, representing divinity. The figure in the centre is dressed half in blue and half in red, symbolising the shared divine and human nature of Christ. The single cup sits between the three figures. Facing us in the icon there is space for another person, any and every person who gazes on the icon.

In the garden of Gethsemane, Jesus prays to the Father: 'Let this cup pass from me' (verse 39), but then, in obedience to God's will, takes up the cup of suffering. In the icon, the three figures look at us. We are invited into the circle, and, if we accept, the cup will touch our lips too.

Day by day, O God, may we enter into the company of your kingdom.

The hour before dawn is the coldest and darkest hour of all. The air hangs dank and cold; all is silent as the grave; and there is a seeping smell of fear.

The authorities are fearful. Judas betrays Jesus, surrounded by a large crowd who have been summoned to arrest Jesus because the authorities fear that there might be a violent reaction. And so they come for him in the hour before dawn.

The disciples are fearful. They are so afraid that when Jesus is arrested they run away. Like deer in the grey early morning mist, reacting to an unexpected movement, they smell fear and run.

In contrast, Jesus shows no fear. He accepts his fate first by telling Judas to do what he has come to do; then by his rejection of the use of the sword as a means of defence; then also through his testimony that God could save him; and finally in his assertion that scripture must be fulfilled. Jesus is not contaminated with the smell of fear, even in the face of death.

The aroma of the precious pure anointment which the woman poured over him sustains him in a time of fear. Assurance of God's love wins out.

Day by day, O God, may we overcome the fears of discipleship.

The smell of fear

Matthew 26: 47–56

The sound of silence

Matthew 26: 57–75

It was a sunny October day and I enjoyed the walk through the streets of Edinburgh to a meeting in a local church. The sky was clear blue and I admired the beautiful colours of the fallen leaves on the pavement – red, orange, brown and green. At the meeting, after a warming cup of coffee we gathered, seated in a circle with some candles burning in the middle. A woman had been asked to lead the opening worship. As she led the prayers she gave thanks to God for what she had enjoyed on the way to the meeting – not the colour of the autumn leaves but the sound of the leaves crunching under her feet, the rustling of the wind in the trees, the sound of passers-by chattering and the sound of the birds heard through the intermittent traffic. She was blind, and the beauty of God's world spoke to her that morning through sound.

Imagine the sound effects in the trial of Jesus: a sound of cloth ripping, the sound of spitting, of punching and slapping. In the courtyard outside, it is the jarring sound of Peter's Galilean accent which is picked on; and then the cock's crow is heard; and finally the sound of bitter tears. The true nature of this shameful episode is betrayed by its sounds. In contrast, listen to the silence of Jesus, echoing the silence of God.

Day by day, O God, may we listen for you in silence.

The healing touch

Matthew 27: 1–10

In 2009, the relics of St Thérèse of Lisieux toured Britain. Thérèse entered a convent at the age of 15 and is revered for her devotion, simplicity, and above all her love. In 1897, aged 24, she died of tuberculosis. Over 100,000 people went to see her relics as they toured Britain, and this week, as I write, the relics are on display in Westminster Cathedral. Many people would consider that queuing to visit relics is just sentimental piety, laughable even. But for others it meets a need. In our sceptical age, there is a widespread longing for something that takes us outside ourselves, feeds our spiritual yearnings and touches the soul.

The sense of touch is very powerful for good or ill. The repentant Judas holds the pieces of silver in his hand. He can feel the weight of the coins in the palm of his hand, and for these he has betrayed Jesus. He can't bear to touch them any longer. He throws the coins to the floor of the temple. The chief priests pick up the contaminated money. They hold the silver coins in their hands while they decide what to do with it. The blood of Jesus is on their hands too.

In contrast, a loving touch touches our heart. Thousands queued to be in touch with St Thérèse. When Jesus is taken from them, his followers long to reach out and touch him, the women to hold his feet and Thomas to touch his side.

Where and how have you experienced touch over the past week?

Day by day, O God, may we receive your healing touch.

Readings in Matthew 26–28

Trial

Notes based on the New Revised Standard Version by

Barbara Calvert

For Barbara's biography see p. 321.

Preparation for the week

The final week in our reading through Matthew's Gospel is also the final week in the Christian year. We are on the verge of Advent, but not there yet. Before Advent, which looks to the coming of Christ, we have to complete the story of his life – and his resurrection.

Again, the material is familiar to us, so we seek to look at it through fresh eyes, exploring contemporary images to help us enter more deeply into its meaning for today.

Like last week, why not read through the story from Matthew 27:11 to the end, in readiness for the daily reading of the most central story of the Christian faith?

A South African production company, Isango Portobello, from a township of Cape Town, performed at the Garrick Theatre in London. *The Mysteries*, based on the medieval Chester Mystery Plays, told the Bible story from creation to resurrection – in just over two hours! Every member of the cast was on the open-plan stage for the whole performance, acting, singing, making music and dance, sound effects, all with minimalist props. The story was told in several different languages: Xhosa, Zulu, Afrikaans and medieval English, but the familiar stories needed no text. This succinct, vibrant, colourful, imaginative retelling of the Bible narrative was a reminder of the basic story of God's relationship with humankind.

Pauline Malefane, a distinguished black opera singer, played the part of God, her stunning performance revealing the nature of God as creator, powerful yet compassionate, trustworthy, exercising true love with justice. Humankind comes out of the story less well. In Cain and Abel, the Garden of Eden, battles and conflicts, the massacre of the innocents, the arrest, trial and crucifixion of Jesus, we are reminded of the constant tendencies of humankind's self-serving nature. Faithlessness, jealousy, fear, cowardice, pride, fickleness and faintheartedness are the depressingly repetitive themes in which we can see ourselves all too clearly. So too, in today's reading we recognise the jealousy of the chief priests and scribes, the fear of Pilate's wife, and the cowardice of Pilate as he fails to take a stand for justice.

When and where have biblical stories come alive for you?

Day by day, O God, deliver us from evil.

The story of human frailty

Matthew 27: 11–26

Readings in Matthew   Barbara Calvert

**Jesus
identified**

Matthew 27:
27–44

Football, a sport enjoyed by millions, also experiences and mirrors many problems. In the newspapers and on television, stories and photos of football violence have given the sport a poor image. The violence is both physical and verbal. Verbal abuse is sometimes racially motivated and sometimes just callous and cruel, though many football teams, like my local Charlton Athletic, are working hard at community relationships in the belief that football can also become a means of change in society. Following a recent match when some atrocious taunting had taken place, the Arsenal manager said 'one starts to say something stupid, everybody follows, even intelligent people. People lose their identity altogether.'

This is what happened in today's story. In the hours before Jesus' death, the people who mock and jeer Jesus lose their identity. The cohort of soldiers, the bandits, the chief priests, the scribes and the elders, all join in the verbal abuse, even 'those who passed by' (verse 39). Only Simon of Cyrene, the blameless carrier of the cross, remains above all this.

But, in the midst of the taunting, they unwittingly identify Jesus. The sign fastened above the cross identifies Jesus as the 'King of the Jews' (verse 29). This taunt ironically comes to confirm what Christians believe about Jesus. And the crucifixion, a cruel mocking death, becomes a more powerful image than the cruel taunting of the people, for it has the power to change hatred into love.

Day by day, O God, help us to discover our true selves.

The description of the dying Jesus, though brief, is full of symbolism. Jesus is offered wine in accordance with Psalm 69:21: 'They gave me poison for food, and for my thirst they gave me vinegar to drink.' Jesus cries out from the cross, 'My God, my God, why have you forsaken me?' in the words of Psalm 22:1. At the point of death, the curtain of the temple is torn in two, overcoming the separation of God from God's people. The tombs are opened and the saints raised, an apocalyptic sign of the end. The writer is determined that we should be in no doubt that the death of Jesus is rooted in scripture. To ensure that we can be quite confident of the narrative, we are told that the women who have been with Jesus ever since Galilee, later to be witnesses to the resurrection, witnessed all these events.

The writer of Matthew's Gospel wants the reader to trust not just feelings but also certainties. When the earthquake moves the ground beneath our feet, when all seems lost, when life is tearing itself apart, the message is to trust not what you feel but what you are sure of. As Jesus hangs on the cross, as his life flows out from him, he calls out to a God he can be sure of. He may feel the absence of God, but he is still certain of God, a certainty that holds him beyond his own essence and existence.

Of what are you most certain, beyond feelings or experience?

Day by day, O God, increase our trust.

The facts of the case

Matthew 27: 45–56

A rough hewn stone

Matthew 27: 57–60

A few years ago, as the twentieth century was drawing to a close, communities looked for appropriate ways to mark the occasion. In Britain, the much derided Millennium Dome was chosen for a national focus of celebration. A large tent-like structure, which for the year 2000 was the venue for a programme of exhibitions and displays, it did not catch the national mood. The exhibitions are long since forgotten, and although the Dome is still there it does nothing to inspire or stir the soul. Local communities, however, were often more successful in finding a symbol to mark the passing of 1000 years. In marked contrast to the flimsy, ephemeral nature of a tent, many communities across the country chose a large, granite stone. On the common just along the road from my house sits such a stone. Rough-hewn from the earth, solid, grey, permanent, it sits, immovable, marking the passage of time.

In the story of Jesus' burial, a new character enters the story, Joseph of Arimathea, described as being already a disciple of Jesus. He is sufficiently important to be able to ask Pilate for the body of Jesus. Watched by the women, Mary Magdalene and the other Mary, the focus of the burial becomes not the people in this story but the stone. Joseph of Arimathea rolls it across the front of the tomb, a great stone, marking not just the passage of time but a new day continuing through all eternity.

Day by day, O God, build your church as a living rock.

From the southern-most tip of the Mull of Kintyre in Scotland, on a fine day it is possible to look across the ocean and see Ireland. If you had stood on this point around the year 563 CE, you might have spotted a small wooden boat in which sailed a monk called Columba, with a few companions, crossing from the shores of Donegal in the north-west tip of Ireland. From the Mull of Kintyre Columba began his missionary journey to Iona, and then across Scotland and into England, said to be one of the most significant events in the early Christian history of the British Isles. Embedded in a rock on the shore of the Mull of Kintyre is a clear footprint, which tradition has it is the footprint of Columba.

When the risen Jesus appears to Mary Magdalene and the other Mary, we have a picture of the two women taking hold of the feet of the risen Jesus, and then running off to tell the other disciples what they have seen. Their actions are a symbolic reminder of the nature of the Christian faith and discipleship – a way of life, nurtured through being at the feet of Jesus, leading to following in his footsteps. In authentic Christianity, worship of Jesus leads to 'continuing his work and living his way', as Walter Wink put it, in his book *Engaging the Powers* (Fortress, 1992).

Day by day, O God, guide us in your footsteps.

They took hold of his feet

Matthew 28:1–15

Good news for all

Matthew 28: 16–20

In the last few years, Europe has seen once again the rise of far right, fascist, racist ideology. The British National Party (BNP) gained supporters by exploiting people's fears of unemployment, the collapse of the global economy and immigration. Leaders of far-right factions are able to use the internet to draw disgruntled and disparate people together, and in just a few months the English Defence League (EDL) emerged. In the 1930s, Oswald Moseley's 'black shirts' marched in Jewish areas stirring up racial hatred; in a similar way, the EDL marched in Muslim areas.

The black British theologian Anthony Reddie went along to a rally in a Muslim area of Birmingham to challenge EDL supporters. Some of them were waving placards claiming to defend Christianity; so Reddie told them that he was a Christian. 'Christianity is for white people,' they said. When Reddie pointed out to them that Jesus was not English, he was Jewish, they replied disbelievingly, 'No he's not.'

In this final passage of his Gospel, Matthew, writing for a Jewish Christian community, is determined there will be no mistake. The good news of the gospel is for Jews and Gentiles alike. This final scene takes place on a mountain, and is like an enthronement of the heavenly king. Jesus has all authority in heaven and on all the earth. He commands the disciples to go and make disciples of all nations. The commission is all-inclusive.

Day by day, O God, open our eyes to see Christ in everyone.

Salvation history

1 Salvation belongs to God

Preparing for the week

I once joked that the best form of defence if cornered in a dark alley was to turn and call out loudly: 'Brother, are you saved?' Any would-be assailant would surely flee from a mad evangelist, giving thanks for a lucky escape. Fortunately I have never had to test the theory. But that salvation should be spoken of, even in jest, as something that might frighten away an attacker, says how muddled popular understanding of salvation has become.

Too often the question, 'Are you saved?' leads to dividing people into 'those loved by God' and 'those whom God would like to love, but hasn't yet', or worse, 'those whom God looked at and decided were unloveable'. This is not the kind of salvation to which Jesus and his disciples gave witness in their lives of healing, truth-telling hospitality. It is certainly not the kind of sacrificial love that Jesus showed on the cross, the place and time when God's loving pursuit of humanity found its end.

Salvation means being saved from harm, rescued from evil of all kinds, and being challenged and nurtured in our lives right now. To paraphrase Amos 5:24 and Psalm 27:13, salvation means the time when justice rolls like water and we see the goodness of God in the land of the living. Being saved is not about a moment when we shouted or prayed enough that God finally decided to look our way, or we followed a set of rules to keep God sweet. Living as a 'saved' people means being adopted into God's 'salvation history', our lives taken to God's purpose a little more each day.

Notes based on the New Revised Standard Version by

Jennifer Smith

The Revd Dr Jennifer Smith is a Methodist minister serving in West London. Originally from the USA, she has lived in the UK since 1993, and travels annually for teaching and church work in Nigeria.

Preparing the way: judgement and soap

Malachi 3:1–4

Reading this passage, I get the image of a thick-armed woman washing clothes in a river. She twists and slaps the cloth, beating it with strong soap to prepare it for wearing again. God's judgement has rightly got a bad name, as it has been perverted to justify poor treatment of those who threaten power, or do not fit an 'appropriate' lifestyle. Yet preparing the way for salvation requires judgement: naming the dirt in our common life that needs washing. It is a sharp thing, judgement. Not for nothing is this passage often read by Christians in the same breath as they speak about John the Baptist, preparing the way for Jesus by calling people to account: 'you brood of vipers' (Luke 3:7)!

That thick-armed woman Malachi brings to mind is not just washing individual souls, but the stains of war, poverty, unfulfilled potential and unshared resources. God's salvation is deeply personal, but it is not private. Saying this, I mean that although God's salvation touches our most intimate parts, it is about the healing of our whole history and society and each of us within it.

Spend some time with the image of God as a thick-armed woman, washing clothes in a river. Imagine sitting beside her as the ills of the world pass through her hands. What is she murmuring as she works?

Create in me a clean heart, O God: renew a right spirit within me.

In the 1862 poem that we know as 'The Battle Hymn of the Republic', Julia Ward Howe wrote of God's vengeance:

He is trampling out the vintage where the grapes of wrath are stored,
He has loosed the fateful lightning of his terrible swift sword.

A committed reformer and abolitionist, Howe wrote to rally support for the American Union, then locked in civil war with the slave-owning states of the Confederacy. Her poem used imagery of Isaiah 63 to underscore the inevitability of God's salvation for those oppressed.

For her ninetieth birthday in 1978, my Vermont great-grandmother, Julia Pease Smith, wanted her extended family to sing her this hymn, from memory. I remember learning the verses over long hours in the car on the drive north. Because of its warlike imagery, some people struggle to sing it today. But to extend the scriptural metaphor, as the author John Steinbeck did, if the conditions of history store up 'grapes of wrath', the day will come when the vintage must be drunk; the day of God's coming as saviour to the people 'in all their distress' (verses 8–9) is sure.

I don't think my great-grandmother wanted to re-open the wounds that shaped the culture of her girlhood, but I do think she wanted us all to know that we were part of God's salvation work in history, and that it was not finished.

O God, bring justice swiftly where oppression grows, and save us from distress.

Salvation history   Jennifer Smith

Deliverance belongs to God

Psalm 3:1–8

A personal re-writing of Psalm 3:5–6:

> *I lie awake and worry;*
> *I wake again to re-play hurt, for my portion in*
>   *the Lord is all used up.*
> *I am never wholly unafraid, I see those*
>   *who love me and even then, imagine*
>   *insults on their lips.*

But maybe this is not quite as at odds with the whole text as first appears: when the Psalmist calls, 'Rise up . . . deliver me, O my God' (verse 7), I hear the plea of one who feels abandoned by God despite assertions of easy sleep. God does not seem to have arisen overnight, and evil is still real.

One benefit of having weathered some adversity and lain awake is the repeated experience that morning comes. I have found trust in God to be a wilful choice, easier as I pass through more dark nights that end in daylight. To say, and come to know without saying, that deliverance belongs to God is to acknowledge the limits of my power. It is to offer God not only my need, but also my sense of abandonment. And if my own, then that of the world around me.

If you keep a diary, look back over it for a time that was very stressful or troubling, that is now past. Try to remember how each day felt. Pray for the memory of each day, for yourself and others who were involved.

O God of wakeful hours, ease my fear. Calm my restless limbs, soften my thoughts and edge me into sleep.

Jennifer Smith   Salvation history

Consider a classified advertisement slotted in between 'personal services' and 'plumbers' in a local newspaper:

PERSONS BEING SAVED WANTED. Not many who are wise by human standards, not many powerful, not many of the 'better' sort. Human weakness, foolishness desirable.

It is easy to parody Paul's words in 1 Corinthians to be a 'duffer's charter' in church, even to excuse incompetence because 'God chose what is foolish in the world to shame the wise' (verse 27), along with the weak, low and despised. This is not what Paul intended, and not what being caught up in God's salvation history is about.

A better demonstration of what Paul meant lies with the tactics of Dr Martin Luther King Jr in the African-American civil rights movement mid-way through the last century. Dr King and non-violent marchers walked into police barricades knowing they would be cut down by batons, fire hoses and dogs before arrest and excoriation in the press. African-American children endured abuse and bullying to desegregate schools and lunch counters. Foolishness, to expose children and those black folk, already vulnerable because of the racism of their society! Weakness, not to fight back when trampled on! Pointless conflict, stirring things up! Such is the wisdom of God.

Grant us the serenity to accept the things we cannot change, the courage to change the things we can, and the wisdom to know the difference.

Adapted from a prayer attributed to
Reinhold Niebuhr

God's wisdom, our foolishness

1 Corinthians 1: 18–31

Salvation history

Jennifer Smith

Teaching an old dog new tricks

John 3:1–7

I once adopted a border collie called Jedediah. Like his namesake, nineteenth-century American 'mountain man' Jedediah Smith, he would cheerfully evade capture across three counties if a door got left open. In the end arthritic hips did what my attempt to train him could not, and he grudgingly stayed closer to home.

It is possible to get into a rutted way of being that works more or less. More and less, at times. If the dog wanders, keep the doors shut – play safe and accommodate the world as it is because I don't have time today to change it. Writ large, this can give us communities, nations and economies that are all bound up by what they cannot do, despite the best intentions.

Salvation history is nothing less than God's pursuit of justice and mercy from creation across the scriptures to the cross, out of the empty tomb and into the world. To be born from above is to be adopted into that history, to find one's own life taken up in God's purpose each day. No wonder Nicodemus was incredulous: we cannot do it ourselves, but only through God's grace. Whether one identifies more with the wandering dog or the frustrated closer of doors, no tricks: only new life.

Is there something you have been avoiding sorting out? Write down the steps to doing it, and take the first one.

O God, give me grace to be born again, to be adopted into your salvation history, to live freely as your beloved child.

Jennifer Smith   Salvation history

There is a story told by the character Alyosha in Fyodor Dostoevsky's *Brothers Karamazov*, called the 'Grand Inquisitor'. Jesus returns and is arrested for disturbing the peace: the Grand Inquisitor, a powerful church leader, comes to his cell to explain why his coming with salvation interferes with the mission of the church, and why he must die again. Here is a church asleep, showing the ironic tragedy of human sinfulness.

Before I scoff, do I truly look for God's salvation to come? Do I look for the day when all my striving and possessions become meaningless, when justice is done and the world changes? I fear there is more than a little of the Grand Inquisitor in me.

Jesus speaks to his disciples of the signs of the day of salvation as the new shoots on the fig tree, signalling summer. He warns them over and again to keep awake, to remain watchful for the coming kingdom. This is not to whip us into anxiety, but to remind us that the world is not finished. We too should be watchful for the signs of new life, even as we are afraid to leave the old behind.

Salvation is near

Mark 13:24–37

'. . . *we do not know how to pray as we ought, but that very Spirit intercedes for us with sighs too deep for words*'

Romans 8:26

Holy Spirit, stay wakeful in my heart: look for buds of new life in me, and breathe them into flower. Give me grace to look for your coming this day, knowing salvation is near.

Salvation history   Jennifer Smith

Salvation history

2 Salvation with a difference

Notes based on the New Revised Standard Version by
Carlton John Turner

Carlton John Turner is an Anglican priest from the Bahamas, with a background as a Spanish teacher. From 2008 to 2009 he completed an MA in Applied Theological Studies at the Queen's Foundation, Birmingham, England. He is married to Carla and looks forward to growing as a contextual theologian.

Preparing for the week

Salvation is an ambiguous, even a dangerous word. It has been used to prescribe who is within God's favour and who isn't. However, the biblical tradition makes it clear that, from beginning to end, God is redeeming the entire creation, including human beings. Moreover, the incarnation of Jesus Christ teaches us that besides being ongoing, salvation is an ever-present reality. It is neither other-worldly nor restricted to a particular class of persons, but is open to all who respond to the invitation sealed in blood by Jesus the Christ.

The notion of salvation has had a particular history within the Caribbean. On the slave plantations, slaves were indoctrinated with the notion that salvation was a purely spiritual event concerning the soul's destination, and therefore the horrors of daily life were of no importance. In fact, slaves were encouraged to accept their bondage gladly, seeing it as God's will for their lives. Even in the second decade of the twenty-first century, such an idea is still current within Caribbean Christianity.

As we move through our reflections this week, may we be challenged to consider ways in which God's kingdom will come 'on earth' as it is in heaven. Whatever salvation means, it must make some positive difference in the everyday living of God's people.

Just as creation was an act of God bringing order out of chaos, this oracle by the prophet Zephaniah sounds a similar note. It begins by speaking of judgement, bondage and disaster, yet it ends in victory and restoration. However, the emphasis of the oracle is on an active, warrior God who positions himself between both extremes and fighting for peace, deliverance and renewal.

The Caribbean has been a region that has known sustained chaos; deliverance and restoration are its deepest cries. Here in the Bahamas we are experiencing unprecedented violence and national chaos, in the face of which there is a pervasive feeling of hopelessness. It is in these times that, as a country and as a region, we are drawn to Zephaniah's God in whose powerful agency is our restoration and hope.

Lord, help us to have the faith to rely upon your agency in the midst of our struggles. You are the mighty one, and for this we forever praise you!

A restoring God

Zephaniah 3: 14–20

Salvation history   Carlton John Turner

Righteousness and peace kissing

Psalm 85:1–13

Christians throughout the ages have identified with the words of the Psalms. In them we find the deepest cries surging up out of people's real lives. In Psalm 85, the desire for righteousness and peace are not merely words to create some aesthetic effect, but the objects of a heart-wrenching request. This psalm is the desperate plea from one who has but one cry left.

As I write this, we in the Bahamas have had our 76th murder for the year. In a country of some 300,000 persons we have seen this statistic rise yearly, with crimes becoming more heinous each year. The courts are overrun. The prison is overrun. Chaos is erupting. Righteousness and peace are not simply words, but our ultimate cry. Nonetheless, we who continue to cry for righteousness and peace also remember that our God *is* righteousness and peace, and wherever he reigns these two things shall always embrace.

Lord, please hear the cries of your children who seek peace in the midst of chaos. Bring your righteousness in the midst of violence and abuse.

Carlton John Turner   Salvation history

Salvation here and now

Luke 2:1–20

The birth of a child always puts a reality check on our notions of time. As I write this reflection my wife is pregnant. Amidst feelings of fear, anxiety and joy, I am consumed with thinking about the kind of world our child will be born into. What kind of world do I want for my child? What kind of man should I be for my child, for my family? At the same time I am very conscious that the answers to such questions lie in the here and now. To be the best I can for my child and my family in the future requires me answering that question now; making the right decisions now.

Luke 2 records the defining moment of the saviour's birth. It was a day that peace came to the earth. It was a peace that the angels sang about: 'Glory to God in the highest heaven, and on earth peace among those whom he favours' (verse 14). This peace was not a future promise but a present reality. The kingdom of God is always in the present. Salvation is always in the here and now.

Lord, give us the grace to see your saving hand in the present, whether in the mundane or the miraculous.

Salvation history   Carlton John Turner

Healing and salvation

Luke 17:11–19

God's healing is indiscriminate! Out of the ten lepers that came to Jesus for healing, the much-loathed Samaritan is healed as well as the others. As both a leper and a Samaritan, he would have been doubly feared and loathed. Interestingly, it is that one leper who comes back to give thanks for his healing.

In the Caribbean there is great need for healing. For starters, lifestyle diseases such as heart disease, diabetes, HIV and AIDS seem to have become epidemic. Also, health care is in desperate need of reform since beds are overrun, and medicine is often too costly for people to afford.

However, there is a deeper form of healing needed. While Christianity holds that grace is unmerited and unlimited, there are deep divisions within Caribbean societies. Some of these divides are ethnic, some racial, some economic, some religious, and some cultural. Jesus' healing of the Samaritan, the 'other', reminds me that the embrace of the other is the deeper healing sought. We need healing from our ungratefulness and pride.

Lord, deliver us from our pride and ungratefulness and allow us to see your face in the other.

The time has come

Galatians 4:4–7

I love the words 'in the fullness of time' (verse 4); they remind me that time is not mine to manipulate. Also, time bears witness to truth. Time will always bear witness to God, who is truth itself. It is in the fullness of time that salvation came to the world in the person of Jesus Christ. If we look to John's Gospel, Jesus is portrayed powerfully as the one bringing ultimate truth to humanity.

We live in a world that is increasingly forgetting this truth. As the world has become increasingly secularised, God, even any notion of God, is pushed aside. The present generation is being taught that the human being is the ultimate source of truth and that human beings control time. In response to this I am reminded of an old song that is very popular in Bahamian society and which says, 'Many things about tomorrow, I don't seem to understand, but I know who holds the future, and I know who holds my hand.' ('I know who holds tomorrow', written and composed by Ira Forest Stanphill.)

God is still the God of time and will act when, where and however God wishes.

Lord, help us to remember always that you alone are God, and we are your favoured children within your beloved creation.

Salvation history   Carlton John Turner

Salvation with a difference

Mark 1:1–8

An image that is often associated with the Holy Spirit is that of fire. The coming of the Holy Spirit on the day of Pentecost is characterised by the imagery of 'divided tongues, as of fire' resting on the heads of believers (Acts 2:3). We see this imagery of fire in Matthew 3:11, where Jesus is spoken of as baptising with the Holy Spirit and with fire. Today, the imagery of fire speaks very powerfully to a contemporary context, as we hear reports of global warming, war, poverty and extreme violence. Yet while the fire of the Holy Spirit serves to bring new life, the fire of the present age works to bring death and destruction.

Salvation is actual, not theoretical. It is in the little as well as the large things. It is demonstrable in every act of kindness, mercy and sacrifice. It comes when transformed hearts begin to live transformed lives. While John's baptism was a sign of turning away from sin, Jesus' baptism was to bring the deepest transformation of all – people would be 'fired up' by the Holy Spirit to bring peace to the world.

A salvation that is to make any difference in our present world is one in which lives are filled with the Spirit of God.

Lord, help us to yield to your Spirit so that our lives, and the lives of everyone we meet, may be engulfed by the flames of your love.

Carlton John Turner   Salvation history

Salvation history

3 Singing salvation

Preparing for the week

This week we concern ourselves with 'singing salvation'. But I wonder how many of us really think of salvation as something to sing about. Of course, as we shall see, Isaiah has given us a song to sing in chapter 40. But, for many of us, the notion of salvation has more to do with the theological acrobatics of the mind, and little to do with the engagement of our bodies.

During this week, we will continue to look at a notion of salvation that brings body and soul together, that yearns for depth and breadth, and crosses the divide between believer and non-believer. We will try to open up biblical passages beyond narrow interpretations without denying their power and purpose. We will journey together challenging our assumptions and comforting our insecurities as we allow ourselves to dwell for a moment in the divine presence.

Sometimes my most powerful experiences have come from making music with others. We are often transported into a world beyond our own when we listen to music and hear the songs of others. So let us see what happens when we sing salvation together.

Notes based on the New Revised Standard Version and *Good As New* by

Mike Holroyd

Mike Holroyd works in the disability sector as a team manager, and is also a theologian and musician. Mike directs a small choir and is passionate about using our singing voices to express the full range of human emotions.

Hope in desolation: God is coming

Isaiah 40:1–11

I have, on a few occasions, sung these words of Isaiah 40 as the solos 'Comfort Ye' and 'Every Valley' from Handel's *Messiah* – and what a privilege it has been. Amazing promises indeed, but are we really ready to allow the rough places to be smoothed over, the valleys exalted and the mountains made low? Sometimes the rough places offer us an opportunity to get a foothold and keep our balance amongst the jagged edges. Perhaps the valleys offer us some security where we sense protection and anonymity. Or making an even bigger mountain out of an existing mountain may have become our life's purpose!

Isaiah's prophecy brings us the kind of hope that can only be achieved through considerable hard work. As individuals, churches or societies we will only begin to experience salvation or enlightenment once we become conscious of and deal with the rough places that we hold on to, the valleys that we hide in, and the mountains that we locate in our eschatological scenery.

God breaks into our lives in a million different ways each day, but will we be awake enough to notice? Will we be free enough to notice the coming of God in others, and will we be available to embrace the presence of God throughout God's creation? Salvation is very much a communal experience, but we each need to take responsibility for realising it.

Pray today that you might be more conscious of our salvation.

Mike Holroyd   Salvation history

It is all too easy to read Psalm 116 with a sense of failure – how could my faith ever live up to that of the writer of this psalm? It is not clear what disaster had befallen the psalmist, but the New Revised Standard Version seems fairly sure that the writer experienced some severe illness, and this does seem a reasonable assumption.

Perhaps the greatest clue to further exploring our theme of salvation is verse 6, which could be paraphrased as 'God protects those who have run out of resources to protect themselves.' We should first be clear that this does not mean that God does not protect those who are not at their wits' end. But, there is an important counter-cultural lesson here, one that flies in the face of our economic systems and political constructs. It is that it is often those who have had the roughest deal in life who have the most profound understanding of salvation – God has quite literally saved them from conflict, drugs, alcohol, isolation and many other a death-dealing reality. Such salvation is not some theological conjecture emanating from the lips of religious luminaries, but a real experience of restoration and new beginnings.

This psalm encourages us to recognise God's saving power in the here and now – not primarily through a formula or belief, but through a real engagement with the source of all being.

Become aware today of your oneness with creation – what is your salvation song?

Lifting the cup of salvation

Psalm 116:1–19

Salvation history

Acts 13:14b–26

I was not particularly good at history at school. My early experience of history was more about learning dates, and less about learning lessons. What it means to learn our history from biblical texts is of course a complex matter – it's quite interesting and disturbing at times to note what happens to communities of faith when they look to scripture for proof of historical accuracy or exegetical precision. The power of scripture as communicated to us through the Holy Spirit comes into its own when we listen to the story within and beyond the text. That is not to deny the 'happenedness' of various events within the biblical narrative, but it is to say that so often the greater truths are found in the unravelling of stories in our own contexts. It is there we discover layer upon layer of meaning which draws us deeper into God.

Paul's appeal here is not a folk song, harking back to how good the old days were – indeed his references back to forty years in the wilderness and the crucial role of David as king can hardly be interpreted as an exemplary moralistic framework for modern living. The appeal here is to learn from the songs of old – that salvation pops up in all sorts of unlikely places, that God's faithfulness goes far beyond what we could ever imagine, and that the process of being saved is much more about God and far less about us.

What lessons from history are you learning today? Pray in and through them.

Mike Holroyd   Salvation history

I remember one horrible moment years ago when a fiery preacher visiting my church proclaimed, 'Thousands of people every minute are going to a lost eternity because they haven't heard of Christ.' This is not the message of a God who longs for the whole of creation to be reconciled; who does everything possible to bring wholeness to God's beloved broken people; who yearns for complete companionship with every creature so much that even the dead are invited into the new realm of God. And then we hear such offensive formulas as 'dead people who lived before the time of Christ could not be saved because they had no chance of hearing of him'. This leads to the absurd conclusion that we should actually not share Jesus with anyone, since they would be better off not knowing, rather than being in danger of making 'the wrong choice'.

We have an urgent song to sing to people who are seeking instant absolutes. The message that is timeless, beyond all generations, is that God is on our side – and in this context 'our' does not simply refer to me, or you, or us Christians, but refers to the whole human family within God's creation. How amazing is this? How utterly divine is this? God crashes through our sinful ability to divide and exclude, by saving the world. Our task is to know this salvation, and to help others do the same.

Timeless salvation

1 Peter 3:18–22

Pray for a wider, deeper sense of God's salvation in the church.

Salvation history   Mike Holroyd

353

Salvation as a feast

Luke 14:15–24

My temptation when reading such a passage as this is to dwell on the exclusive statements rather than the inclusive one. So, we have a story here full of hope and God's graceful generosity, and I tie myself up in knots about the people who have had their chance and blown it! Of course, if this was the truth that the parable was drawing our attention to, then this may well be a legitimate response. But this parable is, of course, not about God giving up on those who have had their chance. God never gives up, and frequently tells us not to give up.

No, this parable is about God's amazing welcome – a demonstration that all, all, all are welcomed to the banquet. A meal is a time for sharing, a time for putting aside our differences and celebrating the fact that the things that we have in common are far more important than that which divides us. This is what is so profound about the eucharist, as long as it is seen as a shared meal rather than the expression of a doctrine. Doctrines are, of course, important because they offer us signposts on life's journey, but it is the sharing of a meal together that brings us all more in touch with our salvation and enables us to join in with the song of the universe.

Pray for all with whom you will share a meal in the coming days.

Mike Holroyd   Salvation history

I have written about 'Mary's Song' for *Words for Today* in previous years, but the power of the Magnificat never ceases. The miracle is that Mary is chosen to embody salvation before she understands and, therefore, believes in it. Scripture is utterly silent about the three-year theology degree that Mary had to undergo to prepare her for this moment! For some reason, we are not given details of the membership classes and pastoral placements that Mary had to attend!

Her calling was to embody salvation – this was a physical act involving pain, borne in her flesh and blood, not a cognitive reception of some ideology, or at least not in the first instance. Salvation is primarily incarnational – that is, it is rooted in the everyday experiences of humankind. Salvation is about living life to the full, rejoicing in our unity with our human family, celebrating our unique purpose within the whole of creation, and embracing the priority of the common good over individual gain.

Sometimes we have to lose ourselves in the embodiment of God's plans in order that we can indeed find ourselves once again. This is the essence of the song of Mary, and it is the song that I want to dare to sing with you day by day, in order that together we may just start to be able to embody God's salvation for the purposes of the whole universe.

Let us help each other today to raise our voices in prayer and in song.

Mary's song of God's salvation

Luke 1:46–55

Salvation history   Mike Holroyd

Salvation history

4 Salvation beyond boundaries

Notes based on
The Message by
Eugene H
Peterson
(NavPress, 2002)
by
Jenny Warbrick

Jenny Warbrick lives
in the Midlands, UK.
An experienced
history teacher, she is
now a freelance
educational writer
and trainer. Jenny
runs the Sunday
school at her local
Anglican church, is
married to the vicar
and has two children
aged 12 and 15.

Preparing for the week

Salvation. Rarely has a word provoked such fierce debate, inspired so many books or led people to die defending their interpretation of it. From the Latin *salvare*, it means 'saving of the soul' and is a central tenet of Christian doctrine. The readings this week contain images which may help to clarify what God's salvation means for you personally, and challenge you to develop as a Christian within your own community of faith and beyond its boundaries.

Read Isaiah and reflect on whether there are aspects of yourself that you dislike which prevent you embracing God's love. John may help to illuminate the darkness of failing to understand or accept God's promise of salvation in Jesus. Use Galatians to consider how Jesus' sacrifice makes you feel, and how that impacts on your life. Salvation for all is a generous offer. Are you as accepting as God of those who are different from you? Like Joseph, we all face challenges in life. How we respond to them can reveal hidden qualities in us and shape our future. Finally, may the excitement, impulsive worship and extravagant generosity of those archetypal boundary-crossers, the wise men, inspire you this Christmas.

This passage is bursting with vivid imagery. The prophet uses four of the senses to describe the happy, loving relationship God seeks with humanity, and to reassure the exiled Israelites that they are not abandoned, but treasured by God. Joyful song, a jewelled tiara, cascades of blossom and the intimacy of being 'in the palm of God's hand' poetically convey the affection and longing God has for each one of us and all his people. However, this can leave us feeling a bit inadequate if we don't feel that joyful, glamorous or special and can't reciprocate.

Assurance of salvation

Isaiah 61: 10 – 62:3

A TV celebrity-stylist helps women feel comfortable in their own bodies. After making them confront their physical reality, he gradually rebuilds their self-image based on self-acceptance, without dieting or cosmetic surgery. It is a remarkable and moving transformation. We are often our worst critic and God our best advocate. God made us, accepts us and loves us with a passion and commitment similar to a couple deeply in love, who find it hard to believe their partner's devotion. We don't have to believe we are precious, but simply accept that God thinks we are.

List all the things you don't like about yourself. Confess these to God, light a candle and then burn the piece of paper. Pray that you will learn to accept yourself for what you are; worthy of God's love and promise of salvation.

Salvation history   Jenny Warbrick

God's love, God gave

John 3:4–21

Imagine this encounter between Jesus and the respected Jewish teacher as a black and white film and you will appreciate the stark visual contrasts. Nicodemus has ventured out under cover of darkness; perhaps afraid to be seen fraternising with this maverick preacher or embarrassed to be asking him questions. His failure to understand as Jesus explains the idea of spiritual rebirth is like a dark cloud over him. It is as if Jesus is speaking another language.

As a teacher, I can relate to Jesus' exasperation; trying to explain a difficult concept to a child can be very frustrating when they can't grasp it, no matter how hard you try. But his message is simple: God loved the world so much that he gave it a priceless gift, his only Son, and 'by believing in him, anyone can have a whole and lasting life' (verse 16). It doesn't need to be dressed up in complex theological language. Jesus illuminates the darkness of misunderstanding with a powerful image of 'God-light' streaming into the world through him. Many people fear 'painful exposure' of their sins and run to hide. But Jesus is trying to reassure us that if we just step out from our dark corner into God's radiant light, he will not judge us, but guide our path.

Holy Spirit, may you shape us within so that we may reflect a little of God's light in our own lives.

Jenny Warbrick   Salvation history

'Under new management' – the sign outside the newly refurbished pub or restaurant is an invitation (or desperate marketing ploy!) to encourage you to venture inside. It makes you curious about possible changes in decor, staff and menu, and you are tempted to try it sometime. Rob Lacey, writing in *The Word on the Street* (Zondervan, 2003) uses this phrase to describe how it feels to live a new life based on faith in Christ. It illustrates how clear it should be to others that your lifestyle has changed, once you have accepted God into your life.

God's love is for all

Galatians 2: 15–21

Writing to the early Christians in the Roman province of Galatia, Paul is anxious to explain that strict adherence to the Jewish law is not the answer to a right relationship with God. Strict adherence to the law might have been his former way to salvation, but once Jesus came and sacrificed himself, external coercion was replaced by internal freedom.

The choice to trust Jesus Christ is open to everyone, without exception. No qualifications are required, no forms need to be filled in, there is no selection process. Just the free gift of love . . . if you dare take it. Because it should come with a warning: this gift could seriously change your life.

Reflect on verse 21. How does Christ's personal sacrifice for you make you feel? How does your faith make a visible difference to your life? Pray for help to make it even clearer.

Salvation history   Jenny Warbrick

God's salvation for all

Romans 10:1–13

I was really looking forward to the performance of Monteverdi's *Vespers* in Coventry Cathedral. It would be a stunning setting for an amazing piece of music, accompanied by original seventeenth-century instruments. So when I found myself miserably confined to bed and too ill to go, I was bitterly disappointed. My husband and mother-in-law went on their own. But on their return, I was somewhat cheered to learn that on the cathedral steps they had been able to give my ticket to a woman waiting hopefully for a last-minute return. She had been thrilled.

In this letter Paul is trying to explain to his fellow Jews that the good news of salvation they have been longing for is not exclusively for them. A hard message to swallow, perhaps, for God's chosen people. But faith is not only an event for ticket-holders. Paul wants the Jews to throw open the doors to the Gentiles waiting outside, or perhaps just passing. This concept of salvation *beyond boundaries* must surely challenge our interpretation of whom salvation is for in today's society. Tickets are free to anyone who acknowledges Jesus as their Lord and Saviour and wants a relationship with him, regardless of religious, racial or socio-economic background, sexual orientation or educational qualifications. Let us extend to everyone a warm welcome to God's extended family.

Examine your heart for prejudice of any kind. Pray for God's help in working to change your attitudes.

Jenny Warbrick

Salvation history

This passage was the basis of the first Godly Play story I ever heard – 'The Good Shepherd' – and it made a profound impact. For those who haven't heard of it, Godly Play is a method of storytelling pioneered by Jerome Berryman, an American, that explores Bible stories using ritual and 2- or 3-D resources. It allows the audience to enter into the story in their own imagination and then wonder out loud about it. Originally conceived as a way to spiritually engage pre-school children, it is as powerful for adults who may re-encounter familiar stories.

Being brought up in an urban environment, the Good Shepherd was a metaphor I hadn't related to much before. But to see the simple wooden figure of Jesus calling his sheep by name as he led them out of the sheepfold made his personal re-lationship with me very real. When he led his sheep to green grass and clear blue water, his care and nourishment of me was in no doubt. When the sheep passed through rocky places of danger, it was clear that however frightened I felt, he would reassure me, and if I got lost, he would never stop searching for me. Jesus' offer of a 'better life than [you] ever dreamed of' is a tantalising one. And surely worth sharing.

Good Shepherd, show me ways to share my faith with those who have not yet heard your voice.

Hidden potential

Matthew 1:18–25

Being made redundant, whether expected or not, is a harsh blow to one's self-esteem. Joseph must have felt similarly 'out of a job'. He no doubt thought himself a good judge of character in choosing Mary, only to feel totally betrayed by the discovery that she had been unfaithful to him and – worse – was carrying someone else's child! It is hard to imagine how humiliated he must have felt. But a testing situation can bring out hidden strengths in a person. As with redundancy, it is how Joseph responded that defines him and signals his future.

Matthew tells us that Joseph was a 'noble' man, and initially he plans a secret divorce, which will spare Mary public disgrace. However, he is still wrestling with his conscience when an angel reassures him in a dream that the child is 'Spirit-conceived'. Jesus' pre-ordained name means 'salvation' as he is destined to 'save his people from their sins'. Joseph's lack of hesitation in marrying Mary demonstrates a remarkable trust in God. As a result, Joseph's life goes off in a completely different direction (literally!) and he takes on a new role as family protector; on the journey to Bethlehem and later in the escape to Egypt.

When faced with unexpected challenges, respond positively, trust in God and see where it leads you . . .

Pray for those facing redundancy or a difficult situation this Christmas, that they might discover their hidden potential.

Jenny Warbrick   Salvation history

Herod's kingship is based on fear. He was 'terrified' to learn of the scholars' arrival. This reveals that despite his glamour and power, he is fundamentally insecure. His hypocritical pretence at devotion in front of the wise men and blatant lie that he seeks the child in order to worship him, illustrates the flawed nature of his human authority. Interestingly, the scholars do not seek Herod out. They are summoned to the palace. We don't know how they reacted, but can imagine they felt obliged to follow his instructions. Only when empowered by a dream do they have the courage to flout Herod's authority, but fearing the consequences, leave the territory 'without being seen' (verse 12).

Jesus' kingship is different. Affirmed by the star which 'hovered over the place of the child' (verse 10), (it reappeared only *after* the wise men left the palace!), the nature of his authority can be judged by others' response. Even before they meet him, the wise men were so excited they 'could hardly contain themselves' (verse 10). When they enter the house, they are 'overcome' and their first impulse is to kneel and worship Jesus. One could interpret their generous gifts as symbols of their own wealth, piety and perhaps sadness that their pilgrimage had come to an end.

Lord Jesus, may we be excited as we celebrate your birth. May our first impulse be to worship, and may our lives be full of generous acts of service to others.

Genuine kingship

Matthew 2:1–12

The good news

Notes based on the Revised Standard Version by

Ruth Shelton

Ruth Shelton is a poet and theologian who teaches adults with learning difficulties in a city-based Further Education College.

Preparing for the week

Mark's Gospel begins with the voice of Isaiah speaking across the ages with bold instructions, which these days might conjure up images of bulldozers, cranes and concrete mixers. It is not an unfamiliar sight on the TV to see groups of protesters who don't want houses or roads built on their local green space.

Prevailing notions of spirituality seem to privilege the experience of silence, the contemplative way of life and natural landscapes over our urban desert of noise, activity, buying and selling. We seem to be saying, 'Keep the city, work, advertising, taxi horns and bus queues out of my spiritual space.' But for Jacob, Moses and Elijah, for John the Baptist and Jesus, the desert was a harsh place where faith was tested to the limit. The whole people of Israel stumbled, lost their way and starved in the desert for forty years. It was far from a place of escape, any more than the synagogue was a place of peace and harmony in Mark's account below. In 'Choruses from the Rock', T S Eliot reminds us that:

> The desert is squeezed in to the tube-train
>   next to you
> The desert is in the heart of your brother

One way of thinking about spirituality is to describe it as paying attention to the everyday, to be ready to see our location with new eyes, and to encounter the divine in its places and people. The meditations below offer a chance to experiment, letting the buildings, churches, city squares and streets of our lives speak of the good news of the one who dwells among us.

People think of me as silence itself, but I have heard many voices cry out in despair, anger, release, prayer. I am a place, neither town nor country, on the fringes, where people come to escape, to hide, to find . . . what? The wild man was one of many who found me, and then many found him.

I became a place of bustle, gathering. Human beings came from the city, the full became empty and the empty became full.

Nothing was ever the same again, but you know that, because you too, are here.

The streets came to me and with them, the holiness of our strange God.

The desert speaks

Mark 1:1–8

> *God of the wild places,*
> *help me to find you.*
> *You live in the wilderness of my own life;*
> *my trampled holy ground.*

For further action and thought

At some point this week during your regular prayer time, pray with a street map of your community or street in front of you. Visualise the house, the streets, the people, and hold them before God, or walk through your neighbourhood paying attention to what is around you.

The good news   Ruth Shelton

The river Jordan speaks

Mark 1:9–15

I know heaven and hell, year in, year out. Heaven is when I am rushing, impelled by my own selfhood, gloriously swollen with water for the towns and villages, for all who come with their buckets and pails. Hell is when despairing people try to end their lives in me, widows sobbing in the reeds, families throwing flowers from the banks. Hell too, when I am dry, children staring at the cracked riverbed, knowing it's pointless to stay, unable to go home.

This strange day, my waters broke upwards as a man rose out of me, smiling and wiping his face with his hands. At the same moment, my brother the sky broke open and I heard the voice of God.

Hell was there too. I could smell it, but the man went straight off, not even dry yet, further into the desert, to face up to hunger and thirst and to demand that the hungry will be fed, and the thirsty drink pure water for ever.

> God, the source of life,
> break the defences of my spirit.
> I will pour down the dusty streets; into
> cupped and waiting hands.

Question for reflection

Where are the deserts and wildernesses in my own life, in my context and locality?

Ruth Shelton   The good news

Sometimes you catch fish, sometimes you don't. That can mean life or death. Sometimes I'm terrifying, and the sky darkens, a boat is lost, someone's son or brother is drowned. Sometimes, I am too calm, and the men sit gazing uneasily at the sun. It's a life of risk, a life on the shores of life, and yet without it, Galilee would not survive.

Today, first Simon and Andrew left their nets, and later the same day, James and John as well. The other fishermen thought it was strange, like madness, but I know fishermen, and they looked as if they had found something that they had been doing all along.

The sea of Galilee speaks

Mark 1:16–20

God of work and labour,
*   call me to my own life.*
I will follow you to the margins, and speak
*   your name there.*

Question for reflection

How can I learn to pay attention to the signs of faith, courage and hope in my everyday encounters?

The good news   Ruth Shelton

The synagogue speaks

Mark 1:21–28

We are used to strangeness within these walls. The mad, the bad, the lost and lonely come here every day. But there was something about this voice, although not loud, ringing round, bouncing against the constraint of my walls. Even the dice-players and pigeon-sellers were listening. We are used to demons too, but the way the new preacher stood in front of the man, calm, unsmiling! It was if he was saying, 'We have had enough of this now.' Human, devil, spirit or stone (and most of us are a mixture), we recognised this voice.

My stone floors creaked with memories, my pillars stirred with the unleashed prayers of centuries past.

And perhaps we were used to our own madness, our familiar little devils. They were part of us. His friends bundled him away afterwards . . .

I fear for him because he has taken something from us, something we didn't need, but we thought that we did.

God of health and healing,
  give me a new voice to address my fears.
My crutches and props will fall way; I stand
  before you, whole as you made me.

For further thought and action
If you are thinking about moving house or job, or find yourself dreaming about a change, think and pray carefully why this is.

Bread and wine was ready on the table but there was no one to serve it. The new arrivals milled around for a bit, but the atmosphere was awkward: there was something missing. The man called Jesus was looking around and then he went upstairs.

He came down again a little time afterwards with Peter's mother-in-law on his arm. Her head was held high. She welcomed the guests. She sat next to Jesus, and when he asked her, she broke the bread and passed it around, and poured the wine. It was such a joyful gathering, with laughter and stories, that people were peering in through my door. It was as if the town and I were the same place, sharing the feast. I had no walls.

He left soon afterwards, pressing through the crowds, and I am waiting for him to return, my doors always open.

*God of all women and all who serve,
    raise them high.
I will see your presence at the feast; I will
    always welcome the stranger.*

Question for reflection
Why am I placed where I am, in my home, my job, my social network?

The town gate speaks

Mark 1:40–45

There had already been a lot of coming and going. Crowds pressing into the town, and then leaving for another place. A man who slipped through my gates at dusk, but who always came back, sometimes with a sad air. And there are always the lepers, forbidden to come in, yet needing to be near. The man I told you about who kept coming and going, as if he wasn't quite sure whether he wanted to be alone or not, was a bit like the lepers in that way.

One day I heard him raise his voice. He had been talking with lepers and he was holding one of them by the shoulders. The man's head fell back and he shouted something, angrily. The leper ran off, rather speedily for someone who was meant to be ill.

I heard talk that he had been healed. Crowds pushed through me, and back, trying to find the man. It seemed to me that no one had been angry enough about the lepers, they were just there, and that this man's shout to the heavens had changed something, and people knew it, without knowing what or why.

God of the voiceless,
make me angry about injustice and
oppression.
I will go to the boundaries of my
experience; I know I will find you there.

For further action and thought

Gather a small group of people in your neighbourhood together to identify the needs of the community. Is there one small thing that you can do something about? Or join with others already doing something?

All about IBRA

IBRA readings

The list of readings for the whole year is available to download from www.christianeducation.org.uk/ibra. You are welcome to make as many copies as you like.

IBRA books

Both extraordinary value at £8.50 each in the UK, with writers from around the world and many different Christian traditions.

IBRA samplers

From time to time IBRA publishes samplers using notes from *Light for our Path* and *Words for Today*, suitable for introducing new readers or for use with Bible study groups. Please contact us at the address below for availability.

IBRA Rep discount

If you live in the UK and purchase 6 or more copies of IBRA books, you can sign up as an IBRA Rep which entitles you to 10% discount off all your IBRA purchases. Just tick the IBRA Rep box on your order form and we'll do the rest.

IBRA International Fund

The IBRA International Fund enables the translation, printing and distribution of IBRA Bible notes and readings. For more details, see page 73. You can make a donation when ordering your books.

IBRA, 1020 Bristol Road, Selly Oak, Birmingham, B29 6LB.

International Bible Reading Association

A worldwide service of Christian Education at work in five continents

HEADQUARTERS
1020 Bristol Road
Selly Oak
Birmingham
B29 6LB
United Kingdom

www.christianeducation.org.uk
ibra@christianeducation.org.uk

and the following agencies:

GHANA
IBRA Secretary
Box GP 919
Accra

asempa@iburstgh.com

INDIA
All India Sunday School Association
Plot No 8,
Threemurthy Colony
6th Cross, Mahendra Hills
PB no 2099
Secunderabad – 500 026
Andhra Pradesh

sundayschoolindia@yahoo.co.in

Fellowship of Professional Workers
Samanvay
Deepthi Chambers
Vijayapuri
Hyderabad – 500 017
Andhra Pradesh
fellowship2w@gmail.com

NEW ZEALAND
Epworth Bookshop
157B Karori Road
Marsden Village
Karori
Wellington 6012

Mailing address:
PO Box 17255
Karori
Wellington 6147

sales@epworthbooks.org.nz

NIGERIA
Hinderer House
The Cathedral Church of St David
Kudeti
PMB 5298 Dugbe
Ibadan
Oyo State

SOUTH AND CENTRAL AFRICA
IBRA South Africa
6 Roosmaryn Street
Durbanville 7550
biblereading@evmot.com

If you would like to advertise in *Words for Today* please contact our Marketing Department at:

IBRA
1020 Bristol Road
Birmingham
B29 6LB

telephone:
0121 415 2978

email:
marketing@christianeducation.org.uk

INTERNATIONAL BIBLE READING ASSOCIATION

1020 Bristol Road, Selly Oak, Birmingham B29 6LB, United Kingdom

You can order using this form or through your local IBRA rep, or online at http://shop.christianeducation.org.uk, or by email to sales@christianeducation.org.uk or by phone on 0121 472 4242

Please return this form to
IBRA, 1020 Bristol Road, Selly Oak, Birmingham B29 6LB

Order form for 2012 books

Name: _____

Address: _____

_____

_____

_____ Postcode: _____

Telephone no: _____ Email: _____

Postage in the UK is free. Payments in pounds sterling, please. If you are ordering from overseas and require more than one copy please contact us for a discounted price.

Code		Quantity	Price	Total
UK customers				
AA110201	Light for our Path 2012		£8.75	
AA110202	Words for Today 2012		£8.75	
	I am an IBRA Rep (see page 369)		10% off	
	I am ordering 6+ books and would like to become an IBRA Rep		10% off	
Europe				
AA110201	Light for our Path 2012		£12.00	
AA110202	Words for Today 2012		£12.00	
Rest of the world				
AA110201	Light for our Path 2012		£15.00	
AA110202	Words for Today 2012		£15.00	
			Subtotal	
	Donation to the IBRA International Fund			
			Total	

☐ **I enclose a cheque (made payable to IBRA)**

☐ **Please charge my MASTERCARD/VISA/SWITCH** (delete as appropriate)

Card Number: ⬚⬚⬚⬚⬚⬚⬚⬚⬚⬚⬚⬚⬚⬚⬚⬚⬚ **Issue Number:** ⬚⬚

Expiry Date: ⬚⬚ ⬚⬚

Security number (last three digits on back): ⬚⬚⬚

Signature: _____

IBRA themes for 2012

Faces of the Divine
Creating God
Divine Lover
Incarnating Saviour
Faithful Companion
Inviting Host

Readings in Mark (1)
Jesus: teacher and healer 1
Jesus: teacher and healer 2

Trees
Trees in the Old Testament 1
Trees in the Old Testament 2
Trees in the Old Testament 3
Trees in the Old Testament 4
Trees in the New Testament
The tree of shame is made the tree of glory

Readings in Mark (2)

Readings in 1 Corinthians
The centrality of the Easter message
The people of God
Understanding the body, the church
The nature of love

Jerusalem
Jerusalem: City of David
Jerusalem: the Holy City

Readings in 1 Samuel
The calling of Samuel
King Saul
David
The death of Saul

Fathers
Fathers and children
Perplexities of fatherhood
Care and counsel

Readings in Mark (3)
Who is this?
He is ...

Not to the swift
Running with an attitude
Live the ongoing race

Missing the mark
Prophets, kings and judges
Disciples and congregations

Genesis 37–50
'Listen to this dream that I dreamed'
'One in whom is the spirit of God'
'It was not you who sent me here, but God'
'Though you intended to do harm to me, God intended it for good'

Jewish festivals
The biblical pattern
Jewish festivals today
The festivals in the ministry of Jesus and the life of the Christian

Readings in Mark (4)
Following Jesus 1
Following Jesus 2

Eyes of God
God sees us where we are
God seeks us out
The watchful God
Face to face with Jesus

1 & 2 Thessalonians
Keep awake and sober
Never tire of doing right

Wisdom
The identity and character of wisdom
The acts of wisdom in creation and history
The call of wisdom
Jesus Christ, the wisdom of God